John Heneage Jesse

Memoirs of celebrated Etonians

Including Henry Fielding, the Earl of Chatham. Vol. 2

John Heneage Jesse

Memoirs of celebrated Etonians

Including Henry Fielding, the Earl of Chatham. Vol. 2

ISBN/EAN: 9783337282783

Printed in Europe, USA, Canada, Australia, Japan

Cover: Foto ©Andreas Hilbeck / pixelio.de

More available books at **www.hansebooks.com**

MEMOIRS

OF

CELEBRATED ETONIANS:

INCLUDING

HENRY FIELDING.
THE EARL OF CHATHAM.
HORNE TOOKE.
HORACE WALPOLE.
GEORGE GRENVILLE.

THOMAS GRAY.
GEORGE SELWYN.
LORD NORTH.
EARL OF BUTE.
EARL TEMPLE.

ETC. ETC. ETC.

By J. HENEAGE JESSE,

AUTHOR OF "MEMOIRS OF THE REIGN OF GEORGE III.," "THE COURT OF THE STUARTS," ETC.

IN TWO VOLUMES.—Vol. II.

LONDON:
RICHARD BENTLEY AND SON,
Publishers in Ordinary to Her Majesty.
1875.

LONDON:
PRINTED BY WILLIAM CLOWES AND SONS,
STAMFORD STREET AND CHARING CROSS.

CONTENTS.

	PAGE
RICHARD OWEN CAMBRIDGE	1
DR. EDWARD BARNARD, Head Master and Provost of Eton	10
HORACE WALPOLE, EARL OF ORFORD	17
NATHANIEL FORSTER, D.D.	49
JOHN MONTAGU, EARL OF SANDWICH	54
ROBERT GLYNN, M.D.	86
GEORGE AUGUSTUS SELWYN	89
FIELD-MARSHAL THE RIGHT HON. HENRY SEYMOUR CONWAY	122
LIEUTENANT-GENERAL JOHN MARQUIS OF GRANBY	143
LIEUTENANT-GENERAL SIR WILLIAM DRAPER, K.B.	150
SIR GEORGE BAKER, BART., M.D.	157
CHRISTOPHER ANSTEY	162
ANTHONY CHAMPION	168
ADMIRAL RICHARD EARL HOWE, K.G.	170
DAVID DALRYMPLE, LORD HAILES	194
THE REVEREND GEORGE GRAHAM	198
GENERAL VISCOUNT HOWE, K.B.	200
CHARLES WATSON-WENTWORTH, MARQUIS OF ROCKINGHAM, K.G.	219
THE REVEREND JOHN FOSTER, D.D.	231

		PAGE
FREDERICK LORD NORTH, K.G., EARL OF GUILFORD	.	234
SHUTE BARRINGTON, Bishop of Durham . . .	.	286
GEORGE STEEVENS	.	294
JOHN HORNE TOOKE		302
JONATHAN DAVIES, D.D.	.	327
CHARLES MARQUIS CORNWALLIS . . .	.	329

MEMOIRS

OF

CELEBRATED ETONIANS.

RICHARD OWEN CAMBRIDGE.

ALTHOUGH neither a profound scholar, nor gifted with the very highest order of either poetical or conversational powers, Richard Owen Cambridge was nevertheless distinguished by a happy universality of agreeable qualities and parts, which alike rendered him respected by the learned, and led to his being welcomed as a delightful companion in every society in which he mixed. "Mr. Cambridge," writes Madame D'Arblay, "has the best stock of good stories I almost ever heard; and, though a little too precise in his manner, he is always well-bred, and almost always entertaining. Our sweet father [Dr. Burney] kept up the ball with him admirably, whether in anecdotes, serious disquisitions, philosophy, or fun; for all which Mr. Cambridge has both talents and inclination." Neither did this agreeable impression become impaired by closer intimacy. "I admire him more and more," subsequently writes the same lady, "and think all that is formal in him wears off upon acquaintance, and all that is pleasant grows more and more conspicuous."[1]

Richard Cambridge, the son of a Turkey merchant, was born in London on the 14th of February, 1717. His father dying while his child was still an infant, bequeathed him to the joint guardianship of his surviving parent, and of his maternal uncle, Thomas Owen, to whose property he, a few years afterwards, succeeded, and whose surname he then assumed in addition to his own.

At Eton, and, indeed, throughout his long life, the accomplished author of 'The Scribleriad' seems to have devoted himself in desultory, in preference to close and deep duties; thus qualifying himself to be esteemed an elegant rather than a profound scholar, and though far from neglecting or underrating the value of classical erudition, deriving his chief delight from the perusal of English poetry, of works of imagination, and of such books as throw a light on human character and on human nature. Happy for him, at all events, it was that not only was he endowed with a keen relish for intellectual occupation, but that he enjoyed a private fortune amply sufficient to exempt him from the labours and interruptions which must have been his lot had he been constrained to follow a settled profession.

[1] Madame D'Arblay's 'Diary and Letters,' vol. ii. pp. 214, 241.

From Eton, in 1734, Richard Cambridge passed as a Gentleman Commoner to St. John's College, Oxford, and thence, in 1737, without having taken a degree, to Lincoln's Inn, where it was then his intention to study for the Bar. This design, however, appears to have been defeated by his marriage, in 1741, at the age of twenty-four, with a Miss Trenchard, second daughter of George Trenchard, Esq., of Woolverton, in Somersetshire, a lady who, for more than the next sixty years, was destined to be the sharer of his happiness and the consoler of his sorrows. He now removed with his bride to his family seat, Whitminster, in Gloucestershire, where, principally occupying himself with his favourite literary pursuits, he continued to reside for the next seven or eight years. Of his other modes of employing himself in the country we may incidentally mention that, though caring little or nothing for the sports of the field, he nevertheless arrived at such expertness in the use of a bow and arrow, that, we are told, "the head of a duck, swimming in the river, was a favourite mark which he seldom missed." The fact is, that this exceptional accomplishment, of which he thus became such an adept, was first of all recommended to his fancy, partly by his having at one time made the history of archery his study, and partly by his having amused himself with forming a collection of ancient and modern weapons connected with the art, which collection he subsequently presented to Sir Ashton Lever's museum. Another noteworthy feature in the habits of this excellent person was the total abstinence from wine which he enjoined on himself, thus setting an example of sobriety to the hard-drinking squires in his neighbourhood, to which his contemporary, Lord Chesterfield, in 'The World,' has paid graceful tribute. " Cantabrigius," writes his lordship, in a paper deprecatory of intemperance, "drinks nothing but water, and rides more miles in a year than the keenest sportsman. The former keeps his head clear; the latter his body in health. It is not from himself that he runs, but to his acquaintance, a synonymous term for his friends. Internally safe, he seeks no sanctuary for himself, no intoxication for his mind. His penetration makes him discover and divert himself with the follies of mankind, which his wit enables him to expose with the truest ridicule, though always without personal offence. Cheerful abroad, because happy at home, and thus happy, because virtuous." The fact that Mr. Cambridge was himself the author of no fewer than twenty-one charming papers in 'The World,' induces, when taken into consideration with Lord Chesterfield's connection with that work, a presumption that from this common association with its pages may have sprung that intimacy between these two accomplished essayists, the existence of which the tenor of the Earl's eulogy seems to imply.

On the death of his uncle Owen, in 1748, Mr. Cambridge, at the age of thirty-one, took a house in London, to which, after a residence there of about two years, he added, as an appanage to it, a villa charmingly situated in the midst of the classical meadows of Twickenham. Here, with Richmond Hill rising in the distance, and the Thames flowing gracefully beneath it, he passed, with the exception of occasional and unimportant intermissions, the remainder of the long and tranquil career which lay before him; still devoting himself to the literary tastes and to the literary labours which had been the delight of his youth. Adopting, as the vehicle of his humour, the famous mock hero of Pope, Swift, and Arbuthnot, he had lately composed, in his retirement at Whitminster, his afterwards celebrated satirical poem, 'The Scribleriad,' which he now (1751) gave to the world. Nor was this the only fruit of his literary labours which he ventured to submit to the judgment of the public. He was also the author of 'A History of the Coromandel War,' as well as of a variety of poems, of the merits of which the following lines, written during the ferment of the great French Revolution of 1789, may, we think, be accepted as a fair specimen :—

"THE PROGRESS OF LIBERTY.

"What progress does Liberty make every week!
How quick from Versailles has she reached Martinique!
And, so soon will her power all th' Indies subdue,
We shall see her dominion extend to Peru;

For now to her standard so great the resort is,
Her conquests she's spreading much quicker than Cortez.
At the rate she goes on, she will soon be possest
Of all hearts that too long have been slaves in the West.
Then eastward she'll bend; 'tis but crossing the ocean;
And she'll put the *poissardes* of Morocco in motion;
Now turning Algiers and the kingdoms piratical
Into popular boroughs and states democratical.
In Egypt a new Constitution and laws
Shall end the contention of Beys and Bashaws.
But how shall we pass by the strict Dardanelle?
How teach such inveterate slaves to rebel?
How impress on the children of Predestination
Those maxims which tend to such strange reformation?
That tyranny turn to a free common weal
To *états-généraux* and a *hôtel-de-ville*?
How make the Visier such a poor renegade,
As to change his three tails for a Christian cockade;
Should Constantinople embrace the idea,
Sure nothing will easier yield than Crimea;
For we know that the mighty Tartarian Cham
Submitted to Russia as meek as a lamb.
Content to resign on the very first notice,
Bag and baggage he sailed o'er the Palus Mæotis.
From the Crim' the divinity lands at Oczakow,
Then, hey! for her favourite veto at Cracow!
If she meet, in her road, hyperborean Kate,
She may chance to persuade that sublime autocrate,
Ere she quits this vain world, to adopt her opinions
And present her to all her extensive dominions.
Now in haste over Sweden and Denmark she wanders
To see how her pupils are acting in Flanders,
From thence to Great Britain she travels with speed,
And, perched on the pillar in famed Runnymead,
She surveys the whole Island, and finds it in awe
Of no power upon earth, but of justice and law;
With no wrongs to redress, and no rights to restore,
She has all she can wish, and she asks for no more."[1]

"Have you"—writes Horace Walpole to the Countess of Ossory, on the 12th of December, 1789[2]—

[1] Chalmers's 'Works of the English Poets,' vol. xviii. p. 298.
[2] 'Letters,' vol. ix. p. 240; ed. 1857.

"Have you seen Mr. Cambridge's excellent verses, called 'The Progress of Liberty'? They were printed last Wednesday in a newspaper called *The Times*, but there ascribed to a young lady. They are as happy a composition, in their way, as 'Bonner's Ghost.'"

From the reign of George II. till late in the reign of George III., Mr. Cambridge's villa at Twickenham became the hospitable rendezvous of the scholar, the statesman, the philosopher, and the wit. Thus, for instance, penned in the days when these classical reunions took place, we are indebted to James Boswell for an account of an interesting party which assembled here in 1775, at which were present, besides Boswell himself, Dr. Johnson, Sir Joshua Reynolds, James Harris, the author of 'Hermes,' and Gibbon, the historian;[1] but it is with Boswell's observations on their host that we have here principally occasion to concern ourselves. "If," he writes, " a beautiful villa on the banks of the Thames, a numerous and excellent library, which he accurately knows and reads, a choice collection of pictures, which he understands and relishes, an easy fortune, an amiable family, an extensive circle of friends and acquaintance, distinguished by rank, fashion, and genius, a literary fame, various, elegant, and still increasing, colloquial talents rarely to be found, and, with all these means of happiness, enjoying, when

[1] Croker's 'Boswell's Life of Johnson,' p. 451, &c.; ed. 1848.

well advanced in years, health and vigour of body, serenity and animation of mind, do not entitle [him] to be addressed *fortunate senex!* I know not to whom, in any age, that expression could with propriety have been used." [1]

Thus gently and gracefully descended this cheerful philosopher and devout Christian into the vale of years. He had at an early period of his life attentively investigated the evidences of the truths of Christianity, and happily the convictions at which he had then arrived continued to afford him comfort to the last. It was not to be expected that he should be exempted from the ailments incidental to old age, but providentially they were recompensed to him by many blessings. " He was considerably advanced in his eighty-third year," writes his son, " before he was sensible, to any considerable degree, of the infirmities of age ; but a difficulty of hearing, which had for some time gradually increased, now rendered conversation troublesome, and frequently disappointing to him. Against this evil, his books, for which his relish was not abated, had hitherto furnished an easy and acceptable resource ; but, unfortunately, his sight also became so imperfect that there were few books he could read with comfort to himself. His general health, however, remained the same, and his natural good spirits and cheerfulness of temper experienced no alteration. Having still the free use of

[1] Croker's 'Boswell's Life of Johnson,' p. 722.

his limbs, he continued to take his usual exercise, and to follow his customary habits of life, accepting of such amusement as conversation would afford from those friends who had the kindness to adapt their voices to his prevailing infirmity; and that he still retained a lively concern in all those great and interesting events which were then taking place in Europe, may be seen in some of his latest productions. But as his deafness increased, he felt himself grow daily more unfit for the society of any but his own family, into whose care and protection he resigned himself with the most affectionate and endearing confidence, receiving their attentions, which it was the first pleasure of his children to pay him, not as a debt due to a fond and indulgent parent, but as a free and voluntary tribute of their affection. In the contemplation of these tokens of esteem and love, he seemed to experience a constant and unabating pleasure, which supplied, in no small degree, the want of other interesting ideas."

Patient, uncomplaining, and tenderly considerate of those around him, succumbing rather to the gradations of a gentle decay than to any dominant malady, Richard Owen Cambridge expired, without a sigh, at his favourite villa, on the 17th of September, 1802, in his eighty-sixth year. His widow, by whom he left two sons and one daughter, survived him less than four years; dying on the 5th of September, 1806.

DR. EDWARD BARNARD,
HEAD MASTER AND PROVOST OF ETON.

"That gifted creature, Barnard, Provost of Eton," as Judge Hardinge designates him, was the son of a clergyman of the Church of England, of whom little more seems to be known than that he resided at Luton, in Bedfordshire, of which place he was Vicar. His son, Edward, was born in March, 1717. He was educated on the foundation at Eton, but, having been inhibited from King's College by superannuation, entered at St. John's College, Cambridge, of which society he in time became a fellow. "I never," writes Judge Hardinge, "could learn that he was there considered as a deep scholar in Philosophy, in Divinity, or even in Classics; but I have understood that he was, in the early part of his life, admired for eloquence, for wit, for spirit, and for that kind of genius whose acute perceptions, taste, and sense catch, half intuitively, the essence of learning, without labour in the pursuit. His wit made him formidable to the dull; and like other wits, he felt himself privileged, at the expense of

Lord Chesterfield's rules, to dart his lightning upon the culprit." [1]

"A merrier man,
Within the limit of becoming mirth,
I never spent an hour's talk withal:
His eye begets occasion for his wit;
For every object that the one doth catch
The other turns to a mirth-moving jest,
Which his fair tongue, conceit's expositor,
Delivers in such apt and gracious words
That aged ears play truant at his tales
And younger hearings are quite ravished;
So sweet and voluble is his discourse." [2]

In 1738, Edward Barnard took his degree as B.A.; in 1742, as M.A.; and, in 1750, as B.D. It would seem to have been about the year 1747 that he became private tutor at Eton to the two sons of the Hon. Thomas Townshend, an accomplished scholar, who, in as many as six Parliaments, represented the University of Cambridge in the House of Commons, and whose eldest son was, in 1783, created Baron, and, in 1789, Viscount Sydney. Of the two boys, Barnard's favourite would seem to have been the younger, Henry, a youth of the highest promise and of heroic courage, who became a Lieutenant-Colonel in the first Regiment of Foot Guards, and who, in 1762, fell, beloved and lamented by the whole army, at the battle of Wilhelmstadt, in Germany. Subsequently, at the instigation of Mr. Townshend, Barnard was induced to take charge of a third pupil, George

[1] Nichols's 'Lit. Anecdotes,' vol. viii. p. 543.
[2] 'Love's Labour Lost,' act ii. scene 1.

Hardinge, the future Judge, to whose communications to Nichols we have been from time to time so much indebted for valuable information relating to Eton men. "In 1752," writes the Judge, "I found him at Eton, and at the same house in which I was to board; so that," he adds, "I had an early access to his wonderful talents and powers. He was like Shakespeare's Yorick, a little more disciplined, and guarded by a controlling spirit, which kept all resentment as well as reply at bay. He discovered with sagacity, in those around him, themes of ridicule which he never spared; but admired, without envy, talents or virtues. It has often at this late period astonished me, that in that limited sphere he could have displayed such a dignity of manner, and such effect of character, as to govern every scene connected with him, notwithstanding this playful turn for a joke, and this talent for *making fun*, as we used to call it, even of those whom he admired and loved. I have seen him very often make some of these personages *laugh at themselves* in his presence, led on by him. He was at the same time friendly, compassionate, and humane."[1]

It could scarcely have been much more than two years after young Hardinge had become his pupil that Barnard, on the resignation of Dr. Sumner, in 1754, succeeded, after a warm contest, in carrying off the Head Mastership of Eton from a formidable

[1] Nichols's 'Lit. Anecdotes,' vol. viii. p. 544.

antagonist, Thomas Dampier, then Lower Master, and afterwards Dean of Durham. Moreover, other advantages and distinctions followed this advancement. In 1756, the degree of D.D. was conferred upon him; about the same time he was presented to the Rectory of St. Paul's Cray, in Kent; in 1760, he was appointed a Canon of Windsor; and, lastly, George III., " struck " with his character and abilities, not only made him one of his chaplains, but is said to have at one time had it in contemplation to appoint him Preceptor to the Heir apparent, afterwards George IV.

Dr. Barnard had presided no long time as Head Master of Eton before the improved condition and prosperity of the school began to bear satisfactory testimony to the tact, firmness, and other qualifications which he possessed for the post. The eulogium, indeed, in his epitaph in the chapel of Eton College, " *Scholæ Etonensis disciplinam et famam per annos undecim auxit et stabilivit*"—does no more than justice to the obligations which he conferred on Eton. From three hundred, which was the average number of boys before his time, he increased the number to upwards of five hundred. " Dr. Barnard," writes his old schoolfellow, Horace Walpole, in 1762, " is the Pitt of Masters, and has raised the school to the most flourishing state it ever knew."[1] He introduced into the machinery of the school a new spirit and a

[1] 'Letters,' vol. iv. p. 32.

purer classical taste. His manner was dignified
and imposing; his talent for command pre-eminent.
His voice and delivery, though naturally musical and
soft, could, if necessary, be raised to a "sort of
mock thunder." Popular, moreover, as he was
with his pupils, he knew as well how to make
himself feared as how to make himself loved. His
little occasional episodical discources from his *rostrum*
are said to have been masterpieces of eloquence,
taste, and feeling. "When," writes Judge Hardinge,
"he gave out a subject for prose or verse, to hear
him was a feast." Of the impressively dramatic
effect produced at times by these expositions, an
interesting example is recorded by his old pupil, the
Judge. "We had lost," he writes, "one of our
schoolfellows, an only son, the heir to an opulent
estate—a youth admired and beloved—at the age of
thirteen or fourteen. He was drowned. Barnard,
just after this event, came to us in school. He was
in tears for half an hour; heard us construe without
listening; broke off abruptly, and was going to part
with us, when, recollecting that he was to give a
subject—with a forcible action, the impulse of the
moment, which Garrick never surpassed—he said, as
if looking at the watery bier—

'His saltem accumulem donis'—

burst from us, and said no more. It made us understand that our subject was a monody on this youth."[1]

[1] Nichols's 'Lit. Anecdotes,' vol. viii. p. 546.

"Heu miserande puer! si qua fata aspera rumpas,
Tu Marcellus eris. Manibus date lilia plenis:
Purpureos spargam flores, animamque nepotis
His saltem accumulem donis, et fungar inani
Munere."—*Æneid*, Lib. vi. 882-886.

Another prominent feature in the system of this accomplished disciplinarian was an antagonism to all kinds of foppery and dandyism on the part of his scholars; an antagonism afterwards rendered famous by one of his old pupils, Christopher Anstey, in his inimitable 'New Bath Guide,' in a passage in which Mrs. Danglecub is made to express her surprise—

" That parents to Eton should send
Five hundred great boobies their manners to mend,
When the master that's left it[1]—though no one objects
To his care of the boys in all other respects—
Was extremely remiss, for a sensible man,
In never contriving some elegant plan
For improving their persons, and showing them how
To hold up their heads, and to make a good bow;
When they've got such a charming long room for a ball,
Where the scholars might practise, and masters and all;
But, what is much worse—what no parent would chuse—
He burnt all their ruffles, and cut off their queues;
So he quitted the school in the utmost disgrace,
And just such another 's[2] come into his place."

On the 25th of October, 1765, Dr. Barnard was elected to succeed Dr. Stephen Sleech—a name but little known to fame—in the Provostship of Eton. He was now, in addition to other causes for congratulation, enabled to indulge to the full, and without any longer jeopardizing his dignity in the

[1] Dr. Barnard.
[2] Dr. John Foster, Dr. Barnard's successor as Head Master.

eyes of his pupils, that love of fun, anecdote, and repartee, which lent its chief charm to his delightful conversational powers. "As Provost," writes Judge Hardinge, "I was often his guest;" and he adds— "In powers of conversation, whether tête-à-tête or in a mixed company, I never yet knew his equal."[1]

Of Dr. Barnard's married life we unfortunately know but little. "He married," continues Judge Hardinge, "a charming young woman, but of too delicate a constitution. He lost her very soon. By her he had a son, who is [1814] in Orders, an excellent and clever man." We meet also with traces of the existence of a sister, who, after the death of his wife, would seem to have presided at times, if not habitually, at the head of her brother's table. Judge Hardinge describes her as having been as hard-featured as the Provost himself, but "remarkably sensible and pleasing."[2]

Dr. Barnard died on the 2nd of December, 1781, aged sixty-four years and nine months. The monument to his memory in Eton College Chapel was erected by his only son; the Latin inscription upon it not being rendered the less interesting from the fact of its having been the composition of Jacob Bryant, who, it may be remembered, had, in their boyish days, rescued his schoolfellow, the late Provost, from a watery grave.

[1] Nichols's 'Lit. Anecdotes,' vol. viii. pp. 547, 549.
[2] Ibid., vol. viii. p. 549.

HORACE WALPOLE, EARL OF ORFORD.

"I WAS born," writes Horace Walpole, "in Arlington Street, near St. James's, London, September 24th, 1717, O.S. My godfathers were Charles Fitzroy, Duke of Grafton, and my uncle Horatio Walpole; my godmother, my aunt Dorothy, Lady Viscountess Townshend."[1] Horace Walpole, the "Prince of epistolary writers," as he has been happily styled, was the third and youngest son of Sir Robert Walpole, who, for nearly a quarter of a century, dispensed the patronage of Church and State in this country, as one of the most powerful Prime Ministers who had ever guided her councils. In the dispensation of that patronage, Sir Robert's sons, and Horace in particular, were certainly not overlooked. As regards Horace, indeed, his lack of fortune as a younger brother was pretty liberally made up for before he was twenty-one, in the shape of Government sinecures. "Soon after," he writes, referring to the month of August, 1737, "my father

[1] 'Short Notes of My Life;' Walpole's 'Letters,' vol. i. p. lxi.; ed. 1857.

gave me the place of Inspector of the Imports and Exports in the Custom House, which I resigned on his appointing me Usher of the Exchequer, in the room of Colonel William Townshend, January 29th, 1738; and as soon as I came of age, I took possession of two other little patent places in the Exchequer, called Comptroller of the Pipe and Clerk of the Estreats."[1] And again Horace writes, "My father died March 28th, 1745; he left me the house in Arlington Street in which he died; 5000*l.* in money, and 1000*l.* a year from the collector's place in the Custom House, and the surplus to be divided between my brother and me."[2] Altogether he seems to have been in the enjoyment of no fewer than five sinecure offices, the combined salaries of which amounted, according to his own showing, to 3900*l.* a year; according to the calculations of the Commissioners of Inquiry, to 6300*l.*, and, in the round estimate of his biographers, to 5000*l.* a year.

The mother of Horace Walpole—a woman of great beauty—was Catherine, daughter of Sir John Shorter, to whose fortune it fell to fill the post of Lord Mayor of London at the memorable epoch of the Revolution of 1688. He was also the father of another daughter, Charlotte, married to Francis Lord Conway, by whom she became the mother of Francis, first Marquis of Hertford, and of Field Marshal Henry Conway.

[1] 'Short Notes of My Life;' Walpole's 'Letters,' vol. i. p. lxii.
[2] Ibid., vol. i. p. lxiv.

A favourable trait in Horace Walpole's nature, as also in that of his friend and schoolfellow, Gray, was the warm devotion which he felt for his mother; a devotion which, in spite of the prevalence of certain painful rumours to the detriment of her fair fame, continued apparently unimpaired till she was no more. The fact is, that according to the fashionable scandal of the last century, Horace Walpole, instead of being the son of Sir Robert, owed his birth to Carr, Lord Hervey, eldest son of the first Earl of Bristol, and brother of John Lord Hervey, whose affectations and personal infirmities are so unenviably perpetuated in Pope's notorious satire. Neither were there wanting circumstances to cast a colour of probability over the imputation. Not only, for instance, is Sir Robert said to have treated his youngest son with marked neglect; not only have we the candid admission of the latter in one of his early letters that his father had hitherto manifested "no partiality" for him, but we have also the significant facts, that while Horace bore, on the one hand, no resemblance, either in mind or body, to the great Minister, he was, on the contrary, distinguished by the delicate appearance and effeminate tastes which characterized a preceding generation of the Herveys.

"Sir Robert," writes Lord Wharncliffe, "scarcely took any notice of him till his proficiency in Eton School, when a lad of some standing, drew his attention, and proved that, whether he had or had not a right to the name he went by, he was likely to do it honour."

Of a constitution so delicate as to require the tenderest nurture—petted and caressed, moreover, as the son of a powerful Prime Minister and of a beautiful woman of fashion—we need scarcely be surprised if we find the subject of this memoir not only becoming the spoiled child of the nursery and the schoolroom, but in some measure remaining a spoiled child in his riper years. That the person most to be blamed for the over-indulgence from which this defect sprang was no other than Lady Walpole herself, may be inferred from the readiness with which we find her exerting herself to gratify so idle a whim on the part of her idolized child, as that of being presented, when scarcely out of the nursery, to Majesty, in the person of King George 1. "This childish caprice," writes Walpole, "was so strong, that my mother solicited the Duchess of Kendal to obtain for me the honour of kissing his Majesty's hand before he set out for Hanover. A favour so unusual to be asked for a boy of ten years old, was still too slight to be refused to the wife of the first Minister for her darling child; yet not being proper to be made a precedent, it was settled to be in private, and at night." Accordingly, on the night of the accorded introduction, the child was committed by its mother to the care of Melusina de Schulemberg, Countess of Walsingham, the alleged niece, but putative daughter of the Duchess of Kendal by George I., who occupied apartments on the garden-floor of St. James's Palace, communicating with those of her aunt, the Duchess, with whom the King had engaged himself to sup. Thus installed, so as to be forthcoming at a moment's summons, the child, on its being announced that his Majesty had descended to supper, was led by Lady Walsingham into the Duchess's ante-chamber, where she and the King were alone together. The figure of the latter when, nearly sixty years afterwards, Walpole recalled it to his memory, was still as distinctly visible to him as if he had seen it but yesterday. " It was that of an elderly man," he said, " rather pale, and exactly like his pictures and coins ; not tall ; of aspect rather good than august ; with a dark tie-wig, a plain coat, waistcoat, and breeches of snuff-coloured cloth, with stockings of the same colour, and blue ribbon over all. So entirely was he my object, that I do not believe I once looked at the Duchess, but as I could not avoid seeing her on entering the room, I remember that just beyond his Majesty stood a very tall, lean, ill-favoured old lady ; but I did not retain the least idea of her features, nor know what the colour of her dress was." Having knelt and kissed the King's hand, his Majesty took him in his arms and addressed a few words to him, after which the child was led back by his conductress to her own apartment.[1]

[1] From Walpole we learn that the interview took place on the night

Young as Walpole was at this time—for he had not completed his tenth year—he had nevertheless been for some time established at Eton. "April 26th, 1727," he writes, "I went to Eton School."[1] To Eton, accordingly, he was carried back after his presentation to Majesty; where, a few days afterwards his ear was startled as it caught the voice of the herald proclaiming the death of the aged monarch in whose arms he had so recently been held, and by whose sudden death, therefore, it was only natural that the child should have been sensibly affected; so affected, indeed, as to shed a flood of tears. Many of the spectators, he adds, doubtless attributed them to apprehensions of his father's anticipated downfall from power, but for this surmise, he assures us, they had not the slightest foundation.[2]

It was doubtless in a great measure owing to the delicacy of Walpole's constitution that, to the last day of his Eton career, we find him taking little or no interest in cricket, boating, or in any of the manly diversions which, to the vast majority of his schoolfellows, constituted their chief source of enjoyment. "I cannot say," he writes to George Montagu in May, 1736, "I am sorry I was never quite a schoolboy. An expedition against bargemen, or a match

---

but one before the King began his last journey to Hanover. George I. sailed from England on the 3rd of June, 1727, and expired on the road to Hanover on the 11th of that month.

[1] 'Short Notes of My Life;' 'Letters,' ut supra, vol. i. p. lxi.
[2] Walpole's 'Reminiscences;' 'Letters,' ut supra, vol. i. pp. xciii. xciv.

at cricket, may be very pretty things to recollect, but, thank my stars, I can remember things that are very near as pretty."[1] He alludes probably to that reciprocity of literary tastes, and that intellectual appreciation of each other's society, which, as we have already intimated, threw a grace over the schoolboy alliance of Walpole, Ashton, West, and Gray. Nor, in recording the names of these four friends, must we omit to couple with them others, such as Walpole's two cousins, the Marquis of Hertford, then Lord Conway, and his brother Henry Conway, Cole, George Selwyn, and George Montagu, one and all of whom survived to be his correspondents in later years. Of these, Montagu—a son of Brigadier-General Edward Montagu, and a near relation of the Montagus, Earls of Halifax—happened at this time to have a brother at Eton who composed, with Walpole and George Montagu, a fraternity which they designated "The Triumvirate," and of which Walpole, in one of his letters written shortly after having quitted Eton, makes affectionate mention. "One of the most agreeable circumstances I can recollect," writes Walpole to George Montagu, "is the Triumvirate, composed of yourself, Charles, and your sincere friend."[2] George Montagu died on the 10th of May, 1780, after having for a long period sat in Parliament as member for Northampton, and also long after the unsatisfactory termination of a

[1] Walpole's 'Letters,' *ut supra*, vol. i. p. 5. [2] Ibid.

friendship which, in more propitious days, had drawn from Walpole many of the most delightful of his memorable letters. "I should have been exceedingly concerned for him a few years ago," writes Walpole on the day after his old correspondent's death, "but he had dropped me, partly from politics and partly from caprice, for we never had any quarrel; but he was grown an excessive humorist, and had shed almost all his friends as well as me. He had parts, and infinite vivacity and originality till of late years, and it grieved me much that he had changed towards me, after a friendship of between thirty and forty years."[1] George Montagu had, besides Charles, two other brothers, Edward and John, of whom the former was killed at the Battle of Fontenoy, and the latter served in the Navy. According to a Quarterly Reviewer of fifty years since—"Of Mr. [George] Montagu it is only remembered that he was a gentleman-like body of the *vieille cour*, and that he was usually attended by his brother John—the Little John of Walpole's correspondence—who was a midshipman at the age of sixty, and found his chief occupation in carrying about his brother's snuff-box."[2] "Some of his [Walpole's] friends," writes Judge Hardinge, "were as effeminate in appearance and in manner as himself, and were as witty. Of these I remember two, Mr. Chute and Mr. George

---

[1] Walpole's 'Letters,' *ut supra*, vol. vii. p. 363.
[2] 'Quarterly Review' for April, 1818, p. 131.

Montagu. But others had effeminacy alone to recommend them."[1]

Having, on the 23rd of September, 1734, quitted Eton, Walpole, in March, 1735, established himself at King's College, Cambridge, where he had entered himself a Gentleman Commoner. Of his principal studies while at Cambridge he has given us a short account with his own pen. "I went," he writes, "to lectures in civil law to Dr. Dickens of Trinity Hall; to mathematical lectures, to blind Professor Saunderson, for a short time; afterwards, Mr. Trevigar read lectures to me in mathematics and philosophy. I heard Dr. Battie's anatomical lectures. I had learned French at Eton. I learnt Italian at Cambridge of Signor Piazza. At home I learned to dance and fence; and to draw of Bernard Lens, master to the Duke [of Cumberland] and Princesses."[2] With the exception of having been the author of a copy of Latin verses on the marriage of Frederick, Prince of Wales, which appeared in print in 1736, Walpole would seem to have passed through the University without aiming at high academical distinction, and finally quitted it in 1739, after long intermissions of absence from his studies, without having taken a degree. In the mean time, though, so long ago as the 27th of May, 1731, Walpole had entered himself at Lincoln's Inn, there seems to be

[1] Nichols's 'Lit. Anecdotes of the 18th Century,' vol. viii. p. 526.
[2] 'Short Notes of My Life;' 'Letters,' ut supra, vol. i. p. lxii.

no evidence of his having at any time either lodged or studied law within its walls.

A deeply-felt sorrow, which, as may here be mentioned, had not long since befallen Walpole, was the death, on the 20th of August, 1737, of the mother whom he loved so well, and by whom his love would seem to have been as tenderly reciprocated. Among the sepulchral effigies in the south aisle of Henry VIIth's Chapel at Westminster, not the least striking is a marble statue—copied in Rome from the famous figure of " Modesty "—and piously erected here to the memory of Lady Walpole by her favourite son.

It was in the spring of 1739 that Walpole and Gray proceeded on their notable tour over France and Italy, bearing and forbearing for a while in their daily intercourse with each other, but eventually falling out and parting company, in April, 1741, at Reggio.[1] Here, then, it was that, after Gray's abrupt departure, Walpole had the misfortune to be attacked by a " kind of quinzy " of so violent a character that, but for the accidental and timely arrival at Reggio of the young Earl of Lincoln with his tutor, the Rev. Joseph Spence, famous as the friend of Pope and as the author of ' Polymetis ' and ' Anecdotes of Books and Men,' the result might have been fatal. For five hours those who tended him despaired of his life. "About three or four in the morning," writes Spence, "I

[1] See *ante*, memoir of Gray.

was surprised with a message, saying that Mr. Walpole was very much worse, and desired to see me. I went, and found him scarce able to speak. I soon learned from the servants that he had been all the while without a physician, and had doctored himself; so I immediately sent for the best aid the place would afford, and despatched a messenger to the Minister at Florence, desiring him to send my friend, Dr. Cocchi. In about twenty-four hours I had the satisfaction to find Mr. Walpole better. We left him in a fair way of recovery, and we hope to see him next week at Venice." "If Lord Lincoln," adds Mr. Spence, "had not wandered to Reggio, Mr. Walpole—who is one of the best natured and most sensible young gentlemen England affords—would have, in all probability, fallen a sacrifice to his disorder."[1]

Walpole, on his return to England in the month of September, 1741, had the satisfaction of finding his position in society and circumstances in life in every respect as desirable as his most sanguine hopes had any right to anticipate. His father was still Prime Minister; he himself had recently been chosen to represent Callington in Parliament; his income was amply sufficient to meet all the wants and luxuries of a young man of family and fashion; the superiority of his natural parts was disputed by none who knew him; and, lastly, he was called away by

[1] 'Short Notes of My Life;' 'Letters,' *ut supra*, vol. i. pp. lxiii. 64.

few or no official duties from the enjoyment of the life of lettered ease which he loved to lead, or from furnishing such contributions to literature and the Muses as he chose to consider not incompatible with his further vocation of a fine gentleman.

Walpole spoke but very rarely in Parliament, and only on one occasion with any effect; that occasion occurring on the 23rd of March, 1742, on the motion for the appointment of a secret committee to inquire into the conduct of Sir Robert Walpole, whom he defended with a warmth and ability which elicited a felicitous compliment from no less competent a judge of oratory than Mr. Pitt. The young member, he admitted, had made a favourable impression on the House; but "if," he added, "it was commendable in him to remember that he was the child of the accused, the House ought to remember, too, that they were the children of their country."[1] Walpole, we may here mention, sat in Parliament successively as member for Callington, Castle Rising, and L ynn, for a period of no fewer than twenty-seven years, finally retiring from the House of Commons at the general election of 1768. The loss of his senatorial position seems to have caused him but little regret. "The comfort," he writes from Arlington Street, on the 12th of March in this year, "I feel in sitting peaceably here, instead of being at Lynn, in the high fever of a contested election, which, at best,

[1] 'Letters,' *ut supra*, vol. i. p. 148.

would end in my being carried about that large town like a figure of a Pope at a bonfire, is very great. I do not think, when that function is over, that I shall repent my resolution. What could I see but sons and grandsons playing over the same knaveries that I have seen their fathers and grandfathers act? Could I hear oratory beyond my Lord Chatham's; will there ever be parts equal to Charles Townshend's?"[1]

In the mean time, in the month of February, 1742, Sir Robert Walpole had been driven from power; on the 9th of that month he was created Earl of Orford; and on the 18th of March, 1745, he died. He was succeeded in the earldom by Horace's elder brother, Robert, who had been created Baron Walpole in his father's lifetime.

In the year 1747, Walpole took it into his head to hire, and the following year, to purchase, of a Mrs. Chevenix, the proprietress of a fashionable London toy-shop, a small villa situated in the picturesque outskirts of the classical village of Twickenham, about a quarter of a mile from Pope's famous villa and immemorial grotto. Everything about his new residence but its uneuphonious name, which happened to be " Chopped Straw Hall," appears to have charmed him, and accordingly when, some time afterwards, he discovered in an old deed that it had formerly gone under the name of Strawberry

[1] 'Letters,' *ut supra*, vol. v. p. 90.

Hill, he was only too well pleased to restore to it its ancient and more harmonious appellation. From this inconsiderable beginning, then, it was that, by means of much enlarging and gothicizing, there arose that familiar castellated pile, and here was formed that heterogeneous collection of archæological relics and choice articles of *virtu*, with which, from this time, we find the tastes and pursuits of Walpole so closely and constantly associated. Of his new dwelling, Walpole writes to Sir Horace Mann, on the 5th of June, 1747 : " The house is so small that I can send it you in a letter to look at. The prospect is as delightful as possible, commanding the river, the town, and Richmond Park; and, being situated on a hill, descends to the Thames through two or three little meadows, where I have some Turkish sheep and two cows, all studied in their colour for becoming the view." And again, three days afterwards, Walpole writes to his cousin, Henry Conway, from Strawberry Hill itself : " It is a little plaything-house that I got out of Mrs. Chevenix's shop, and is the prettiest bauble you ever saw. It is set in enamelled meadows, with filigree hedges :—

'A small Euphrates through the piece is roll'd,
And little finches wave their wings in gold.'[1]

Two delightful roads, that you would call dusty,

[1] " And little *eagles* wave their wings in gold."—
Pope to Addison, occasioned by his Dialogues on Medals.

supply me continually with coaches and chaises; barges, as solemn as Barons of the Exchequer, move under my window; Richmond Hill and Ham Walks bound my prospect; but, thank God! the Thames is between me and the Duchess of Queensberry.[1] Dowagers, as plenty as flounders, inhabit all around, and Pope's ghost is just now skimming under my window by a most poetical moonlight."[2]

Walpole's memorable art collection—his historic pictures, his marbles, his rare books, his priceless engravings, his mediæval armour, his unique gems and enamels—have long since been dispersed far and wide; yet, happily, his fantastic villa still remains to regale us with a thousand memories of the beaux and beauties of former days, as well as to remind us of a remarkable man, who, though his writings may not have greatly tended to improve the moral condition of mankind, has nevertheless bequeathed to posterity an exhaustless mine of sparkling wit and harmless intellectual enjoyment.

Walpole was still engaged in enlarging and gothi-

---

[1] Katherine Hyde, Duchess of Queensberry—the lovely "Kitty" of Prior's muse, as well as rendered celebrated by the verse of Pope and Gay—resided at this period in a small house in Ham Walks. Walpole, having one day called upon her, and found that she was out airing in her carriage, addressed to her the following not very ingenious lines:

"To many a Kitty, Love his car
Would for a day engage;
But Prior's Kitty, ever fair,
Retains it for an age."

[2] Walpole's 'Letters,' *ut supra*, vol. ii. pp. 85, 86.

cizing his new purchase, when an adventure befell him which, but for the merciful dispensation of Providence, might have cut short at once his occupation and his life. He was returning to London through Hyde Park from Holland House, about ten o'clock on a moonlight night in the month of November, 1749, when, as related by Walpole himself, his chariot was stopped by two armed desperadoes, one of whom, it appears, was the then celebrated and "fashionable" highwayman, McLean, immortalized by Gray in his "Long Story."[1] "The pistol of one of them," he writes, "going off accidentally, grazed the skin under my eye, left some marks of shot on my face, and stunned me. The ball went through the top of the chariot, and if I had sat an inch nearer to the left side, must have gone through my head."[2] Yet, writes Walpole, the whole affair was conducted with "the greatest good breeding on both sides."[3]

The career of McLean was, for a person of his class, a remarkable one. So lively, for instance, was the interest taken in him by the fair sex, that when apprehended and condemned to death the following year, not only did women of fashion visit and sympathize with him in his condemned cell, but, according to Soame Jenyns, "some of the brightest eyes" shed

[1] "A sudden fit of ague shook him;
He stood as mute as poor McLean."

[2] 'Short Notes of My Life;' 'Letters,' *ut supra*, vol. i. p. lxii.
[3] 'The World,' No. 103, of 19th December, 1754.

tears for him.[1] "His father," writes Walpole, "was an Irish dean; his brother is a Calvinist minister in great esteem at the Hague. He himself was a grocer [in Welbeck Street], but losing a wife that he loved extremely about two years ago, and by whom he has one little girl, he quitted his business with two hundred pounds in his pocket, which he soon spent, and then took to the road with only one companion, Plunket, a journeyman apothecary, my other friend, whom he has impeached, but who is not taken. McLean had a lodging in St. James's Street, over against White's, and another at Chelsea; Plunket one in Jermyn Street; and their faces are as known about St. James's as any gentleman who lives in that quarter, and who perhaps goes upon the road too. McLean had a quarrel at Putney bowling-green two months ago with an officer, whom he challenged for disputing his rank; but the captain declined, till McLean should produce a certificate of his nobility, which he has just received." "As I conclude he will suffer, and I wish him no ill," continues Walpole, "I don't care to have his idea, and am almost single in not having been to see him. Lord Mountford,

---

[1] Note to 'The Modern Fine Lady,' a Poem:
   "She weeps if but a handsome thief is hung."
"The chief personages," writes Walpole, "who have been to comfort and weep over this fallen hero are Lady Caroline Petersham and Miss Ashe; I call them Polly and Lucy, and asked them if he did not sing:
   'Thus I stand like the Turk with his doxies around.'"
Walpole's 'Letters,' ut supra, vol. ii. p. 219, and note.

at the head of half White's, went the first day: his aunt was crying over him : as soon as they were withdrawn, she said to him, knowing they were of White's—' My dear, what did the Lord say to you?—have you ever been concerned with any of them ? ' Was not it admirable ? What a favourable idea people must have of White's! And what if White's should not deserve a much better ?"

Of Walpole as an author, or more especially, we should have said, of Walpole as a poet, we may content ourselves with observing that his verses are, generally speaking, of a sufficiently light and ephemeral character to preclude criticism ; of his better-known, however, and more ambitious writings, his first prose work, the ' Odes Walpolianæ,' published in 1752, furnishes us with a graphic description of his father's stately mansion, Houghton Hall, in Norfolk, and of its noble collection of pictures, afterwards purchased of the third Earl of Orford by the Empress Catherine of Russia. In 1757, Walpole set up his private printing-press at Strawberry Hill, the first-fruits of which were an impression of Gray's odes, with prints and vignettes by Bentley. The following year he published his ' Catalogue of Royal and Noble Authors ; ' in 1761 appeared the 'first volume of his ' Anecdotes of Painting in England,' and, in 1763, his ' Catalogue of Engravers.' He next produced, in 1764, his famous fiction ' The Castle of Otranto ; ' in 1768, he privately printed his powerful but harrowing tragedy, 'The Mysterious Mother,' and, the same year, published his ingenious 'Historic Doubts on the Life and Reign of King Richard III.' Lastly, we should mention, that the publication of two other of his more important works—his 'Memoirs of the Reign of King George II.,' and his 'Memoirs of the Reign of King George III.,' as well as of his "incomparable" 'Letters,' were delayed till after his decease.

"It is the fashion," writes Lord Byron, "to underrate Horace Walpole; firstly, because he was a nobleman, and secondly, because he was a gentleman; but, to say nothing of the composition of his incomparable 'Letters' and of the 'Castle of Otranto,' he is the 'Ultimus Romanorum,' the author of the 'Mysterious Mother,' a tragedy of the highest order, and not a puling love-play. He is the father of the first romance and of the last tragedy in our language, and surely worthy of a higher place than any living writer, be he who he may."[1] Yet Walpole himself, by some strange perversion, was either unable, or affected to be unable, to discover the merit of productions which, as he must have been well aware, had afforded delight to thousands. "I do not," he said, " look upon myself as an author. I may say, without the vain affectation of modesty, that I have done nothing. My 'Catalogue of Royal and Noble

[1] Preface to 'Marino Faliero;' Byron's 'Works,' vol. xii. p. 62; ed. 1833.

Authors' almost any bookseller could have drawn up. My chief compilation, the 'Anecdotes of Painting in England,' is Mr. Vertue's work, not mine."[1] That Walpole, indeed, may have rated at their just value the moderate amount of learning and philosophy which are displayed in his works may not be at all improbable; but, on the other hand, that he really thought meanly of his own unquestionable abilities and delightful style, we cannot for a moment conceive. For instance, while professing to underestimate his 'Anecdotes of Painting in England,' no one knew better than Walpole himself that the work was indebted for its chief charm, not to Vertue's MSS. from which it was compiled, but to his own grace of style, to the fund of agreeable information which he had amassed, and to his own graphic delineations of character. The fact is, that a dread lest his reputation as a fine gentleman should become confounded with, and should suffer by its association with that of an author by profession, seems not only to have perpetually haunted his mind, but to have involved him in many inconsistencies. No man, for instance, valued literature more, or was apparently more ambitious of achieving literary celebrity, yet a contempt for authors and authorship everywhere creeps out in his writings. No man, again, could profess profounder indifference to hostile criticism, yet probably few men have ever suffered more keenly

[1] 'Walpoliana,' p. 162.

from the stings of vulgar critics whom he affected to despise. Again, careless of results as he would have desired to be thought, the fate even of his most insignificant fugitive pieces was watched by him, after they had quitted his hands, with an interest which he was but ill able to conceal. Lastly, while professing to devote himself to a careless existence of fashion and pleasure, he was in fact passing laborious hours in endeavouring to achieve that very literary reputation which he affected so much to contemn. "Pray, my dear child," he writes to Sir Horace Mann, in his happiest style, "don't compliment me any more upon my learning; there is nobody so superficial. Except a little history, a little poetry, a little painting, and some divinity, I know nothing. How should I? I who have always lived in the big busy world; who lie a-bed all the morning, calling it morning as long as you please; who sup in company; who have played at pharaoh half my life, and now at loo till two or three in the morning; who have always loved pleasure; haunted auctions—in short, who don't know so much astronomy as would carry me to Knightsbridge, nor more physic than a physician, nor in short anything that is called science. If it were not that I lay up a little provision in summer, like the ant, I should be as ignorant as all the people I live with. How I have laughed, when some of the magazines have called me the *learned gentleman!* Pray don't be like the magazines."[1]

[1] Walpole's 'Letters,' *ut supra*, vol. iii. p. 288.

Nor was it in his literary capacity only that Walpole's contradictions of character manifested themselves. Inconsistency was, in fact, one of its leading features. Thus, though one of the largest sinecure-holders in England, we find him avowing himself a financial reformer. Again, fragile as was his lath-and-plaster villa at Twickenham—of which it was facetiously said that he had survived three sets of battlements—we find him entailing it on his heirs with as much mindfulness to perpetuity as if it had been Alnwick or Warwick Castle. No one could affect a profounder contempt for royal personages, yet no one seemingly took a greater pleasure in chronicling the trifling doings of kings, or in dividing his winnings at a loo-table with princesses. "The Duke of Gloucester," writes Gilly Williams to George Selwyn, "has professed a passion for the Dowager Waldegrave [Walpole's niece] : he is never from her elbow ; this flatters Horry Walpole not a little, though he pretends to dislike it."[1] Again, though, even in his dealings with Art, Walpole could be penurious almost to meanness, he could on other occasions be liberal even to magnificence. Three times, for example, twice in the instance of Marshal Conway, and once in the instance of Madame du Deffand, he not only offered to share his fortune with his friends in their hour of exigency, but pressed it upon them with a warmth and earnestness which

[1] 'Selwyn Correspondence,' vol. i. p. 334.

it seems difficult to misinterpret into mere hyperbole. Lastly—though so advanced a Whig as to write *Major Charta* on a fac-simile of the death-warrant of Charles I., and to hang it up in his bed-chamber—the French Revolution no sooner threatened to extend its levelling principles to England, than the fine-weather Republican betrayed as much consternation as might have been expected in an ordinary alarmist.

Walpole's caprices, and they were many, may or may not have made him enemies, but at all events they lost him many friends. He quarrelled, not only with Gray and George Montagu, but with Ashton, Mason, and, lastly, with an amiable friend of later years, Judge Hardinge. On Montagu, indeed, we have seen Walpole laying the blame of their rupture, but then Montagu's version of the affair, it must be remembered, still remains undivulged. He, Walpole, was harsh and ungracious at times to his blind old friend, Madame du Deffand, who idolized him; he was severe to another friend, Bentley, to whose taste and talents he was so much indebted in the construction and adornment of Strawberry Hill; and, lastly, Muntz, the clever Swiss painter, whom he maintained on a paltry salary at Strawberry Hill, Walpole, as he himself tells us, unceremoniously "turned out of doors."[1] Though not exactly embracing a case in point, these instances of harshness recall naturally to our memories Walpole's much-

[1] Walpole's 'Letters,' *ut supra*, vol. iii. p. 266.

impugned conduct towards the unhappy poet, Chatterton; but happily, on this point, censure must be admitted to have fallen far more heavily on him than he deserved. In the dispassionate judgment, indeed, of Sir Walter Scott, Walpole's treatment of the "marvellous boy" was "perfectly defensible,"[1] and in Sir Walter's judgment we are inclined to concur.

In strong contrast to the more frivolous and capricious features of Walpole's character, stood out the political sagacity and foresight which we frequently find doing credit both to his heart and head. He generously and strenuously resisted the indefensible and merciless execution of Admiral Byng; in the very infancy of George Grenville's fatal measure for taxing the American Colonies he foresaw and foretold those national disasters and disgraces of which so few others had the wisdom to see that it was the prelude; and lastly, to his infinite honour be it recorded, he was one of the earliest and most indignant denouncers of the system and horrors of the detestable African slave trade. "We have been sitting," he writes, while still a member of the House of Commons, in 1750, " this fortnight on the African Company. We, the British Senate—that temple of liberty, and bulwark of Protestant Christianity—have, this fortnight, been pondering methods to make more effectual that horrid traffic of selling negroes. It has appeared to us, that six and forty thousand of

[1] 'Memoirs of the Novelists,' vol. i. p. 312.

these wretches are sold every year to our plantations alone! It chills one's blood; I would not have to say one voted for it, for the continent of America."[1]

Of Walpole, as he appeared among his lilacs and laburnums at Strawberry Hill, we have a graphic sketch from the pen of one of his fellow-residents at Twickenham, Miss Letitia Hawkins, a daughter of Dr. Johnson's friend and biographer, Sir John Hawkins. The sketch in question is, indeed, not only interesting as the portrait of a distinguished man, but, as Sir Walter Scott observes, " affords the most lively idea of the person and manners of a Man of Fashion about the middle of the last century."[2] " His figure," writes Miss Hawkins, " was not merely tall, but, more properly, long and slender to excess; his complexion, and particularly his hands, of a most unhealthy paleness. His eyes were remarkably bright and penetrating, very dark and lively. His voice was not strong, but his tones were extremely pleasant, and, if I may so say, highly gentlemanly. I do not remember his common gait. He always entered a room in that style of affected delicacy, which fashion had then made almost natural; *chapeau bras* between his hands, as if he wished to compress it, or under his arm; knees bent, and feet on tip-toe, as if afraid of a wet floor. His dress in visiting was most usually, in summer, when I most saw him, a

---

[1] Walpole's 'Letters,' *ut supra*, vol. ii. p. 197.
[2] 'Memoirs of the Novelists,' vol. i. p. 310.

lavender suit, the waistcoat embroidered with a little silver, or of white silk worked in the tambour, partridge silk stockings and gold buckles, ruffles and frill generally lace. I remember, when a child, thinking him very much under-dressed, if at any time, except in mourning, he wore hemmed cambric. In summer no powder, but his wig combed straight, and showing his very smooth, pale forehead, and queued behind; in winter, powder."

Walpole's conversation, as might perhaps have been expected from him, would seem to have been that of a man who is in the habit of writing epigrams in prose, and of conversing as he writes. Miss Berry, indeed, extolls his conversation as having been " as singularly brilliant as it was original;"[1] but then Miss Berry, it must be borne in mind, knew him only in the last years of his life, when all his attentions and flatteries were lavished on her charms. Another contemporary and less partial criticiser of Walpole's conversational powers, who knew him longer, and scarcely less intimately, was Judge Hardinge. "When," he writes, "I became familiar with his effeminacy of manners, it was lost in his wit, ingenuity, and whimsical but entertaining fund of knowledge." Subsequently, however, the Judge somewhat qualifies his admiration. "Though he was elegant and polished," continues the Judge, "he was not, I think, *well-bred*, in the best view of that

[1] 'Social Life in England and France.'

phrase. He demanded a full stretch of admiring homage to his *bons-mots*, and rather lectured in a series of prose epigrams, than conversed playfully and so as to put the hearer quite at his ease. One left him, at least I did, fatigued, though charmed with his enlivening sallies."[1]

Walpole, despite his being ruffled by occasional caprices and affectations, appears to have descended uncomplainingly and gracefully into the vale of years. To Hannah More he writes, on the 2nd of July, 1789, on the verge of seventy-two: "And who has more cause to be thankful to Providence for his lot. The gout, it is true, comes frequently, but the fits are short, and very tolerable; the intervals are full of health. My eyes are perfect; my hearing but little impaired; chiefly to whispers, for which I certainly have little occasion; my spirits never fail; and though my hands and feet are crippled, I can use both, and do not wish to box, wrestle, or dance a hornpipe. In short, I am just infirm enough to enjoy all the prerogatives of old age, and to plead them against anything that I have not a mind to do."[2]

It was now about eighteen months previously to the date of this letter, that, in the drawing-room of his friend, Lady Herries, Walpole first formed the acquaintance of those two fair and accomplished sisters, Miss Mary and Miss Agnes Berry, for whose

---

[1] Nichols's 'Lit. Anecdotes of the 18th Century,' vol. viii. p. 525.
[2] Walpole's 'Letters,' *ut supra*, vol. ix. p. 188.

amusement it may be needless to observe that he subsequently composed his charming octogenarian 'Reminiscences of the Courts of George I. and II.,' and with whose graceful friendship and fascinations the happiness and the weakness of his closing years became so intimately interwoven. Their father, Mr. Berry, a gentleman of moderate private fortune, and of intellectual tastes, had spared no pains to endow them with those refined accomplishments which, from girlhood to an almost patriarchal age, continued to surround them with troops of affectionate intimates and friends. "Mr. Berry," writes Walpole to Lady Ossory, "carried his daughters for two or three years to France and Italy, and they are returned the best-informed and the most perfect creatures I ever saw at their age. They are exceedingly sensible, entirely natural and unaffected, frank, and being qualified to talk on any subject, nothing is so easy and agreeable as their conversation, nor more apposite than their answers and observations. The eldest, I discovered by chance, understands Latin, and is a perfect Frenchwoman in her language. The younger draws charmingly, and has copied admirably Lady Di's [Diana Beauclerk] gipsies, which I lent, though for the first time of her attempting colours. They are of pleasing figures; Mary, the eldest, sweet, with fine dark eyes that are very lively when she speaks, with a symmetry of face that is the more interesting from being pale. Agnes, the younger, has an agreeable, sensible countenance, hardly to be called handsome, but almost. She is less animated than Mary, but seems, out of deference to her sister, to speak seldomer, for they dote on each other, and Mary is always praising her sister's talents."[1] Again, more than three years afterwards, Walpole writes to Lady Ossory : "In short, they are extraordinary beings, and I am proud of my partiality for them; and since the ridicule can only fall on me, and not on them, I care not a straw for its being said that I am in love with one of them; people shall choose which : it is as much with both as either, and I am infinitely too old to regard the *qu'en dit-on.*"[2] Notwithstanding, however, this disclaimer of " partiality " on the part of Walpole, we need only very cursorily glance over his correspondence at this period, to satisfy ourselves how entirely the elder sister was his favourite, if not his passion. So long, for instance, as her home was near his, either in London or the neighbourhood of Twickenham, he seems to have enjoyed as much happiness and contentment as old age has a right to expect; while, on the other hand, if absent with her father in Italy, if paying visits to friends in Yorkshire, or to other places, we find him from time to time either expressing himself inconsolable during her absence, or else anticipating her return with something very much resembling the impatient ardour of a youthful lover.

[1] Walpole's 'Letters,' *ut supra*, vol. ix. p. 153. [2] Ibid., vol. ix. p. 374.

On the 5th of December, 1791, Horace Walpole, by the death of his eccentric nephew, George, third Earl of Orford, succeeded to his kinsman's earldom and to his crippled estates. The coronet, which thus devolved on him, he professed, and apparently in all sincerity professed, to regard in the light of an encumbrance and an infliction. Business he had never loved; and accordingly when, with his new accession of rank, he found himself involved in endless consultations with lawyers, in the investigation of complicated accounts in dry questions of the validity of mortgages and leases, and . in other uncongenial duties, can we wonder that the change which was thus necessitated in the occupations and habits of a *virtuoso* in his seventy-fifth year, should have proved almost intolerable? Blessed, moreover, with every comfort and luxury that money can provide—surfeited with the adulation of fine ladies and literary triflers—what additional happiness, or what importance worth attaining, could an empty title confer on him? Subscribing himself, somewhat affectedly, " Uncle to the late Earl of Orford," it was not till several months after his nephew's decease, that the "new old lord," as he pleasantly styled himself, could bring himself to sign his proper title at the foot of his correspondence; neither did he ever take his seat in the House of Lords. " Surely," he himself writes, "no man of seventy-four, unless superannuated, can have the smallest pleasure in sitting at home, as I always do, and being called by a new name."

Walpole's last letter to Mary Berry—a letter in which, by-the-by, he speaks of himself as a "superannuated old Etonian"—is dated the 15th of December, 1796; his last letter to his old correspondent, the Countess of Ossory, bearing date the 15th of the following month. Hitherto, old age had laid its hand lightly on him, and accordingly if, in the latter of these communications, we discover evidence of an irritability denoting pain or discontent, we must ascribe it to the more frequent and severer attacks of gout, by which, during the last few months of his life, he was unhappily afflicted. Still, not only did his favourite villa, with its rare archæological treasures and its cherished library continue to afford him as much gratification as ever, but it was not without the greatest reluctance that the old philosopher, as he was pleased to consider himself, could be induced, at the earnest desire of his friends, to consent to remove thence to London, in order to be near the best medical advice. When, at length, he quitted it, it was, as he himself felt convinced, never to return. Happily, the closing weeks of his life were cheered by the affectionate and unwearying attentions of the two young ladies, whose society had now so long constituted the chief attraction of his declining years. "When not immediately suffering from pain," writes Miss Mary Berry, " his mind was tranquil and cheerful. He was still capable of being amused, and of taking some part in conversation; but during the last weeks of his life, when fever was superadded to his other ills, his mind became subject to the cruel hallucination of supposing himself neglected and abandoned by the only persons to whom his memory clung, and whom he always desired to see. In vain they recalled to his recollection how recently they had left him, and how short had been their absence: it satisfied him for the moment, but the same idea returned as soon as he had lost sight of them. At last, Nature sinking under the exhaustion of weakness, obliterated all ideas but those of mere existence, which ended, without a struggle, on the 2nd of March, 1797." Walpole died at his house, No. 11 Berkeley Square, in his eightieth year. His remains were interred with those of his renowned father in the family burying-place in Houghton Church.

NATHANIEL FORSTER, D.D.

NATHANIEL FORSTER, one of the most learned Greek, Latin, and Hebrew scholars of his time, was born on the 3rd of February, 1718, at Stadscombe, in the parish of Plymstock, Devonshire, of which place his father, the Reverend Robert Forster, was minister. His mother was Elizabeth, sister of Nicholas Tindal, the translator of Rapin's History of England.

Having, at the age of thirteen, reached the head of the large and flourishing grammar-school at Plymouth, Nathaniel Forster was transferred to Eton, whence, after a novitiate of apparently only sixteen months, he was removed to Pembroke College, and afterwards to Corpus Christi College, Oxford, of which latter Society he became a Fellow in 1739. In October, 1735, he took his degree of B.A; in February, 1838, as M.A., and in April, 1746, as B.D. It was not till 1750 that he received the degree of D.D. Notwithstanding his extensive scholarship and indefatigable industry, his merits remained for many years, if not unrecognized, at least unrewarded by

Church preferment. Thus, although admitted to Deacon's orders as early as the year 1739, it was not till July, 1749, that, at the recommendation of Archbishop Secker, then Bishop of Oxford, he obtained from Lord Chancellor Hardwicke the small Rectory of Hethe, in Oxfordshire. About the same time, he was introduced by the Bishop to that great and good prelate, Dr. Joseph Butler, Bishop of Bristol, who, on his translation to the see of Durham in 1750, not only appointed him his domestic chaplain, but, by honouring him with his friendship and high opinion, justified him in fostering sanguine hopes of future and early advancement in his profession. Any such hopes, however, as he may have been cheered by, were destined to be frustrated by the death of the excellent Bishop, who, having in the mean time nominated him his executor, with a bequest of two hundred pounds, expired at Bath in his arms in June, 1752. " Poor Forster, whom I have just received a letter from," writes Bishop Hurd to Bishop Warburton, " is overwhelmed with desolation at the loss of his master." Thus disappointed and dispirited, he returned to Oxford, where he was preparing to prosecute his classical studies with undiminished ardour, when he was once more drawn from his retirement by the favour of a third prelate, Dr. Herring, Archbishop of Canterbury, who, in July, 1752, appointed him one of his chaplains, and whose intimate friend and correspondent he subsequently became. From this period his prospects began to improve. In February, 1754, he was nominated by his former benefactor, Lord Chancellor Hardwicke, to a prebendal stall at Bristol; and in the autumn of the same year was presented by his patron, the Archbishop, to the valuable vicarage of Rochdale in Lancashire.

This latter preferment would seem to have demanded from its new vicar all the tact, temper, and good sense at his command. "Dear Forster," writes the Archbishop to him, "I question whether you will thank me for saying that I am glad I have sent you to Rochdale; and the more so, as there is so much party rage abounding there. I know you will try what prudence and integrity will do, to serve God and the King, and to allay these unchristian and mischievous animosities."[1] And again, in similar affectionate terms, the Archbishop on another occasion writes to him—" Don't be anxious; it hurts me to see you so. I esteem you, and if God continues my life, I will befriend you as soon, and in the best manner that I can."[2] According to Dr. Whitaker, in his 'History of Whalley,' Dr. Forster's abode at Rochdale was of no long duration.

On the 15th of May, 1755, Dr. Forster was elected a Fellow of the Royal Society; on the 12th of the following May, he was appointed chaplain to King George II.; and in 1757, through the interest of the second Earl of Hardwicke, then Viscount

[1] Nichols's 'Lit. Anecdotes,' vol. ix. p. 294.   [2] Ibid.

Royston, was nominated preacher at the Rolls Chapel.

Besides several other learned publications, Dr. Forster was the author of a remarkable dissertation on the authenticity of the celebrated disputed passage in Josephus relating to the Saviour; a dissertation which elicited from Warburton the high encomium that it was "the best piece of criticism" of the period in which it was composed.

The character of Dr. Forster, as delineated by his contemporaries, was that of a mild, benevolent man, endowed with good discernment and a perfect command over his temper. Thus eminently well qualified to discharge the duties of the sacred profession which he had undertaken, he was enjoying in the prime of life every prospect of rising to its highest ranks, when, in the month of August, 1757, his happiness and worldly prosperity bade fair to receive a still further increase by his contracting a marriage with a lady—described as "of great merit and possessed of considerable fortune"—Susan, widow of John Balls, Esq., of Norwich. But, unhappily, by this time his close application to study had so seriously undermined his constitution as to justify the most gloomy apprehensions of his friends. His end, indeed, was fast approaching. Previously to his marriage he had provided himself with a home for his bride in Craig's Court, Charing Cross, in which abode, after the enjoyment of little more than two months' connubial felicity, he expired on the 20th of October, 1757, in the fortieth year of his age. His remains were interred in the neighbouring church of St. Martin in the Fields; his widow erecting a monument to his memory in the Cathedral Church of Bristol, the Latin inscription upon which was the composition of Dr. Hayter, successively Bishop of Norwich and London.

Dr. Forster's widow, it should be mentioned, re-married Philip Bedingfield, Esq., of Ditchingham, in Norfolk.

JOHN MONTAGU, EARL OF SANDWICH.

THE subject of this memoir was born in the parish of St. Martin's in the Fields, London, on the 3rd of November, 1718. He was the great-great-grandson of the first and celebrated Earl of Sandwich, whose body, recognizable by the insignia of the Order of the Garter, was found floating on the waves after the great sea-fight with the Dutch in 1672, and great-grandson, through his grandmother, of John Wilmot, the libertine Earl of Rochester. In 1722, when only four years old, he lost his father, Edward Richard, Viscount Hinchinbroke; and in October, 1729, when he had nearly completed his thirteenth year, he succeeded his grandfather as fourth Earl of Sandwich.

In his earlier days, John Earl of Sandwich, as in the case of his schoolfellow and future political colleague, Lord Halifax, afforded high promise of attaining that moral and intellectual superiority which, but for the libertinism which they severally contracted in their riper years, might in both instances have enabled them to transmit honoured names to posterity. Not only, at Eton, was Lord Sandwich distinguished by his proficiency in classical literature, but in the Eton List for 1732—where he stands the head boy of the Fifth Form—we find his name preceding those of Jacob Bryant, Horace Walpole, Gray, West, Barnard, and Cambridge, notwithstanding one and all of these gifted youths were his seniors in point of age. "He was versed in modern languages," writes his friend, Cradock, "as well as in the Greek and Roman classics; he spoke French and Italian fluently, and I have reason to believe he was equally conversant with the German and the Spanish."[1]

In 1735, at the age of seventeen, Lord Sandwich removed from Eton to Trinity College, Cambridge, where he and Lord Halifax are said to have been the first noblemen who publicly declaimed in the College Chapel. After a residence of about two years at the University, he departed with his friend Brabazon Ponsonby, afterwards first Earl of Bessborough, on a voyage round the Mediterranean; visiting on his route Sicily, Malta, Turkey, Egypt, Italy, and other countries washed by its classic waters, and carrying off from Rome the Swiss painter, John Stephen Liotard, whom he induced to accompany him to Constantinople, with the object of securing sketches by him of the remarkable places and costumes which might attract them during their wanderings. When,

[1] Cradock's 'Literary and Miscellaneous Memoirs,' vol. i. pp. 152, 153.

after an absence of about two years, the young lord returned to England, he had at all events qualified himself for election to the Dilettanti Club and the Antiquarian Society; bringing home with him plans and drafts of the Pyramids; more than fifty Greek inscriptions which he had industriously transcribed; two mummies and eight embalmed ibises from the catacombs of Memphis; a large quantity of Egyptian papyrus; fifty intaglios; five hundred medals, and other rarities. But what he apparently most prided himself upon was his discovery, "among some rubbish and lumber in a sort of wood-yard" at Athens, of a remarkable marble, which, having been purchased and presented by himself to Trinity College, Cambridge, excited, under the name of the *Marmor Sandvicense,* much interest and curiosity among the learned; proving to bear date the year 374 before Christ, and to contain a minute account of the receipts and disbursements of the three magistrates deputed by the people of Athens to celebrate the feast of Apollo at Delos in the one hundred and first Olympiad.[1] Moreover, besides rendering these services to archæology, Lord Sandwich not only composed a very creditable account of his 'Voyage,' which, after his decease, was published, with a memoir of his life, by his chaplain, the Reverend John Cooke,[2] but could scarcely have attained his

[1] Nichols's 'Lit. Anecdotes,' vol. iv. pp. 496, 497, 663.
[2] 'A Voyage performed by the late Earl of Sandwich round the Mediterranean in the Years 1738 and 1739:' London, 1799.

majority when, under his auspices and presidentship, was formed the Egyptian Club, composed of gentlemen who had either visited Egypt, or who took an interest in Egyptian antiquities.[1]

It was probably immediately on his coming of age, in 1739, that Lord Sandwich took his seat in the House of Lords, joining at the same time that resistless political phalanx which ultimately succeeded in driving Sir Robert Walpole from power. Here he had scarcely played his part for more than twelve months, when, during a debate on naval affairs, we find him delivering himself with a spirit and force which evoked the warm admiration of at least one of his brother Peers. "My Lords," spoke Lord Bathurst, "the two noble young Lords [Sandwich and Halifax] who opened this debate, spoke with such dignity, such strength of argument, and such propriety of expression, that I began to imagine myself in an old Roman or Lacedæmonian senate; and therefore," added Lord Bathurst sarcastically, "I must return thanks to the noble Duke [Newcastle] who spoke last, for he has brought me back to a British House of Peers."[2] Lord Sandwich, it is true, could at no period of his long Parliamentary career plume himself on possessing the

"Eloquiam ac famam Demosthenis aut Ciceronis;"

yet, nevertheless, there were features in his oratory,

[1] Nichols's 'Lit. Anecdotes,' vol. v. p. 334.
[2] 'Parl. Hist.' vol. xi. p. 787.

from which many of his contemporaries might, with advantage to their audience, as well as to themselves, have taken profitable lessons. In the House of Lords, for instance, he rarely rose to speak except on pressing occasions of moment or necessity; that is to say, unless he had either something important or interesting to communicate, some accusation to rebut, some fallacy to expose, or some falsehood to refute. Happy in the selection of his words, terse, compendious, and impressive, few members of the Upper House found readier or more attentive listeners than Lord Sandwich. Moreover, he not only bore with patience and good temper the incessant charges of malversation and ministerial neglect which in later years were brought against him by party animosity, but sustained with spirit and composure even the fiercest invectives of the dreaded Chatham, and, indeed, at least on one occasion encountered him with success.[1] Conciseness in writing, he seems to have held in no less estimation than conciseness in speaking. If any naval officer, was one of his dicta when First Lord of the Admiralty, had occasion to write to him, and would conclude his communication without turning over the first page, he should receive an immediate answer to his letter; but otherwise the officer must expect him (Lord Sandwich) to consult his own time in replying to the communication.

[1] See Walpole's 'Memoirs of the Reign of George III.,' vol. iv. p. 321.

Lord Sandwich was still only twenty-two years of age, when, on the 7th of March, 1741, he married Judith, third daughter of Charles, first Viscount Fane of the kingdom of Ireland, by whom he became the father of John, fifth Earl of Sandwich. Not only was his union with this lady apparently productive of happiness to neither party, but from its failure to confer happiness upon him probably sprang those irregularities which marked Lord Sandwich's later matrimonial career. To Sir Horace Mann, Horace Walpole writes on the 9th of February, 1766: "Your old friend, Lord Fane, is dead, and has left three thousand pounds a year to poor Lady Sandwich, who cannot enjoy it. She is shut up; the family blood and her misfortunes have turned her head."[1] Lady Sandwich, it may be mentioned, survived her lord more than five years, dying, apparently at an advanced age, on the 20th of August, 1797.

Lord Sandwich's earliest initiation into the civil employments of the State dates from the 27th of December, 1744, when, consequent on the appointment of his friend, John Duke of Bedford, to be First Lord of the Admiralty, he was nominated to be second at that Board, with his old schoolfellow, George Grenville, and the celebrated Admiral, afterwards Lord, Anson for his junior colleagues. The following year, on the famous landing of Prince Charles Edward in Scotland, Lord Sandwich's activity in raising men in defence of the

[1] Walpole's 'Letters,' vol. iv. p. 477.

reigning family obtained for him, on the 27th of September, 1745, a captaincy in the Duke of Bedford's provincial regiment, which was followed by a colonelcy in the Duke of Montagu's Ordnance Corps, on the 22nd of November following; and subsequently by successive army promotions till he reached the rank of General, on the 25th of May, 1772.[1]

Lord Sandwich was still retaining his seat as a Junior Lord of the Board of Admiralty, when, in the month of August, 1746, at the age of twenty-seven, he was sent to Breda as Minister Plenipotentiary to negotiate a treaty for a general peace, which treaty was subsequently signed by him at the Congress of Aix-la-Chapelle on the 7th of October, 1748. The satisfactory manner in which he discharged this important service, seems to be sufficiently attested by the short autograph State Paper in which George II. notifies to the States General the recall of his Minister: "We have thought proper," writes the King, "to recall our Minister Plenipotentiary the Earl of Sandwich, in order that he may exercise the important post which we have conferred upon him in these kingdoms, as a recompense for the faithful and zealous services which he has rendered us."[2]

The important post here glanced at by the King

---

[1] Cooke's Memoir of Lord Sandwich, prefixed to 'Voyage Round the Mediterranean,' p vi. and *note*.

[2] Ibid. pp. viii. ix.

was the presiding seat at the Board of Admiralty, a post conferred upon Lord Sandwich on the 26th of February, 1749, while he was still only in his thirty-first year. "The Admiralty," writes Walpole, "was the favourite object of Lord Sandwich's ambition; and his passion for maritime affairs, his activity, industry, and flowing complaisance, endeared him to the profession, re-established the marine, and effaced great part of his unpopularity. No man in the Administration was so much master of business, so quick or so shrewd; and no man had so many public enemies who had so few private, for, though void of principles, he was void of rancour, and bore with equal good humour the freedom with which his friends attacked him, and the satire of his opponents."[1] Not less favourable is the verdict pronounced on the deserts of this much-abused statesman by one who not only lived on terms of intimacy with him, but who was peculiarly well qualified to form a correct estimate of his merits—Charles Butler, the author of the 'Reminiscences.' "Lord Sandwich," he writes, "might serve as a model of a man of business. He rose early; he often appointed the Reminiscent to attend him at six o'clock in the morning; and his time, from that hour till a late dinner, was wholly dedicated to business. He was very methodical; slow, but not wearisome; cautious, but not suspicious; rather a man of sense than a man of

[1] Walpole's 'Reign of George III.' vol. iv. p. 257.

talent; had much real good nature. His promises might be relied on. His manners partook of the old Court; and he possessed, in a singular degree, the art of attaching persons of every rank to him. Few houses were more pleasant or instructive than his lordship's. It was filled with rank, beauty, and talent, and every one was at ease."[1] Pleasing, however, as were these qualities, they were not, as must already have been made manifest to the reader, without their drawbacks. "He was a most profligate and abandoned character," writes Lord Chesterfield, "but with good abilities;"[2] nor, if confined to a later stage of his life, would these harsh words on the part of his brother Earl appear to have been unmerited.

Having resigned the post of First Lord of the Admiralty in June, 1751, Lord Sandwich remained without employment in the State till December, 1755, when he was nominated Joint Vice Treasurer of Ireland. In April, 1763, on George Grenville being constituted First Lord of the Treasury, he was re-appointed First Lord of the Admiralty in his room, and, in August following, was nominated one of the principal Secretaries of State, which office he resigned on the formation of the Rockingham Administration, in July, 1765.

It was not apparently till during the prominent

[1] Butler's 'Reminiscences,' p. 71.
[2] Chesterfield's 'Letters,' edited by Earl Stanhope, vol. ii. p. 479.

part taken by Lord Sandwich in the arbitrary prosecution of Wilkes, in 1763, that the unpopularity ascribed to him by Walpole, combined with the character for gross libertinism imputed to him by Lord Chesterfield, led, as was the case, to his name becoming a byword of public reproach. George Grenville, it may be remembered, had been scarcely more than a week or two at the head of the Treasury, when the publication of the famous forty-fifth number of the 'North Briton' provoked him to commit his rash and short-sighted measure of declaring war against Wilkes and the Press. Nor was this the only weapon which ministers were prepared to employ against the unsuspicious demagogue. Wilkes, as could have been no secret to Lord Sandwich, had recently printed, if he had not actually composed and published, an obscene and blasphemous poem, entitled 'An Essay on Woman,' composed in imitation of Pope's 'Essay on Man.' As Pope had inscribed his poem to Henry St. John, Lord Bolingbroke, commencing it with the words—

"Awake, my St. John!" &c.,

so was this impure production inscribed by Wilkes to a beautiful courtesan of the day—

"Awake, my Fanny!" &c.[1]

---

[1] The spurious editions of the 'Essay on Woman,' make the poem commence—
"Awake, *my Sandwich!* leave all meaner joys;" &c.
"My Fanny" was Fanny Murray, the daughter of a musician at Bath, and successively mistress of the Honourable John Spencer, better

The grossest portion of this gross production was the notes, which were not only written in imitation of Bishop Warburton's 'Commentaries upon Pope's Works,' but most irreverently professed to be from the pen of that right reverend prelate.

To obtain a copy of this work, and by its means to prosecute and crush the popular demagogue as a branded blasphemer and libeller, was now the paramount object of Grenville and his colleagues. Had their zeal originated in a true regard for the interests of religion and morality, one might have half forgiven the means, however unworthy they might be, by which the Ministry attempted to secure his conviction. But, as it happened, nothing could be much more unjustifiable than those means. Wilkes, it should be borne in view, had made not the slightest attempt to foist his impure 'Essay' on the public. No young mind could be said to have been tainted by its obscenities; no single Christian faith had been disturbed by its profaneness. As Lord Sandwich must have well known, only thirteen copies of it had been printed, and of these the circulation had been restricted to a corresponding number of congenial spirits, doubtless as hardened in debauchery as Wilkes himself. Moreover, with the express object of *preventing* publicity, he had printed the work at a private press

---

known as "Jack Spencer," and of Beau Nash. She was married to a person of the name of Ross, and died in 1770. 'Notes and Queries,' Second Series, vol. iv. pp. 1, 41.

of his own at his residence in Great George Street, Westminster; thus, it should be added, entailing on ministers no slight difficulty in obtaining a copy for the purposes of prosecution. Lord Sandwich, indeed, had in all probability received a presentation copy, but, though he had undertaken to lead the attack in the House of Lords against Wilkes, what man could be so entirely lost to all sense of honour, as to convert into a legal instrument of prosecution and oppression the confidential gift of a friend? Another copy had fallen into the hands of Government at the time of the arrest of Wilkes and of the seizure of his papers, but the means by which it had been obtained had been before too high a tribunal too recently denounced to be illegal to permit of its being turned to the exceptional purpose for which it was required. In this dilemma, one Kidgell, chaplain to the profligate Duke of Queensberry, then Lord March, came to the assistance of ministers, and, by means of bribing one of the printers in Wilkes' employ, secured a copy of the poem, which he placed in the hands of the Solicitor of the Treasury.[1]

The day fixed upon for opening the campaign against Wilkes in the House of Lords, was that of the assembling of Parliament, the 15th of November, 1763. On that day, even before the King's speech could well be taken into consideration, Lord Sandwich, as Secretary of State, laid the poem of his unsuspecting

[1] Walpole's 'Reign of George III.,' vol. i. pp. 310, 311.

brother-libertine upon the table of the House, at the same time, in pharisaical language, denouncing it as a most blasphemous, obscene, and abominable libel. At his requisition several of the most offensive passages were read aloud, to the great disgust of many of the peers, and especially of "the good Lord Lyttelton," who is described as groaning in spirit, and entreating that the perusal might cease. But it was Bishop Warburton, the counterfeited author of the infamous notes, who naturally betrayed the greatest anger and disgust. "The blackest fiends in hell," he exclaimed in a paroxysm of rage, "would avoid keeping company with Wilkes;" at the same time begging pardon of Satan for coupling them in the same sentence. Neither did the conduct of Lord Sandwich excite much less disgust and surprise than had been provoked by the profanity and impurities of Wilkes. Not only had they been intimate companions over the bottle, but, within little more than a fortnight, at a club—" composed of players and the loosest revellers of the age "—to which they severally belonged, they had sat together bandying ribald wit and listening to obscene catches.[1] It may or may not have been the case that Lord Sandwich was one of the members of the infamous Medmenham Abbey Club, of which Wilkes was the idol; but, at all events, his close connection with its orgies is more

[1] Walpole's 'Letters,' vol. iv. p. 134. Walpole's 'Reign of George III.,' vol. i. p. 313.

than once referred to in a clever poem of the time, addressed to the Earl himself:[1]

> "The midnight orgies you reveal,
> Nor Dashwood's *cloistered rites* conceal;" &c.[2]

And again:

> "In vain you tempt Jack Wilkes to dine,
> By copious draughts of *chaliced wine*,
> And *anthems* to Moll's Rose;" &c.

Even Lord Sandwich's own friends and supporters, on any allusion being made to his canting philippic in the House of Lords, were scarcely able to repress a titter. "Never before," exclaimed his old associate in profanity, Sir Francis Dashwood, who listened to him, "had he heard the devil preach."[3] The fact is, that not only had he become a scoffer at religion as well as a rake, but about this very time he was expelled from the Beef Steak Club for blasphemy. In the House of Commons, Thomas Townshend proceeded to such lengths as to denounce him as the "most profligate sad dog in the kingdom." The Earl was in the House at the time, a fact of which Townshend seems to have been cognizant; adding

[1] 'Ode to the Earl of Sandwich,' see the 'New Foundling Hospital of Wit,' vol. ii. pp. 97, 100, and vol. iii. p. 134.
[2] Alluding to Sir Francis Dashwood, afterwards Lord Le Despencer, the Father Abbot of this shameless society.

> "Dashwood shall pour, from a communion cup,
> Libations to the goddess without eyes,
> And hob or nob in cider and excise."—
> *Churchill*, 'The Candidate.'

[3] Walpole's 'Reign of George III.,' vol. i. p. 311, *note*.

that he hoped he was present, and that if he was not present, "he was ready to call him so to his face in any company."[1] Out of doors, as well as in Parliament, scorn everywhere pursued the luckless Earl. It happened, for instance, that a few days after the debate in the House of Lords, the 'Beggars' Opera' was performed at Covent Garden Theatre. The play passed off quietly till towards its close, when Macheath exclaims—" That Jemmy Twitcher should peach me, I own surprised me ; 'tis a proof that the world is all alike, and that even our gang can no more trust one another than other people."[2] It would have been a dull audience not to have comprehended at once the affinity between *Jemmy Twitcher* and the apostate Earl, and accordingly there arose simultaneously from gallery, from pit, and from boxes a cry of "*Jemmy Twitcher! Jemmy Twitcher!*'—a name by which, during the remainder of his days, Lord Sandwich became as familiarly known as by the title which he had inherited from his forefathers.[3] Lastly, Wilkes' friend, Charles Churchill, poured down upon him a pitiless storm of rhyming invective:

> " His life is a continued scene
> Of all that's infamous and mean.
> He knows not change, unless grown nice
> And delicate from vice to vice.

---

[1] Walpole's ' Letters,' vol. iv. pp. 317, 325.
[2] Act iii. scene 4.
[3] Walpole's ' Reign of George III.,' vol. i. pp. 313, 314.

> Nature designed him, in a rage,
> To be the Wharton of his age;
> But having given all the sin,
> Forgot to put the virtues in.
> To run a horse, to make a match,
> To revel deep, to roar a catch;
> To knock a tottering watchman down,
> To sweat a woman of the town;
> By fits to keep the peace, or break it,
> In turn to give a p— or take it;
> He is, in faith, most excellent,
> And, in the word's most full intent,
> A true choice spirit we admit;
> With wits a fool, with fools a wit.
> Hear him but talk, and you would swear
> Obscenity herself was there,
> And that Profaneness had made choice
> By way of trump, to use his voice;
> That, in all mean and low things great,
> He had been bred at Billingsgate;
> And that, ascending to the earth,
> Before the season of his birth,
> Blasphemy, making way and room,
> Had marked him in his mother's womb;
> Too honest—for the worst of men
> In forms are honest now and then—
> Not to have, in the usual way,
> His bills sent in; too great to pay;
> Too proud to speak to, if he meets
> The honest tradesman whom he cheats;
> Too infamous to have a friend;
> Too bad for bad men to commend;
> Or good to name; beneath whose weight
> Earth groans; who hath been spared by Fate
> Only to shew, on mercy's plan,
> How far and long God bears with man."[1]

The next incident of any interest in the career of Lord Sandwich was his contesting, in February, 1764 —three months after his parliamentary onslaught on

[1] 'The Duellist,' book iii.

Wilkes—the High Stewardship of the University of Cambridge, with a highly accomplished nobleman, Philip, second Earl of Hardwicke. At the University, the contest, notwithstanding the purely honorary nature of the office, excited an extraordinary amount of interest and ferment. "This silly dirty place," writes Gray, the poet, to Dr. Wharton, "has had all its thoughts taken up with choosing a new High Steward;" yet, as Earl Stanhope observes, "supreme as is the contempt with which the poet speaks of the contest, he was soon drawn into its whirl."[1] "Ambitious industry," writes Walpole, "was never exerted so indefatigably as by Sandwich on this occasion. There was not a corner of England, nay, not the Isle of Man, unransacked by him for votes. He ferreted out the mad, the lame, the diseased from their poor retreats, and imported them into the University. Letters on letters were written, and fawning applications made to all who could influence a vote of any country clergyman.[2] The struggle having by this time assumed the form of a trial of strength between the Government and the Opposition, the leading divines and professional men at Cambridge, notwithstanding the now notorious profligacy of Lord Sandwich, reconciled it to their consciences to support him as the

---

[1] 'Gray's Works,' vol. iv. p. 29; Aldine edition. Earl Stanhope's 'Hist. of England,' vol. v. p. 91.
[2] Walpole's 'Reign of George III.,' vol. i. p. 395.

Government candidate. Happily, the younger men of the University pressed forward to redeem the credit which had thus suffered at the hands of their superiors. Lord Sandwich, for instance, having been invited to dine at Trinity College, he no sooner made his appearance in the hall, than the undergraduates, to the number of forty-four, rose and retired from it, to the great displeasure of their superiors.[1] Such, indeed, on this occasion, was the complaisance of the University dignitaries, and especially of the clergy, as to provoke from Gray his bitter pasquinade, ' The Candidate ; or the Cambridge Courtship,' which is to be met with only in the later editions of his poetry.

> " When sly Jemmy Twitcher had smugg'd up his face
> With a lick of court whitewash, and pious grimace,
> A-wooing he went, where three sisters of old
> In harmless society guttle and scold.
>   ' Lord! sister,' says Physic to Law, ' I declare,
> Such a sheep-biting look, such a pick-pocket air!
> Not I for the Indies!—You know I'm no prude—
> But his nose is a shame, and his eyes are so lewd!
> Then he shambles and straddles so oddly—I fear—
> No—at our time of life 'twould be silly, my dear.'
>   ' I don't know,' says Law, ' but methinks for his look,
> 'Tis just like the picture in Rochester's book ;
> Then his character, Phizzy,—his morals—his life—
> When she died, I can't tell, but he once had a wife.
> They say he's no Christian, loves drinking and w——g,
> And all the town rings of his swearing and roaring !
> His lying and filching, and Newgate-bird tricks ;—
> Not I—for a coronet, chariot and six.'

---

[1] Walpole's ' Reign of George III.,' vol. i. p. 396. The names of the seceding undergraduates may be seen in Churchill's ' Works,' by W. Tooke, vol. iii., p. 161, *note* ; ed. Boston, 1854.

> Divinity heard, between waking and dozing,
> Her sisters denying, and Jemmy proposing.
> From table she rose, and with bumper in hand,
> She stroked up her belly, and stroked down her band—
> 'What a pother is here about wenching and roaring!
> Why, David loved catches, and Solomon w——g;
> Did not Israel filch from th' Egyptians of old
> Their jewels of silver and jewels of gold?
> The prophet of Bethel, we read, told a lie:
> He drinks—so did Noah;—he swears—so do I:
> To reject him for such peccadillos, were odd;
> Besides, he repents—for he talks about G * *—.[1]
>
> [*To Jemmy*]
> Never hang down your head, you poor penitent elf,
> Come buss me—I'll be Mrs. Twitcher myself.'"

Churchill also, in a poem which Lord Bath, a contemporary critic of no common perspicacity, considers to be "the severest and the best" of all his works[2]— returned to the charge against Lord Sandwich with undiminished acrimony and power :—

> "From his youth upwards to the present day,
> When vices, more than years, have marked him gray,
> When riotous excess, with wasteful hand,
> Shakes life's frail glass, and hastes each ebbing sand;
> Unmindful from what stock he drew his birth,
> Untainted with one deed of real worth,
> Lothario, holding honour at no price,
> Folly to folly added, vice to vice;
> Wrought sin with greediness, and sought for shame,
> With greater zeal than good men seek for fame."[3]

> "——skulking round the pews, that babe of grace,
> Who ne'er before at sermon showed his face,
> See *Jemmy Twitcher* shambles!—stop! stop thief!—
> He's stol'n the Earl of Denbigh's handkerchief."—
> *Heroic Epistle to Sir William Chambers.*

[2] 'The Candidate.'   [3] Ibid.

It should be mentioned that, at the close of the contest for the High Stewardship, in consequence of each candidate claiming a majority of one, the question was referred to the Court of Queen's Bench, which tribunal, after a protracted hearing, decided, on the 25th of April, 1765, in favour of Lord Hardwicke.

Lord Sandwich, as we have already stated, held the post of Secretary of State from August, 1763, till the formation of the Rockingham Administration in July, 1765. From this latter date he remained without office till January, 1768, when he was appointed joint Postmaster-General with his old associate in libertinism, Lord Le Despencer; and again, in January, 1771, no long time after the accession of Lord North to the premiership, was, after having previously held the seals as Secretary of State for a few weeks, appointed to his former and favourite employment of First Lord of the Admiralty, which post he continued to fill till March, 1782, when he and Lord North retired together from office. Among his colleagues in the Board Room of the Admiralty, he found seated there, in 1771, the celebrated Charles James Fox, at that time a young man of not quite two and twenty. At this early period, then, it may have been, that Fox first imbibed that seemingly personal aversion to Lord Sandwich, which, at a later date, and after Fox had become the "Man of the People," appears to have coloured the frequent and famous charges brought by him against the Earl in Parliament, on account of alleged gross mal-administration of the affairs of the navy. Unmerited as we believe these attacks to have been, they nevertheless had not only the effect of shaking Lord North's ministry, and of redoubling Lord Sandwich's unpopularity with the masses of the people, but, on one occasion, during the exciting Keppel and Palliser riots in 1779, nearly cost that nobleman his life. It has been asserted that, at the daring assault made at that time by the rabble on Lord Sandwich's residence at the Admiralty, Charles Fox was one of the ringleaders. "It happened at three o'clock in the morning," writes Walpole, " that Charles Fox, Lord Derby, and his brother, Major Stanley, and two or three more young men of quality, having been drinking at Almack's, suddenly thought of making a tour of the streets, and were joined by the Duke of Ancaster, who was very drunk; and, what showed it was no premeditated scheme, the latter was a courtier, and had actually been breaking windows. Finding the mob before Palliser's house, some of the young lords said—' Why don't you break Lord George Germaine's windows?' The populace had been so little tutored that they asked who he was, and being encouraged, broke his windows [in Pall Mall]. The mischief pleasing the juvenile leaders, they marched to the Admiralty, forced the gates, and demolished Palliser's and Lord Lisburne's windows. Lord Sandwich, exceedingly terrified, escaped through the garden *with his mistress, Miss Ray,* to the Horse Guards, and there betrayed a most manifest panic."[1] Among the rioters are stated to have been Mr. Thomas Grenville, afterwards First Lord of the Admiralty, and young William Pitt, afterwards the future famous Premier. "A lady of rank," writes Captain Brenton, in his 'Life of the Earl of St. Vincent,' "assured me that she actually saw Mr. Pitt break her windows."[2] Of the other rioters, the Duke of Ancaster—hereditary Lord Great Chamberlain, and son of the then Mistress of the Robes to Queen Charlotte—is said to have passed the night in the watch-house. In less than five months he was no more.

Whatever share Charles Fox may have had in the attack on the official residences of the Lords of the Admiralty, he followed it up, on the 19th of April, by not only pouring in the House of Commons as fierce a torrent of invective against Lord Sandwich as was ever listened to within the walls of that assembly, but by also moving an address to the King to remove the Earl from his councils and presence for ever. The naval service, Fox insisted, had been neglected in every one of its departments; the treasure which Parliament had voted to maintain

---

[1] Walpole's 'Last Journals,' vol. ii. p. 343. Lord George Germaine was at this time Secretary of State; Sir Hugh Palliser and Lord Lisburne were Lords of the Admiralty.

[2] Brenton, vol. i. p. 24; Earl Russell's 'Memorials of Fox,' vol. i. p. 224; Keppel's 'Life of Admiral Viscount Keppel,' vol. ii. p. 192.

its efficacy had been profligately squandered; the country was in a shamefully defenceless condition. The motion was, not untriumphantly, negatived in Lord Sandwich's favour by a majority of two hundred and twenty-one to one hundred and eighteen.[1] Nevertheless Fox and the Opposition continued to assail him, and, in his person, the Government, with unflagging pertinacity. The last and most famous of these attacks took place on the 7th of February, 1782, almost in the closing hours of the North Administration, when Fox, preparatory to moving for a vote of censure against the harassed Earl, charged him, in a magnificent speech, with being the author of the many naval failures and disasters which had disgraced the country during the late war with the American colonists and their allies. On this occasion, Fox's motion was not only defeated by so small majority as twenty-two, but when, on the 23rd, the discussion was renewed by him, he found that majority reduced to only nineteen. On the 15th of the following month, on the question of a direct vote of want of confidence in ministers, proposed by Sir John Rous, member for Suffolk, they escaped defeat by a majority merely of nine, and on the 20th the entire administration resigned. It may here be mentioned that, from this time, with the exception of a brief tenure of the rangership of the parks during the Coalition Ministry, Lord

[1] 'Annual Register' for 1779, p. 137.

Sandwich never again held employment under Government.

Unhappily, the occurrence of a domestic incident of an unusually tragic character threw a gloom over Lord Sandwich's later years. The circumstance, incidentally mentioned by Walpole, of the Earl's mistress, Miss Ray, having been the companion of his precipitate flight from the Admiralty to the Horse Guards, can scarcely have failed to suggest certain unpleasant surmises to the mind of the reader. That, for instance, less than a century since, a First Lord of the Admiralty should, as Lord Sandwich appears to have done, not only have publicly established his mistress at his official residence at Whitehall, but that bishops and their wives— cognizant though they were that the frail creature to whose unrivalled strains they came to listen, was the paramour of their host and the mother of his children —should unblushingly have sat through the musical and dramatic performances with which the Earl was in the habit of entertaining his neighbours at Hinchinbroke, certainly affords curious evidence of the lax morality of our forefathers. Some years had elapsed since this ill-fated woman, then a beautiful girl of sixteen, had been induced by Lord Sandwich to abandon her calling as a mantua-maker in Tavistock Street, Covent Garden, and to place herself under his protection. Nature had endowed her with an exquisite taste and ear for music, which her noble lover spared no cost in cultivating, placing her under the tuition of Giardina, one of whose most favourite pupils she became. Subsequently, large sums of money were offered, but offered in vain, to tempt her to sing on the stage. Her performances in the private theatricals and oratorios at Hinchinbroke excited never-failing admiration; her execution of the fine air in Jephthah—"Brighter scenes I seek above," is said to have been perfection.

In the fate of Miss Ray, as it is almost needless to state, is involved the tragical incident to which we have just called attention. On the 7th of April, 1779, exactly six weeks after her flight with Lord Sandwich from the Admiralty, she was suddenly deprived of existence by the hand of a young clergyman of the name of Hackman, who shot her through the head, exactly opposite the Bedford Coffee House, under the Piazza of Covent Garden, just as she was about to enter her carriage at the close of the theatrical performances. Vanity, it would seem, had formerly induced Hackman to quit a desk in a merchant's office for the more showy profession of arms. Happening; subsequently, when a lieutenant of the sixty-eighth regiment, to be in command of a recruiting party in Huntingdonshire, he was invited by Lord Sandwich to Hinchinbroke, where he became passionately enamoured of his future victim, whom he in vain endeavoured to persuade to become his wife. He now, apparently in the hope of rendering his position in life more agreeable to her, quitted the Army for the Church, when, having obtained the living of Wiverton in Norfolk, he repeated his proposals, but, in the words of a contemporary brother-clergyman, was unable to bend "the inflexible fair in a black coat more than in a red."[1] Being unable to live with her, he felt that he could not live without her; and accordingly, on the night on which the cruel catastrophe occurred, he had followed her to the theatre with the determination of destroying himself in her presence, and himself only, when, perceiving her accepting with apparent satisfaction the attentions of a young Irish barrister of the name of Macnamara, he was seized with so uncontrollable a fit of jealousy as to despatch her in the manner which has been mentioned. A second pistol-shot, which, before the bystanders had time to arrest his arm, he fired at his own head, failed to prove fatal; and accordingly, having been seized and subjected to the necessary preliminary examination before Sir John Fielding, the magistrate, at the neighbouring Shakespeare Tavern, he was committed by him to take his trial at the Old Bailey.

The remains of Miss Ray were interred by the side of those of her mother in the graveyard of the peaceful village of Elstree, in Hertfordshire, which had given her birth, and where she had probably passed the days of her innocent childhood. A few

[1] The Rev. Dr. Warner: 'Selwyn Correspondence,' vol. iv. pp. 67, 68.

days afterwards—on the 19th of April—Hackman expiated his crime at Tyburn. The anguish and horror of Lord Sandwich, when the tragical fate of the mother of his children was communicated to him, are described as having been excessive. "I could have borne anything," he exclaimed, "but this." For a time he retired to the seclusion of a friend's house in the neighbourhood of Richmond, but apparently without experiencing the relief of which he stood so much in need. In the mean time, Charles Fox was preparing to rehurl his thunder at the broken-spirited Earl, and accordingly he was driven back to London, probably at an earlier period than he had intended to return. When, shortly after his having reached the Admiralty, he was visited by his friend, Cradock, the autobiographer found him in an apartment in which the familiar portrait of his murdered mistress was still suspended over the mantelpiece; the Earl's disconnected speech, and the wretched health which was depicted on his countenance, plainly betraying the severity of the inward struggle by which he was almost prostrated.[1] For a time, society seems to have been all but hateful to him. "His lordship," writes Cradock, "rarely dined out anywhere; but, after a great length of time, he was persuaded by our openhearted friend, Admiral Walsingham, to meet a select party at his house. All passed off exceed-

[1] Cradock's 'Literary and Miscellaneous Memoirs,' vol. i. pp. 146, 147.

ingly well for a while, and his lordship appeared more cheerful than could have been expected; but after coffee, as Mr. and Mrs. Bates[1] were present, something was mentioned about music, and one of the company requested that Mrs. Bates would favour them with 'Shepherds, I have lost my Love.' This was unfortunately the very air that had been introduced by Miss Ray at Hinchinbroke, and had been always called for by Lord Sandwich. Mr. Bates immediately endeavoured to prevent its being sung, and by his anxiety increased the distress; but it was too late to pause. Lord Sandwich for a while struggled to overcome his feelings, but they were so apparent, that at last he went up to Mrs. Walsingham, and in a very confused manner said, he hoped she would excuse his not staying longer at that time, but that he had just recollected some pressing business which required his return to the Admiralty; and, bowing to all the company, rather hastily left the room. Some other endeavours to amuse him afterwards did not prove much more successful."[2]

Lord Sandwich's love for music seems, as may perhaps have been already inferred, to have amounted almost to a passion. The musicians offered up incense to him as their patron; he was the soul of the Catch Club; and one of the directors of the Concerts of Ancient Music. In the oratorios which varied the

[1] Formerly Miss Harrop, a charming singer.
[2] Cradock's 'Memoirs,' vol. i. p. 147.

Christmas festivities at Hinchinbroke, we find him performing on the kettle-drum. The jocular catch, 'Fie! nay, pr'ythee, John,' is said to have been his composition.[1]

The last ten and uneventful years of Lord Sandwich's life present a pleasing contrast to the libertinism and turmoil of its meridian. Those years were almost entirely passed in comparative retirement at Hinchinbroke. "There," writes his friend, Cradock,[2] "he still preserved the same calmness of mind, the same temperate forbearance, as had always before distinguished him, and enjoyed solitude, without writing daily to his friends to boast of his philosophy." In all the relations of his later years Lord Sandwich is described as having been truly amiable. "He was a good and affectionate father," writes his chaplain and biographer, the Rev. J. Cooke; "a kind master to his servants, most of whom were known to live in his service many years. They who were in the habit of living with him had every occasion to observe and admire the sweetness of his temper, which showed itself in continual acts of kindness and benevolent attention to all around him." Another pleasing feature in Lord Sandwich's character was the apparent absence of all malice in his disposition. No statesman of his day had endured more from political persecution and

---

[1] Park's 'Royal and Noble Authors,' vol. iv. p. 403, *note*.
[2] 'Memoirs,' vol. i. p. 152.

party spite, yet seemingly no man could more entirely have forgiven his slanderers and foes. To the wants of the distressed, his hand and heart are said to have been ever open. He was not only constant in his attendance at Divine worship in his parish church at Huntingdon, but he also set the praiseworthy example to his fellow-parishioners of making a point of joining the congregation on Sundays before the commencement of the service, and requiring the same token of reverential deference from the different members of his family. As a magistrate, and as chairman of the quarter sessions, he devoted himself to the duties required of him with his accustomed energy and ability; as a neighbour, his hospitality was generous and his entertainments frequent; "the noble host," to quote the words of his reverend biographer, "inspiring by the easy politeness of his address, his affability and engaging manners, and the charms of his conversation, universal cheerfulnes sand good humour amongst his guests."[1]

Of Lord Sandwich when in his sixty-seventh year there is a pleasing notice from the pen of his old schoolfellow, Horace Walpole. To Lady Ossory the latter writes from Strawberry Hill, on the 21st of June, 1785: "I could not finish my letter yesterday, for Lord Sandwich, who was to breakfast with me, arrived sooner than I expected. He brought Mr.

[1] Memoir prefixed to 'Voyage Round the Mediterranean,' p. xxxii.

Noble with him, the author of the 'History of the Cromwells;' and Mr. Selwyn came to dinner with us, and the latter stayed all night. Lord Sandwich has taken the patronage of Mr. Noble (as Hinchinbroke was the residence of Oliver), and the second edition will be much more accurate and curious than the first. I could not but look with admiration at the Earl, who at our age can enter so warmly into any pursuits and find them amusing. It is pleasant to have such spirits that, after going through such busy political scenes, he can be diverted with carrying a white wand at Handel's Jubilee, and for two years together!"[1]

The little that we know of Lord Sandwich's closing hours in no degree detracts from these more favourable glimpses into his character. About the month of December, 1791, in consequence of a complaint of the bowels, to which he had been periodically subject, making serious and visible inroads on his constitution, he followed the advice of his physician, Dr. Hallifax, and repaired to Bath to try the efficacy of its waters. "Having," continues his chaplain and biographer, "resided there a few weeks without receiving the expected benefit, he returned to his house in town the latter end of February, 1792. He was not sensible of his danger till within a few days before his death, when some very alarming symptoms convinced his mind, not

[1] Walpole's 'Letters,' vol. viii. p. 558.

yet impaired, that his recovery was no longer to be hoped for. He received the intimation with firmness. During even the last stages of his illness he frequently conversed on public affairs, with the same reach of thought and perspicuity of expression as he had at any time been accustomed to do." On the subject, more especially, of the impending horrors of the French Revolution, he expressed himself with such feeling and force as to excite the surprise of his attendant physician. "You speak, my Lord," said Dr. Hallifax, "more like a philosopher and a Lord in Parliament than one on the bed of sickness." [1]

Thus, to quote the words of his friend Cradock, died Lord Sandwich, "with the utmost fortitude and resignation."[2] His dissolution took place on the 30th of April, 1792, in the seventy-fourth year of his age.

[1] 'Memoir,' *ut supra*, pp. xxxix. xl.
[2] Cradock's 'Memoirs,' vol. i. p. 148.

ROBERT GLYNN, M.D.

This "great, disinterested, virtuous, and consummate scholar and physician," the "dilectus Iapis"—

"The loved Iapis on the banks of Cam"

—of the 'Pursuits of Literature,'[1] was born of an old and honoured family at Kelland, near Bodmin, in Cornwall, on the 5th of August, 1719. He subsequently, on succeeding to the property of a relative, took the name of Cloberry, but apparently without it being either adopted by his friends or finding much favour from himself.

In 1737 Robert Glynn was elected from the foundation at Eton to King's College, Cambridge; in 1741 he took his degree as B.A.; in 1745 as M.A.; in 1758 as M.D.; and in 1763 became a Fellow of the College of Physicians. Of his literary achievements while at the University, the only example which has survived its gifted author appears to be his poetical essay on the 'Day of Judgment,'

[1] Dialogue iv. p. 444.

which obtained for him the Seatonian prize in 1757, and the merits of which, from his contemporaries at least, won golden opinions.

Dr. Glynn's first practice as a physician was at Richmond; from which place, however—finding himself perhaps retaining an unalterable prepossession in favour of a college life and the society of his former schoolfellows and college friends—he returned to Cambridge, where he prosecuted, to the acquirement of great credit and pecuniary profit, the active discharge of his professional duties, and where he continued to reside during the long remainder of his existence. Unfortunately, owing to the uneventful uniformity of that existence, the materials for composing the story of his life are confined to little more than brief records of his goodness, his integrity, his benevolence, and the sagacity and humanity displayed by him in the exercise of his professional calling. Of long and distinguished celebrity in the University of Cambridge—eminent on account of his abilities, but still more eminent on account of his virtues—the venerable philanthropist continued to enjoy, to the end of his days, the heart-felt reverence and affection, not only for the middle-aged and of the advanced in years, but also of the young. For many years, we are told, "his tea-table was frequented by young men of the highest rank and character, who have since been raised to the highest offices in Church and State. The suggestions of his experience were so tempered by the urbanity of his manners, that his society had a very visible influence upon the direction of their studies and conduct."[1]

Thus calmly, and thus beneficially to others, the "loved Iapis" descended into the vale of years. "It was happy for those around him," writes Nichols, "that it pleased Providence to extend his life to a very advanced period. His faculties were clear and vigorous within a very short time of his decease. During his illness, sensible of his gradual decay, he expressed nothing but resignation and kindness, and expired without a struggle or a groan."[2]

Dr. Glynn, or rather Dr. Glynn Cloberry, died on the 8th of February, 1800, in the eighty-first year of his age. In obedience to his repeated injunctions, his remains were privately interred between ten and eleven o'clock at night in the chapel vault of his college. By his last will, also, he manifested how sincere was the interest which he took in the college in which he had been educated, by bequeathing to it the sum of six thousand pounds.[3]

There is extant a fine and scarce portrait of Dr. Glynn, engraved by Facius in 1783, after a drawing by the Rev. Thomas Kerrick, to whom, as his friend and executor, he bequeathed a legacy of five thousand pounds.[4]

[1] Nichols's 'Lit. Anecdotes of the 18th Century,' vol. viii. p. 215, and *note*. [2] Ibid., vol. viii. p. 212. [3] Ibid., vol. viii. pp. 211, 212, 216.
[4] Ibid., vol. viii. p. 216, and *note*.

GEORGE AUGUSTUS SELWYN.

PERHAPS no individual in this country has ever achieved for himself a more widely spread celebrity, as far as mere oral wit and conversational pleasantry are concerned, than George Selwyn. The reputation of other celebrated wits has mostly been enhanced by their having distinguished themselves in other branches of intellectual excellence. Villiers Duke of Buckingham; Lords Dorset, Rochester, Chesterfield, and Harvey; Sir Charles Hanbury Williams, Foote, Wilkes, Colman, the late Rev. Sydney Smith and Theodore Hook, were men who had one and all distinguished themselves in the pursuit of literature, and more than one of them shone in the senate. On the other hand, the fame of Selwyn rests entirely on the credit accorded him by his contemporaries for social humour and conversational wit. The House of Commons, in fact, though he sat there during more than a generation, apparently never listened to his voice, while literature is indebted to him for but a solitary epigram :

"ON THE DISCOVERY OF A PAIR OF SHOES ON A LADY'S BED.

Well may suspicion shake its head;
Well may Clorinda's spouse be jealous;
When the dear wanton takes to bed
A pair of shoes—because they're fellows."

George Augustus Selwyn, the scion of an honourable and influential family on the side of both parents, was born on the 11th of August, 1719. His father was Colonel John Selwyn, of Matson, in Gloucestershire, who, after having in his youth served as aide-de-camp to the great Duke of Marlborough, and risen to command a regiment, was returned to Parliament, from which time he for many years figured as a person of considerable note in the fashionable and political circles at the Courts of George I. and II. The mother of George Selwyn was Mary, daughter of General Farrington, of the county of Kent, and Woman of the Bedchamber to Queen Caroline; a lady from whose example of vivacity and wit, as recorded by her contemporaries, her son doubtless drew those brilliant qualities which rendered him the charm of every society into which he entered. She survived till the 6th of November, 1777, when she expired in the eighty-seventh year of her age. In the interesting burial-place of the Selwyns, in the grounds at Matson, is a monument to the memory of the father and mother of George Selwyn. Their epitaph describes them to have been "affectionate parents; kind to their dependents;

charitable to the poor; and faithful and beloved servants to King George II. and Queen Caroline." George Selwyn was their second son.

In the list of Eton scholars for 1732, the name of George Selwyn stands the last but two in the Fifth Form; there occurring above him, in the same Form, the names of Lord Sandwich, of Jacob Bryant, Walpole, Gray, West, Cole, Glynn, and Conway. From Eton he passed to Hertford College, Oxford, apparently with no very high reputation for classical knowledge, and evidently with a strongly prevailing tendency to run a course of extravagance and to pursue a life of pleasure. "Dear George," writes his father to him while at Hertford College in 1740, "I am disposed once more to pay your debts, which is what you have no pretension to ask. Let me know what your Oxford bills amount to, that they may be paid first, and I will remit the money to you; but don't always expect to be answered next post, for I have too much business to answer all letters next post, and yours is of a nature that I think does not merit punctuality."[1] Colonel Selwyn, however, not only paid his son's debts, as is here intimated, but by means of the interest which he enjoyed with the Government at this time, obtained for him the appointment of Clerk of the Irons and Surveyor of the Meltings at the Mint, to which offices he was nominated on the 1st of March, 1740, five months

[1] 'George Selwyn and his Contemporaries,' vol. i. p. 32.

before he became of age. The duties thus imposed upon him he was allowed to have performed by deputy; his own share of them, as appears by information obtained from the Mint, being confined to occasional attendances at the weekly dinners which were formerly held at the public expense for the entertainment of the officers connected with that department.

In 1742, Selwyn, having withdrawn himself from the University for a season, performed the grand tour of Europe, became a member of one or two of the patrician clubs in St. James's Street, and, on his return to Hertford College, as an undergraduate, found himself, at the age of twenty-five, the favoured correspondent, among other persons of distinction, of the popular *bon-vivant* and statesman, Richard Rigby, and of the celebrated poet and wit, Sir Charles Hanbury Williams. "I hope," writes the latter to him, " you divert yourself well at the expense of the whole University, though the object is not worthy of you. The dullest fellow in it has parts enough to ridicule it, and you have parts to fly at nobler game."[1] Had Selwyn, at all events, been contented with merely "*diverting* himself at expense of the University," he would have acted, if not unobnoxiously, at least far less indefensibly than he did. Unfortunately, however, he was tempted to give far more unjustifiable offence to those in authority. It

[1] 'George Selwyn and his Contemporaries,' vol. i. p. 67.

seems to have been very shortly before the organization of the infamous Medmenham Abbey Club, with its impure and blasphemous orgies, that Selwyn, at a tavern wine-party in the summer of 1745, was led to commit an act of impious ribaldry, alike so insulting to the holiest rite of the Church of England, as to the University itself, as to determine the authorities to visit the offender with the severest punishment which it was within their jurisdiction to inflict. It was to no purpose that, in the hope of escaping the stigma attached to expulsion, Selwyn, by resigning his studentship at Hertford College, relieved the University of his presence, and returned to the more congenial society of White's Club. "If," writes to him his friend, Charles Lyttelton, afterwards Bishop of Carlisle, "your late conduct has really been half as bad as it is now represented—I mean with regard to what passed at the tavern—the University has it in her power, and, I am sorry to add, in her inclination, to set a public mark of infamy upon you by affixing a *Programma of Expulsion* on every post within the precincts of her jurisdiction." [1] This power, after due investigation, the University not only resolved to exercise, but proceeded at once to inflict. To Selwyn, for instance, on the 28th of July, 1745, another of his friends, the Hon. Richard Leveson Gower, writes: "By the arrival of Lord Charles Scott from the Convocation, I find that you are expelled publicly,

[1] 'George Selwyn and his Contemporaries,' vol. i. p. 72.

and your name to be fixed up, as usual on such occasions : nothing remarkable happened. There is a strong edict against keeping company with you, and, moreover, that is to be fixed up with the other *programma.*"[1] Having advanced thus much to the discredit of Selwyn, it is but justice to him to have to add that, by several of the dignitaries of the University, his offence was regarded rather as an ill-judged intent to ridicule the external ceremonies and empiricisms of the Roman Catholic Church, than as intended to be a direct and wanton insult to the fundamental truths of Christianity. The Vice-Chancellor, in particular, was charged with having entertained too severe a view of the conduct of the culprit. To Selwyn, after his expulsion, Dr. H. Brookes writes : " In the little I did with a view to silence or soften the prosecution, my judgment went along with me, and I really thought I was consulting the general credit and interest of the University as well as yours. Even now I cannot but adhere to my opinion, that an *éclat* on this unhappy occasion was hurtful to both. Numbers, it seems, entertained very different sentiments. These prevailed, and the censure took place in its utmost extent."[2] To this view of the case it should be further adduced in Selwyn's favour, that previously to his perpetration of the act of unworthy mummery of which he was convicted, his conduct at

[1] 'George Selwyn and his Contemporaries,' vol. i. pp. 76, 77.
[2] Ibid., p. 78.

Oxford had apparently been such as to bear the severest test of academical inquiry. We have the authority, for example, of Dr. Newton, of Hertford College, in a letter seemingly addressed to Dr. Brookes, not only that Selwyn "strictly conformed" to the rules of that society while he continued a member of it, but the Doctor adds—" The upper part of the society here, with whom he often converses, have, and always have had, a very good opinion of him. He is certainly not intemperate, nor dissolute, nor does he ever game, that I know or have heard of. He has a good deal of vanity, and loves to be admired and caressed ; and so suits himself with great ease to the gravest and the sprightliest. I wish, upon the whole, you would persuade the Vice-Chancellor to be content with his going at his own time. He will be little here in the Long Vacation. I will be responsible for his being in good order."[1]

In 1747, two years after Selwyn's expulsion from Oxford, he found himself, at the age of eight and twenty, combining, with the consequences which accrues to a seat in Parliament, a reputation for wit and geniality which rendered him the cynosure of an attached host of admirers and friends. As a member, moreover, of the House of Commons, his constant, though silent, support of the Court party earned for him, in addition to his anomalous appointments at the Mint, the lucrative post of Paymaster

[1] 'George Selwyn and his Contemporaries,' vol. i. p. 93.

of the Works, an office, it is true, which was abolished by Burke's Economical Reform Bill in 1782; but as Mr. Pitt, two years afterwards, conferred upon Selwyn the appointment of Surveyor-General of the Works, the pecuniary loss which he had temporarily sustained was probably not considerable.

On the 27th of June, 1751, died George Selwyn's elder brother, John Selwyn, M.P. for Whitchurch, a young man of considerable merit, and the intimate friend of the accomplished cavalier, Marshal Conway. To the latter, for instance, Horace Walpole writes from Rome on the 23rd of April, 1740 : " As I have wrote you two such long letters lately, I did not hurry myself to answer your last; but chose to write to poor Selwyn upon his illness. I pity you excessively upon finding him in such a situation. What a shock it must have been to you! He deserves so much love from all that know him, and you owe him so much friendship, that I can scarce conceive a greater shock. I am very glad you did not write to me till he was out of danger; for this great distance would have added to my pain, as I must have waited so long for another letter."[1] Colonel Selwyn survived his eldest son but little more than four months; dying on the 5th of November, 1751, in his sixty-second year, and bequeathing to his surviving son, George, the bulk of his property. The latter

[1] Walpole's 'Letters,' vol. i. p. 45.

thus found himself, at the age of thirty-two, in the
desirable possession of the family mansion and estates
of Matson, of a considerable landed property at
Ludgershall, in Wiltshire, as well as of an estate in
Barbadoes, in which island he succeeded in obtaining
for himself the appointment of Registrar of the Court
of Chancery. Moreover, not only was it now in his
power to return whom he pleased to Parliament as
one of the two representatives of the borough of
Ludgershall, but, in addition to this accession of
political influence, the family interest which he
possessed at Gloucester and in its neighbourhood was
sufficiently powerful to enable him to secure his own
return, during a long succession of years, for that
city. Matson, too, was not only a profitable possession, but also a delightful residence. "The vale,"
writes Walpole, who visited Matson in the summer
of 1753, "increases in riches to Gloucester. I stayed
two days at George Selwyn's house, called Matson,
which lies on Robin Hood's Hill. It is lofty enough
for an Alp, yet is a mountain of turf to the very top,
has wood scattered over it, springs that long to be
cascades in twenty places of it; and from the
summit it beats even Sir George Lyttelton's views,
by having the city of Gloucester at its foot, and the
Severn widening to the horizon. The house is small,
but neat. King Charles lay here at the siege [of
Gloucester, in 1643], and the Duke of York, with
typical fury, hacked and hewed the window-shutters

of his chamber as a memorandum of his being there."[1] Twenty-one years from this time, we find Walpole again paying a visit to Matson. To Cole, the antiquary, he writes from there on the 15th of August, 1774. "You will not dislike my date. I am in the very mansion where King Charles the First and his two eldest sons lay during the siege; and there are marks of the last's hacking with his hanger on a window, as he told Mr. Selwyn's grandfather afterwards. The present master has done due honour to the royal residence, and erected a good marble bust of the martyr in a little gallery. In a window is a shield in painted glass, with that king's and his queen's arms, which I gave him."[2]

By his intimate friends, Selwyn was not more admired for his wit than he was beloved by them for his many amiable and endearing qualities. "I have long looked upon you," writes the first Lord Holland to him, "to be like no other man in the world."[3] Not only does Horace Walpole—cynical as he was and prone to quarrel with his friends—uniformly speak with tenderness of his old schoolfellow, whether during his lifetime or after his death, but we find even the worldly and profligate Lord March, afterwards Duke of Queensberry, moved to address him in language of almost feminine affection. "As

[1] Walpole's 'Letters,' vol. ii. p. 354.
[2] Ibid. vol. vi. p. 104; Wraxall's 'Hist. Memoirs,' vol. iii. pp. 55, 56; 3rd edition.
[3] 'George Selwyn and his Contemporaries,' vol. ii. p. 154.

to your banker," he writes to him in 1765, "I will call there to-morrow; make yourself easy about that, for I have three thousand pounds now at Coutts's. There will be no bankruptcy without we are both ruined at the same time. How can you think, my dear George, and I hope you do not think, that anybody, or anything, can make a *tracasserie* between you and me? I take it ill that you even talk of it, which you do in the letter I had by Ligonier. I must be the poorest creature upon earth—after having known you so long, and always as the best and sincerest friend that any one ever had—if any one alive can make any impression upon me when you are concerned. I told you, in a letter I wrote some time ago, that I depended more upon the continuance of our friendship than anything else in the world, which I certainly do, because I have so many reasons to know you, and I am sure I know myself."[1]

The pecuniary aid which, in the foregoing extract, Lord March presses upon his friend, was required on account of a heavy loss recently incurred by Selwyn, either at Almack's or White's, of a considerable sum of money at play. Gaming, indeed, was his prevailing thought, happily, his only deep-rooted vice. Even as late as 1780, when he had reached his sixty-second year, we find him still indulging in that fatal propensity. "The very first time I went to Boodles'," said William Wilberforce, "I won

[1] 'George Selwyn and his Contemporaries,' vol. i. p. 376.

twenty-five guineas of the Duke of Norfolk. The
first time I was at Brookes's, scarcely knowing any
one, I joined from mere shyness in play at the faro
table, where George Selwyn kept bank. A friend
who knew my inexperience, and regarded me as a
victim decked out for sacrifice, called to me, 'What,
Wilberforce, is that you?' Selwyn quite resented
the interference, and, turning to him, said in his
most expressive tone—'Oh, Sir, don't interrupt Mr.
Wilberforce; he could not be better employed.'"[1]
It was probably very soon after this period that
Selwyn effectually and penitentially broke off the
evil habit by which he had so long been enslaved.
"Gaming," was his somewhat tardy discovery and
remark, "was too great a consumer of four things—
of time, health, fortune, and thinking."

With the exception of an alarming accident which
befell Selwyn in 1764, we find year after year of his
easy existence gliding away unruffled by any incident
worthy of being recorded. "George Selwyn,"
writes Walpole to Lord Hertford in March, 1764,
communicating the mischance in question, "has had a
frightful accident that ended in a great escape. He
was at dinner at Lord Coventry's, and just as he was
drinking a glass of wine, he was seized with a fit of
coughing; the liquor went wrong and suffocated him:
he got up for some water at the sideboard, but
being strangled, and losing his senses, he fell against

[1] 'Life of Wilberforce,' by his Sons, vol. i. pp. 16, 17.

the corner of the marble table with such violence that they thought he had killed himself by a fracture of the skull. He lay senseless for some time, and was recovered with difficulty. He was immediately blooded, and had the chief wound, which is just over the eye, sewed up; but you never saw so battered a figure. All round his eye is as black as jet, and, besides the scar on his forehead, he has cut his nose at top and bottom. He is well off with his life, and we with his wit."[1] Selwyn lived to resume his career of luxurious indolence and pleasure. "*I* rise at six," writes his friend, Lord Carlisle, to him from Spa in 1768; "am on horseback till breakfast; play at cricket till dinner; and dance in the evening till I can scarce crawl to bed at eleven. There is a life for you. *You* get up at nine; play with Raton [his dog] till twelve in your night-gown; then creep down to White's to abuse Fanshawe; are five hours at table; sleep till you can escape your supper reckoning; then make two wretches [chairmen] carry you, with three pints of claret in you, three miles for a shilling."[2] Lord Carlisle, it should be mentioned, is not the only friend of Selwyn whom we find bantering him on account of his habit of falling asleep in society. "When you have a quarter of an hour, *awake* and to spare," writes Walpole to him, "I wish you would bestow it on me;" and again Gilly Williams writes to

---

[1] Walpole's 'Letters,' vol. iv. p. 209.
[2] 'George Selwyn and his Contemporaries,' vol. ii. pp. 325, 326.

him: "We hear of your falling asleep standing at the old President's [Henault's], and knocking him and three more old women into the fire." In the House of Commons Selwyn occasionally provoked much merriment, not merely by falling asleep during the debates, but by snoring in concert with the Prime Minister, Lord North.

In 1780, after having been returned to Parliament as member for Gloucester for more than thirty years, Selwyn, owing to the unpopularity of the calamitous American war, of which he had been a staunch supporter, had the mortification of finding himself compelled to withdraw from the approaching contest for the representation of that city. From Gloucester, therefore, which now hanged him in effigy, he beat a retreat to his own close borough of Ludgershall, where his return to Parliament was celebrated with bonfires and ringing of bells.[1] "I know him," writes Sir Nathaniel Wraxall, "with some degree of intimacy, having sat as his colleague in Parliament during more than six years for Ludgershall. But it was not," adds Wraxall, "so much as a man of wit that I cultivated his society. He was likewise thoroughly versed in our history, and master of many curious as well as secret anecdotes relative to the houses of Stuart and Brunswick. As he had an aversion to all long debates in Parliament, during which he frequently fell asleep, we used to withdraw ourselves

[1] Walpole's 'Letters,' vol. vii. pp. 440, 441.

to one of the committee-rooms up-stairs, where his conversation was often very instructive."[1]

It was to Selwyn apparently that Horace Walpole was indebted for his first introduction to the celebrated Madame du Deffand, and to that brilliant circle of which she was the animating genius. In that circle Selwyn's conversational wit seems to have been not less appreciated, nor his society less courted, than at Devonshire House and White's. With all the leading persons of wit, talent, and fashion in Paris he was intimate, and the French language he spoke to perfection. "I shall let Lord Huntingdon know," writes Lord March to him, "that you are thought to have a better pronunciation than any one that ever came from this country." With the Queen of Louis XV., Selwyn was an especial favourite. "I dined to-day," writes Lord March to him, "at what is called no dinner, at Madame de Coignie's. The queen asked Madame de Mirepoix—'Si elle n'avait pas beaucoup entendu médire de Monsieur Selwyn et elle?' Elle a répondu—'Oui, beaucoup, Madame.' 'J'en suis bien aise,' dit la reine." Selwyn's predilection for the society of his French friends sometimes provoked a good-natured remonstrance from his admirers on this side of the Channel. Alluding to Madame du Deffand, the President Henault, and the Duc de Choiseul, Lord March writes in 1766: "Lady Hertford made a

[1] Wraxall's 'Hist. Memoirs,' vol. iii. pp. 55, 57, 58: 3rd edition.

thousand inquiries about you; asked how long you intended to stay, and hoped you would soon be tired of blind women, presidents, and premiers."[1] "Cannot we," writes Gilly Williams to him, "get you an hospital in this island, where you can pass your evenings with some very sensible matrons? and, if they are not quite blind, they may have some natural infirmity equivalent to it."

Selwyn, to a thorough enjoyment of the pleasures of society, to an imperturbable good-humour, to a kind heart, and to a passionate fondness for children, most unaccountably superadded, as is well known, a morbid interest in the details of human suffering, and, it has been confidently asserted, a taste for witnessing criminal executions. Not only is he said to have been a constant attendant on the horrors of the gibbet, but to have taken an absorbing interest in the various details of crime and mortality, in the private history of the criminal, in his demeanour at his trial, in the dungeon, and on the scaffold, and the state of his feelings in the terrible hour of dissolution. In illustration of these remarks, ample and curious evidence might be adduced. "George Selwyn," writes Walpole, "loves nothing upon earth so well as a criminal, except the execution of him;" and again, referring to an anecdote he had just been relating, Walpole writes : " I told this story the other day to George Selwyn, whose passion is to see coffins, and

[1] 'Selwyn Correspondence,' vol. ii. p. 54.

corpses, and executions. He replied, that Arthur More had had his coffin chained to that of his mistress. 'Lord!' said I, 'how do you know?' 'Why, I saw them the other day in a vault at St. Giles's.' He was walking this week in Westminster Abbey with Lord Abergavenny, and met the man who shows the tombs. 'Oh! your servant, Mr. Selwyn; I expected to have seen you here the other day, when the old Duke of Richmond's body was taken up.'[1] Shall I tell you another story of George Selwyn before I tap the chapter of Richmond, which you see opens very *apropos*? With this strange and dismal turn, he has infinite fun and humour in him. He went lately on a party of pleasure to see places with Lord Abergavenny and a pretty Mrs. Frere, who love one another a little. At Cornbury there are portraits of all the royalists and regicides, and illustrious headless, Mrs. Frere ran about, looked at nothing, let him look at nothing, screamed about India paper, and hurried over all the rest. George grew peevish, called her back, told her it was monstrous, when he had come so far with her, to let him see nothing. 'And you are a fool; you don't know what you missed in the other room.'—'Why, what?'—'Why, my Lord Holland's picture.'[2]—'Well! what is my Lord Holland to me?'—

---

[1] The body of the first Duke of Richmond, natural son of Charles II., was removed from Westminster Abbey to Chichester Cathedral in 1750, on the 1st of September in which year Walpole writes.

[2] Henry Rich, Earl of Holland, beheaded in New Palace Yard, Westminster, in 1749, and buried at Kensington.

'Why, do you know,' said he, 'that my Lord Holland's body lies in the same vault in Kensington Church with my Lord Abergavenny's mother?' Lord! she was so obliged, and thanked him a thousand times."[1]

The trials and executions of the Scotch rebel lords, which followed close on Selwyn's removal from Oxford, afforded him ample opportunity of alike gratifying his taste for the humorous and the tragic. At the trials of Lords Kilmarnock and Balmerino, observing what is called a *hatchet-faced* lady[2] looking intently on the rebel lords, he remarked in reference to the humane practice of averting the edge of the axe from the prisoner till *after* conviction— "What a shame it is of her to turn her face to the prisoners before they are condemned!"[3] Again, on some ladies bantering him on his want of sensibility in volunteering to see Lord Lovat's head cut off, "Why!" he said, "I made amends by going to the undertaker's to see it sewn on again."[4] A further similar anecdote of him is recorded by Walpole. "George," writes the latter, "never thinks but *à la tête tranchée* : he came to town t'other day to have a tooth drawn, and told the man he would drop his handkerchief for the signal."[5]

The temptation of witnessing the execution of Damiens, who was broken on the wheel in March,

[1] Walpole's 'Letters,' vol. ii. pp. 222, 223.
[2] Mrs. Bethel, daughter of Samuel, first Baron Sandys.
[3] Walpole's 'Letters,' vol. ii. p. 46.   [4] Ibid., vol. ii. p. 81.
[5] Ibid., vol. ii. p. 95.

1757, for attempting to assassinate Louis XV., is said to have been too strong for Selwyn to resist. " I have been assured," writes Sir Nathaniel Wraxall, "that he went over to Paris expressly for the purpose of witnessing the last moments of Damiens, who expired under the most acute torture for having attempted the life of Louis XV. Being among the crowd, and attempting to approach too near the scaffold, he was at first repulsed by one of the executioners; but having informed the person that he had made the journey from London solely with a view to be present at the punishment and death of Damiens, the man immediately caused the people to make way, exclaiming at the same time 'Faites place pour Monsieur. C'est un Anglais, et un amateur.'"[1] It should here be mentioned that something very like this story is related of another man of unquestionable humanity, the once celebrated traveller and natural philosopher, De la Condamine, who, it is said, contrived to gratify his curiosity by obtaining a place on the scaffold at the time of Damiens' execution. " Est-il des nôtres ?" said one of the executioners to another. " Non," was the reply, " Monsieur n'est qu'amateur."[2]

In justice, however, to Selwyn, it is but fair to mention that, shortly after he was no more, an earnest and affectionate attempt was made by one of his surviving

[1] Wraxall's 'Hist. Memoirs,' vol. iii. pp. 62, 63; 3rd edition.
[2] Walpole's 'Letters,' vol. iv. p. 92, *note*.

friends, probably the Reverend Dr. Warner, to relieve his memory from the imputation of ever having premeditatedly attended a scene of human suffering. The defence in question appeared in the 'Gentleman's Magazine' for April, 1791. The writer of it, after insisting that to a man who, like Selwyn, possessed " one of the most tender and benevolent of hearts," the sight of an execution would have been perfectly abhorrent, proceeds—" I shall content myself with informing you, that this idle but wide-spread idea of his being fond of executions (of which he never in his life attended but at one, and that rather accidentally from its lying in his way, than from design) arose from the pleasantries which it pleased Sir Charles Hanbury Williams and the then Lord Chesterfield to propagate, from that one attendance, for the amusement of their common friends. Of the easiness with which such things sat upon him, you may judge from the following circumstance, which I have heard him more than once relate : Sir Charles was telling a large company a similar story to that of his attending upon executions, with many strokes of rich humour received with great glee, before his face, when a gentleman, who sat next to the object of their mirth, said to him in a low voice—' It is strange, George, so intimate as we are, that I should never have heard of this story before.' 'Not at all strange,' he replied in the same voice, 'for Sir Charles has just invented it, and knows that I will not by contradiction spoil the pleasure of the company he is so highly entertaining.' And such was his good nature in everything."

Now, while acquitting the writer of this defence of intentionally preferring his regard for his friend's memory to truth, we are nevertheless at a loss to account for that apparently utter ignorance on his part of Selwyn's early tastes and habits, which, as far as they concern his alleged passion for witnessing scenes of mortality and horror, are substantiated by the united, and as yet uncontradicted, evidence of his contemporaries. That, at all events, he was present at the decapitation, not only of Lord Lovat, but also of Lords Kilmarnock and Balmerino, there appear strong reasons for believing. On the 13th of August, 1746, for instance, five days before the two latter lords underwent their sentence, a Mr. William Skrine writes to Selwyn: "I know your design of attending the execution of the lords on Monday next; do me the favour to let me hear from you what method you design to take for that purpose, and whether you can assist me in it."[1] The "method," as may be observed by the significance of the address to the following note, dated the next day, was evidently by obtaining admission to one of the houses overlooking the scaffold on Tower Hill:

[1] 'George Selwyn and his Contemporaries,' vol. i. p. 105.

"Tower Hill, 14th August, 1746.

"SIR,

"As you are unknown to my servants, you will please to show them this, when you will be let into my house.

"I am, Sir, your most humble servant,

"S. BETHELL."[1]

A third note to Selwyn, though certainly proving nothing, is nevertheless curiously suggestive.

"Heythrop, July 14th.

"I can, with great pleasure, inform you, my dear Selwyn, that the *head* is ordered to be delivered on the first application made on your part. The expense is little more than a guinea; the person who calls for it should pay it. Adieu, *mon cher mondain*.

"T. PHILLIPS."[2]

Few literary tasks threaten to prove more disappointing in their results than that of collecting the scattered *bons mots* of a celebrated wit, with the view of demonstrating to posterity that he merited the high reputation awarded him by his contemporaries. Many of his happiest sayings are probably lost to us; others, perhaps, have suffered by passing from mouth to mouth; while the peculiar charm of manner and voice, which must have greatly enhanced their

[1] 'George Selwyn and his Contemporaries,' vol. i. p. 105.
[2] Ibid., vol. i. p. 119.

value at the moment when they proceeded from the lips of the utterer, can now of course be accepted only on credit. " Horace Walpole," was a remark of Lord Ossory, " was an agreeable, lively man, very affected, always aiming at wit, in which he fell very short of his old friend, George Selwyn, who professed it in the most genuine but *indescribable* degree." [1] The fact is, that Selwyn's delivery of his good sayings was distinguished by a quaint gravity of voice and countenance, which never failed to force laughter from every one but himself. Horace Walpole more than once alludes to Selwyn's habit of turning up the whites of his eyes, and to the peculiar demureness of his countenance, when giving utterance to some thought of irresistible drollery or wit. This happy peculiarity likewise impressed itself on the mind of Wraxall. "The effect," he writes, "when falling from his lips, became greatly augmented by the listless and drowsy manner in which he uttered them, for he always seemed half asleep; yet the promptitude of his replies was surprising." [2] Under these circumstances, then, should the following imperfect summary of Selwyn's recorded witticisms fail to satisfy to the full the expectations of the present generation, the reader's surprise, it may be hoped, will not prove more considerable than his disappointment.

[1] Walpole's ' Letters,' vol. v. p. 256.
[2] ' Hist. Memoirs,' vol. iii. p. 56.

A gentleman who had been twice passed unrecognized by Selwyn in the streets of London, on meeting him a third time, accosted him with the reminder that they had formerly been acquainted at Bath. "I remember it very well," replied Selwyn, " and when we next meet at Bath, I shall be happy to be acquainted with you again."

A fellow-passenger with him in a stage-coach, imagining from his appearance that he was suffering from illness, insisted upon teasing him with good-natured inquiries as to the state of his health. At length, worn out by the repeated question of "How are you now, sir?"—"Very well, I thank you," replied Selwyn, "and I mean to continue so for the rest of the journey."

He was one day walking with Lord Pembroke when they were besieged by a number of young chimney-sweepers, who continued importuning them for money. Selwyn at length made them a low bow. "I have often," he said, "heard of the majesty of the people; I suppose your highnesses are in court mourning."

It was after a brilliant combat of wit at Earl Gower's dinner-table, between Selwyn and the celebrated Charles Townshend, that, on the party breaking up, the latter carried his antagonist with him in his chariot as far as the door of White's Club. "Good night!" said Townshend, as they parted; "Good night!" replied Selwyn; "and remember this is the first *set down* you have given me to-day."

One night, at White's, observing the Postmaster-General, Sir Everard Falkener, losing a large sum of money at piquet, Selwyn, pointing to the successful player, remarked—" See how he is robbing the mail!"[1]

On another occasion, observing Mr. Ponsonby, the Speaker of the Irish House of Commons, tossing about bank-bills at a hazard table at Newmarket, —" Look," he said, " how easily the Speaker passes the Money Bills."[2]

The beautiful Maria Countess of Coventry, after exhibiting to him a splendid new dress, covered with large silver spangles the size of a shilling, inquired of him how he admired her taste—" Why," he said, " you will be *change for a guinea*."[3]

At the sale of the effects of a late Prime Minister, Mr. Pelham, Selwyn, pointing to a silver dinner-service, observed—" Lord! how many *toads* have been eaten off these plates!"

Walpole, alluding to the uniformity in the system of politics which had prevailed throughout the reigns of the first two Georges, happened to add—" But there is nothing new under the sun." " No," said Selwyn, " nor under the grandson."

Soon after the marriage of Francis Lord North to

[1] Walpole's 'Letters,' vol. ii. p. 315.   [2] Ibid., vol. iii. p. 38.
[3] Ibid., vol. iii. p. 261.

his third wife, Miss Furnese, somebody remarking that it was very hot weather in which to marry so fat a bride—" Oh," replied Selwyn, " she was kept in ice for three days before."[1]

At a dinner party, at which Selwyn happened to meet the much-maligned Abyssinian traveller, Bruce, one of the guests inquired of the latter whether he had met with any musical instruments in Abyssinia. "I think," replied Bruce, after some slight hesitation, "I saw one *lyre* there." "Yes," whispered Selwyn to his nearest neighbour, "and there is one less since he left the country."[2]

Not unfrequently we find his friend, Charles Fox, the subject of Selwyn's wit. A namesake of Fox having been hanged at Tyburn, Fox inquired of Selwyn whether he had attended the execution. "No," was the reply; "I make a point of never frequenting rehearsals."

At the time that Fox, then in the height of his dissipation, was lodging with his friend Fitzpatrick at Mackie's, the oilman, in Piccadilly, somebody at Brookes's hazarded a remark that their being domiciled there would prove the ruin of poor Mackie. "On the contrary," remarked Selwyn, "he will have the credit of having the choicest *Pickles* in his house of any man in London."

Fox, when Minister for Foreign Affairs, in 1783, was boasting at Brookes's of having prevailed upon

[1] Walpole's 'Letters,' vol. ii. p. 257. [2] 'Walpoliana,' p. 20.

the French Court to relinquish their pretensions to the gum trade. " As you have permitted the French to draw your *teeth*," observed Selwyn, " they would be fools indeed to quarrel with you about your *gums*." [1]

A subscription for the relief of Fox's necessities having been proposed to be opened by his friends, and one of them remarking that " he wondered how Fox would take it"—" Take it," said Selwyn, " why, *quarterly*, to be sure."

Occasionally Selwyn's witticisms were, whether directly or indirectly, associated with the House of Commons. When George Grenville, to whom public business, and especially Parliamentary business, was positive enjoyment, once fainted in the House, Selwyn's voice, amidst eager calls for cold water and ammonia, was heard vociferating—" Why don't you give him the Journals to smell to?" [2]

Burke was one day wearying the House of Commons with one of those long speeches which obtained for him the name of the " Dinner-bell," when the late Lord George Seymour, just as he was about to enter the House, encountered Selwyn, who had just quitted it : " Is the House up ?" asked Lord George. " No," replied Selwyn, " but Burke is."

Selwyn having declined to re-nominate Lord George Gordon for the borough of Ludgershall, on

---

[1] Walpole's 'Letters,' vol. vi. p. 311.
[2] Earl Russell's 'Life of Moore,' vol. ii. p. 213.

the ground that the electors would refuse to vote for him, "Oh, yes," replied Lord George, "if you would recommend me, they would choose me if I came from the coast of Africa."—"That," said Selwyn, "is according to what part of the coast you came from; they would, certainly, if you came from the Guinea Coast." "Now, Madam," writes Walpole to Lady Ossory in relating this anecdote, "is not this true inspiration as well as true wit? Had one asked him in which of the four quarters of the world Guinea is situated, could he have told?" Again, in reference to the slender stock of knowledge from which Selwyn drew his wit, Walpole writes—"You will like to hear sayings of George Selwyn. On [Pratt] Lord Camden's son having another place, he said: '*Sat prata biberunt.*' In short, he who never read anything has always a quotation ready and apropos."[1]

Selwyn's love of practical fun seems, like his wit, to have been freely indulged. Alluding to the witty and notorious Audrey Harrison, Viscountess Townshend, Walpole writes to George Montagu in 1766: "On Sunday last George Selwyn was strolling home to dinner at half an hour after four. He saw my Lady Townshend's coach stop at Carraccioli's [the Neapolitan ambassador] chapel. He watched, saw her go in; her footman laughed; he followed. She went up to the altar, a woman brought her a cushion; she knelt, crossed herself, and prayed. He stole up,

[1] Walpole's 'Letters,' vol. viii. p. 261.

and knelt by her. Conceive her face, if you can, when she turned and found his close to her. In his most demure voice, he said : 'Pray, Madam, how long has your ladyship left the pale of our Church?' She looked furies, and made no answer. Next day he went to her, and she turned it off upon curiosity; but is anything more natural?"[1]

Of Selwyn's peculiar style of humour we have another, and only one other, example to record. "The late Duke of Queensberry," writes Wraxall, "who lived in the most intimate friendship with him, told me that Selwyn was present at a public dinner, with the mayor and corporation of Gloucester, in the year 1758, when the intelligence arrived of our expedition having failed before Rochefort. The Mayor, turning to Selwyn—'You, Sir,' said he, 'who are in the ministerial secrets, can no doubt inform us of the cause of this misfortune?' Selwyn, though utterly ignorant on the subject, yet unable to resist the occasion of amusing himself at the inquirer's expense—'I will tell you in confidence the reason, Mr. Mayor,' answered he; 'the fact is, that the scaling-ladders, prepared for the occasion, were found on trial to be too short.' This solution, which suggested itself to him at the moment, was considered by the Mayor to be perfectly explanatory of the failure, and as such he communicated it to all his friends, not being aware, though Selwyn was,

[1] Walpole's 'Letters,' vol. iv. p. 502.

that Rochefort lies on the River Charente, some leagues from the sea-shore, and that our troops had never even effected a landing on the French coast."[1]

A redeeming trait in the character of George Selwyn was his passion for children, a passion pleasingly exemplified in the Selwyn Correspondence by the indications which it contains of his fondness for the offspring of Lords Coventry and Carlisle, and especially for Lady Anne Coventry, afterwards Lady Anne Foley, the daughter of the beautiful Countess Maria. These transient predilections, however, were towards the close of Selwyn's life succeeded by a more remarkable and all-absorbing devotion for another interesting and mysterious child, the "Mie Mie" of the Selwyn Correspondence, whom, with the tardily-obtained consent of her mother, he adopted as his daughter, and brought up under his roof. This child was Maria Fagniani, the putative and recognized daughter of the Marquis and Marchioness Fagniani, and the future wife of the third, and mother of the fourth, Marquis of Hertford. It would be a false affectation of delicacy to pass over in complete silence the mysterious reports which were circulated in the last century respecting the questionable parentage of Selwyn's infantine charge. According to common belief, the Duke of Queensberry and Selwyn severally believed themselves to be the father of the child; this belief being far from

[1] Wraxall's 'Hist. Memoirs,' vol. iii. pp. 56, 57.

weakened when, subsequently, the latter bequeathed her a fortune of 33,000l., and the Duke the great sum of 150,000l., besides other reversions. In the opinion, indeed, of Dr. Warner, the common and intimate friend of the Duke of Queensberry and Selwyn, the arguments in favour of the child having been indebted for its being either to the one or to the other preponderated unmistakably on the side of the Duke. " The more," he writes to Selwyn, " I contemplate his [the Duke's] face, the more I am struck with a certain likeness to the lower part of it; his very chin and lips, and they are rather singular. But you will never be d'accord upon this interesting subject; as I am sorry to be too much convinced; but that you know better than I." [1]

Although, for some years previously to his death, Selwyn had been constantly a sufferer from gout and dropsy, he nevertheless, towards the close of his days, so far recovered from their attacks as to enjoy a grateful respite from pain, and, indeed, a temporary restoration to comparative health. Six months, however, before his end, his ailments returned with such increased violence as to convince him that his case was hopeless. He died penitent, the Bible, at his own request, being frequently read to him during his last illness. His dissolution took place at his own house in Cleveland Row, St. James's, on the 25th of January, 1791, in the seventy-second year of his age.

[1] 'George Selwyn and his Contemporaries,' vol. iv. pp. 133, 134.

To Miss Berry, Walpole writes on that day: "I am on the point of losing, or have lost, my oldest acquaintance and friend, George Selwyn, who was yesterday at the extremity. These misfortunes, though they can be but for a short time, are very sensible to the old; but him I really loved, not only for his infinite wit, but for a thousand good qualities." And again, four days afterwards, Walpole writes— "Poor Selwyn's gone, to my sorrow; and Ucalegon feels it!" "His end," also writes Walpole to Lady Ossory, "was lovely; most composed and rational. From eight years old I had known him intimately, without a cloud between us; few knew him so well, and consequently few knew so well the goodness of his heart and nature."[1]

> "If, this gay favourite lost, they yet can live,
> A tear to Selwyn let the Graces give!
> With rapid kindness teach oblivion's pall
> O'er the sunk foibles of the man to fall;
> And fondly dictate to a faithful Muse
> The prime distinction of the friend they lose.
> 'Twas social wit, which, never kindling strife,
> Blazed in the small, sweet courtesies of life;
> Those little sapphires round the diamond shone,
> Lending soft radiance to the richer stone."

Such was a tribute which, shortly after Selwyn's death, appeared in some of the literary periodicals of the day to the memory of the most fascinating of companions, and one of the most amiable of men. By his will, the 33,000*l*. which Selwyn bequeathed

---
[1] Walpole's 'Letters,' vol. ix. pp. 276, 277, 278.

to Maria Fagniani was to be paid to her either on her coming of age or on her marriage, if married previously to that time, with a reversion of that sum to the children of Lord Carlisle in the event of Mademoiselle Fagniani dying either in her nonage or unmarried. To his nephews, Charles Townshend and Elbro Woodcock, Esquires, Selwyn bequeathed one hundred guineas each; and to his valet, Pierre Michalin, his wardrobe and an annuity of 30*l*. The residue of his real and personal estates he demised to the Duke of Queensberry, with the exception of Ludgershall, which estate, agreeably with the provisions of his father's will, passed to the possession of the Townshend family.

FIELD-MARSHAL THE RIGHT HON. HENRY SEYMOUR CONWAY.

As remarkable for the beauty of his form as for the singular harmony of his voice, Henry Conway united with these qualities the far higher attributes of a man of unsullied virtue, of a skilful and gallant soldier, of an upright and enlightened statesman, and of an accomplished votary of literature and the Muses. "Faith, my lord," was the reply of a brave young scion of the house of Stanhope[1] to the encomiums of his kinsman, Lord Chesterfield, "I believe I have as much courage as other people; [though] indeed, I don't pretend to be like Harry Conway, who walks up to the mouth of a cannon with as much coolness and grace as if he was going to dance a minuet."[2]

Henry Seymour Conway was born in 1720. He

[1] George Stanhope, brother of Philip, second Earl Stanhope, a young soldier, distinguished alike by his high sense of honour, and by the valour which he displayed at the battles of Falkirk and Culloden. He died unmarried, at the age of thirty-six, on the 24th of January, 1754.

[2] Walpole's 'Memoirs of the Reign of George II.,' vol. iii. p. 55, *note*.

was the second son of Francis Baron Conway, and brother to Francis, the second Baron, created, in 1793, Marquis of Hertford. The latter, who passed through Eton at the same time with his brother, Henry, like him also passed through life not without distinction. In 1763, he was sent as Ambassador Extraordinary to the Court of France; and, in 1765, was appointed Lord Lieutenant of Ireland. He died on the 14th of June, 1794, at the age of seventy-five. The mother of the two brothers was Charlotte, daughter of Sir John Shorter, Lord Mayor of London, and sister of Catherine Shorter, the first wife to Sir Robert Walpole. They were thus, as it may not be inexpedient here to bear in mind, first cousins to Horace Walpole, whose affectionate correspondence with the younger brother commenced in 1740, when Walpole was twenty-three and Conway twenty years old, and terminated only in March, 1795, when Walpole was in his seventy-ninth year, and when Conway was sinking into the grave.

Henry Conway could have left Eton no considerable time when, in 1739, he set out on his travels over a limited portion of the continent of Europe. At Paris he was joined by Horace Walpole and by Gray, the poet, in company with whom he subsequently proceeded to Rheims, where they severally took up their abode for about three months. Their next removal was to Geneva, whence Walpole and Gray, having there taken leave of Conway, continued their route by way of Lyons, Turin, and Genoa, to Florence. To what distance, or for what length of time, Conway extended his wanderings, we are ignorant. In 1741, he was returned to the Irish Parliament as member for the county of Antrim, and the same year was elected to the English Parliament for Higham Ferrers.[1] Subsequently Penryn, St. Mawes, Thetford, in Norfolk, and the borough of St. Edmund's Bury, respectively returned him during a long succession of years as their representative to Parliament. But though now introduced into the sphere the best fitted for the exercise of his promising abilities, the House of Commons, all his predilections were at this time in favour of military service, and accordingly the army became the profession of his choice. In 1741, he was appointed Captain-Lieutenant of the 1st Regiment of Foot Guards, with the rank of Lieutenant-Colonel; and in the spring of the following year, sailed from England to join the British army in Flanders. " We crept over the sea," he writes, " in four tedious days, and from thence stepped immediately into a bilander; which bilander is a certain vast fresh-water machine, answering one's idea of the Ark, and filled with just such a motley complement—Dutch, English, German, Flemish, civil, military, male, female, dogs, cats, &c., but all, in appearance, of the unclean kind."[1] In June,

[1] 'Memoirs of the Marquis of Rockingham,' by the Earl of Albemarle, vol. i. p. 382.

1743, Conway was present at the battle of Dettingen; in May, 1744, he was appointed aide-de-camp to Marshal Wade on his succeeding Lord Stair in the command of the British Army in Germany; and again, on the Duke of Cumberland replacing Marshal Wade in that command in 1745, Conway was appointed aide-de-camp to the Duke. Thus, at the Battle of Fontenoy, in May this year, we find the Prince and his aide-de-camp fighting side by side, and severally behaving with distinguished valour. "Mr. Conway, in particular," writes Walpole, " has highly distinguished himself."[1] "As to the behaviour of the Duke, of which I was a witness the whole time," writes Conway himself to Walpole, "I can say I never saw more coolness, nor greater intrepidity than he showed throughout the whole; exposing himself wherever the fire was hottest, and flying wherever he saw our troops fail, to lead them himself, and encourage them by his example. His horse received three wounds, and he one spent ball on his arm, which only made a slight bruise, but did no hurt. For myself, the balls had the same complaisance for me as for the Duke: one only hit my leg after all its force was gone, and my horse, which I rid all day, received only a slight wound in the leg."[2] On the 6th of April, 1746, Conway, at the age of twenty-six, was appointed to the command of the 48th Regiment

[1] 'Letters,' vol. i. p. 352.
[2] 'Rockingham Papers,' *ut supra*, vol. i. pp. 408, 409.

of Foot. Ten days afterwards he was engaged at the battle of Culloden, still apparently serving as aide-de-camp to the Duke of Cumberland. "Mr. Conway," writes Walpole to Sir Horace Mann on the day before the battle, "has got a regiment, for which, I am sure, you will take part in my joy."[1]

The remaining incidents connected with Conway's military career require no length of detail. The gallantry, nevertheless, which he displayed at the battle of Laffeldt, in July the following year, must not be forgotten. "Harry Conway, whom Nature always designed for a hero of romance," writes Walpole, "and who is *déplacé* in ordinary life, did wonders; but was overpowered and flung down, when one French hussar held him by the hair while another was going to stab him. At that instant, an English sergeant with a soldier came up, and killed the latter, but was instantly killed himself. The soldier attacked the other, and Mr. Conway escaped, but was afterwards taken prisoner; is since released on parole, and may come home to console his fair widow."[2] The "fair widow," referred to by Walpole, was Lady Caroline Campbell, widow of Charles Bruce, Earl of Aylesbury, to whom Colonel Conway was married on the 19th of December following. Her father was Lieutenant-General John Campbell, afterwards fourth Duke of Argyle, and her mother one of

[1] Walpole's 'Letters,' vol. ii. p. 15.
[2] Ibid., vol. ii. p. 91.

the loveliest and wittiest ornaments of the Court of
George II., Mary Bellenden :

"Madge Bellenden, the tallest of the land,
And smiling Mary, soft and fair as down."—*Gay.*

"You, Sir," writes Lady Luxborough to Shenstone,
the poet, " have also had an agreeable lady at your
house. I mean the Countess of Aylesbury; whose
charms and whose conduct have always been equally
admired by those I have heard speak of her. I have
been told she was a lover of retirement in her old
lord's time : I do not know what she may be in her
young colonel's. She is, you know, daughter to
General Campbell and to Miss Bellenden, who was
so celebrated when maid of honour to Queen
Caroline. It is no wonder, then, that she is
pleasing." [1]

In July, 1749, Colonel Conway was transferred
from the command of the 44th to that of the 29th
Regiment of Foot; the latter regiment, as we learn
by a letter from Walpole to Sir Horace Mann at
Florence, being at this time stationed in Minorca.
" My chief reason for writing to you," says Walpole,
" is to notify a visit that you will have at Florence
this summer from Mr. Conway, who is forced to go to
his regiment at Minorca, but is determined to reckon
Italy within his quarters. You know how particularly
he is my friend. I need not recommend him to
you ; but you will see something very different from

[1] Walpole's 'Letters,' vol. viii. p. 481, *note.*

the staring boys that come in flocks to you, now, once a year, like woodcocks. Mr. Conway is deservedly reckoned one of the first and most rising young men in England. He has distinguished himself in the greatest style, both in the army and in Parliament. This is for you: for the Florentine ladies, there is still the finest person and the handsomest face I ever saw. No, I cannot say that all this will be quite for them! he will not think any of them so handsome as my Lady Aylesbury."[1]

On the 25th of December, 1751, Colonel Conway was appointed to the command of the 13th Regiment of Dragoons, and, on the 30th of January, 1756, at the age of thirty-six, was promoted to the rank of Major-General. The following year he was employed as second in command in the expedition against Rochefort; a service which, though it proved an unsuccessful one, seems in no degree to have derogated from his reputation, either for military skill or for personal courage. On the 30th of March, 1759, he was advanced to the rank of Lieutenant-General; on the 25th of May, 1772, to that of General; and, on the 12th of October, 1793, towards the close of his life, to that of Field-Marshal. His last active employment was in 1761, when, during the absence of the Marquis of Granby, he commanded the British forces in Germany under Prince Ferdinand of Brunswick, and from which country, the

[1] Walpole's 'Letters,' vol. ii. p. 261.

following year, he was appointed to conduct them to England.

From Henry Conway as a soldier, we now turn to Henry Conway as a statesman. Unquestionably, in the latter capacity he was not without his faults; those faults being irresolution and a proneness to make too great sacrifices to popularity. "To talk to Conway against public opinion," writes Walpole, "was preaching to the winds."[1] On the other hand, his natural talents were considerable; his political integrity was untarnished; his patriotism, sincere and ardent. He was also an able, and, when speaking under excitement, an eloquent and a formidable speaker. Creditable, however, to him, as were General Conway's earlier rhetorical efforts in the House of Commons, it is not till 1764—during the debates on the great constitutional question of the legality of arrest and seizure of papers by "General Warrants"—that we find him delivering the earliest of those fine and effective bursts of oratory with which he henceforth, from time to time, electrified the House. To Lord Hertford, Walpole writes, on the 6th of February in that year: "For about two hours the debate hobbled on very lamely; when, on a sudden, your brother rose and made such a speech, —but I wish anybody was to give you the account except me, whom you will think partial; but you will hear enough of it to confirm anything I can say.

[1] 'Memoirs of the Reign of George III.,' vol. ii. p. 207.

Imagine fire, rapidity, argument, knowledge, wit, ridicule, grace, spirit, all pouring like a torrent, but without clashing. Imagine the House in a tumult of continued applause. Imagine the Ministers thunderstruck; lawyers abashed and almost blushing, for it was on their quibbles and evasions he fell most heavily, at the same time answering a whole session of arguments on the side of the Court. No; it was *unique*. You can neither conceive it, nor the exclamations it occasioned." [1]

For opposing the Government on the question of the legality of General Warrants, General Conway was visited by the Grenville Administration with the severest penalties which it lay in its power to inflict. To his brother, Lord Hertford, he writes on the 23rd of April: "You will, I think, be much surprised at the extraordinary news I received yesterday, of my total dismission from his Majesty's service, both as groom of the bedchamber and colonel of a regiment." The proceeding, indeed, is denounced by him as "the harshest and most unjust treatment ever offered to any man on the like occasion;"[2] yet heavily as he must have felt not only the degradation but the diminution of fortune, he bore the blow with a philosophy which must have excited the admiration even of his enemies. "Mr. Conway," writes Walpole on the 14th of May, "is turned out of the King's bedchamber and out of his regiment. His temper,

[1] Walpole's 'Letters,' vol. iv. p. 179.   [2] Ibid., vol. iv. pp. 228, 229.

patience, resignation, are beyond example. His calmness and content prove how much his mind is at ease. He would not bear his sufferings with such fortitude if his conduct had not been as pure as virtue itself."[1] Nevertheless, a clear indication of his deep sense of the great wrong which had been inflicted upon him was extorted from him, though not till many months afterwards, in the House of Commons. " An accidental debate happening," writes Walpole, " General Conway, to the surprise of everybody, and particularly of me, who had with astonishment beheld his tranquillity, broke out on his own dismission, and attacked George Grenville with a fire, eloquence, and rapidity of passion and bitterness that showed both how much he had resented and how much he had concealed. Very warm words passed between them. Great applause was given to Conway by the Opposition; and the ministers felt that the vengeance they had exerted began to lose something of its sweetness."[2]

"Friends," it has been said, "are born for the days of adversity." Happily for Conway, the wrong which he had sustained at the hands of his enemies was amply counterbalanced by the proofs of tenderness and fidelity which he received from those by whom he had long been beloved and appreciated. It was, indeed, to the credit of human nature that,

[1] Walpole's 'Letters,' vol. iv. p. 235.
[2] Walpole's 'Reign of George III.,' vol. ii. p. 43.

without any previous communication one with the other, Lord Hertford, the Duke of Devonshire, and Horace Walpole severally pressed him to accept an income from them equivalent to the loss which he had sustained. " Horace Walpole," writes Conway to Lord Hertford, " has, on this occasion, shown that warmth of friendship that you know him capable of, so strongly that I want words to express my sense of it."[1] The Duke, it should be mentioned, survived his generous offer only a few months; dying at Spa on the 2nd of October, 1764, at the age of forty-four, and bequeathing to General Conway, by a codicil to his will, the sum of five thousand pounds. "I give to General Conway," runs the codicil, which is in the Duke's own handwriting, " five thousand pounds as a testimony of my friendship to him, and of my sense of his honourable conduct and friendship for me."[2]

On the dismissal of George Grenville from power, and the formation of the weak, though well-intentioned, Rockingham Administration, in July, 1765, General Conway was appointed Secretary of State. In the mean time, Grenville, previously to having been driven from power, had succeeded in carrying his famous and fatal measure, the American Stamp Act, leaving to his successors the ungracious obligation of encountering the burst of grief and indignation with which the arbitrary imposition of taxes

[1] Walpole's 'Letters,' vol. iv. p. 230.
[2] Ibid., vol. iv. p. 280, *note*, 281.

on their country inspired all classes of the American people. From this time the tidings from America became in the highest degree alarming. Not only were associations formed there to exclude the importation and use of British manufactures, but the colonists even arrived unhesitatingly at the resolution of refusing to repay the large sums for which they were in debt to the principal English merchants, on account of goods and wares imported from the mother-country. Thus trade between the two countries was almost destroyed; the merchants of Bristol and Liverpool were reduced to a state of bankruptcy; in the manufacturing towns a third of the artisans were out of employment; while England, no less clamorously than America, demanded a speedy adjustment of the dispute. Such was the critical state of affairs when, on the 21st of February, 1766, General Conway, with all eyes fixed upon him, rose from his seat in the House of Commons, and, as spokesman of the new Ministry, formally moved for permission to bring in a Bill for the immediate repeal of the obnoxious measure of the late Government. The House was crowded with members; the galleries and lobby were filled with merchants from the seaport towns; seldom, within the walls of St. Stephen's, had party feeling run higher, never had a question of more vital national importance been under discussion beneath its roof. That Conway spoke ably and eloquently may be readily imagined. Happily, too, his words carried with them conviction to the House ; and accordingly when, at half past one o'clock in the morning, the House of Commons divided, ministers were declared to be in a large majority, the numbers being 275 to 167. The members dispersed in a state of considerable excitement, Grenville and his friends testifying in no measured terms their indignation at their favourite policy having been bastardized. As the chiefs of the two great political parties retired through the crowd of merchants and other persons who thronged the avenues leading from the House of Commons, they were severally greeted with expressions of applause or of disapprobation according to the part which they had played in the momentous debate. Conway was the first who made his appearance : his fine countenance, we are told, radiant with satisfaction at the triumph which he had achieved for his party, and at the essential service which he had rendered to humanity and to his country. Burke, in a misplaced quotation from the Scriptures, describes it "as it had been the face of an angel."[1] The crowd, as they opened an avenue to allow him to pass, not only thanked and congratulated him, but, as his carriage drove off, honoured him with three rounds of huzzas. Grenville, on the contrary, was received with groans and hisses. Exasperated beyond all power of self-control, he seized one of the most vociferous of the offenders

[1] Acts vi. 15.

by the throat, when, but for the man's pusillanimity, the consequences might have been serious. " Well!" said the fellow, " if I may not hiss, at least I may laugh." Grenville flung the man from his grasp and passed on.

In July, 1766, after a tenure of office of scarcely more than twelve months, the Rockingham Administration succumbed to its own weakness. The almost universal demand of the country, at this time, was for the return of Mr. Pitt, the " Great Commoner," to power; and Conway, in whose breast the welfare of his country was second to no selfish consideration, readily acquiesced in the wisdom of the requirement. When George the Third, for instance, intimated to Conway, in the royal closet, that he had actually sent for Mr. Pitt—" Sir," was Conway's reply, " I am glad of it. I always thought it the best thing your Majesty could do. I wish it may answer. Mr. Pitt is a great man ; but as nobody is without faults, he is not unexceptional." " To Conway alone " (on his retiring), writes Walpole, " his Majesty was gracious, and told him he hoped never to have an administration of which he should not be one."[1] Nor was the King's manner to Conway less "gracious" on his subsequently declining to fill the post of Master-General of the Ordnance. " When the King offered him the Ordnance," writes Walpole, " he desired to be excused ; but offered to do the whole business of

[1] Walpole's 'Reign of George III.,' vol. ii. p. 338.

Master without taking the salary, adding that, if his Majesty would appoint no Master, he thought he could make advantageous improvements in the office. The King told Conway he was a phenomenon; that there was no satisfying other people, but he would not take even what was offered to him."[1]

In the mean time, one of the results of the King's sending for Pitt to the royal closet had been the continuance of Conway as Secretary of State, which post he filled till January, 1768, when he resigned the seals. His next appointment, bearing date the 22nd of October, 1772, was as Governor of Jersey, where, according to Walpole, he "acted in his diminutive islet with as much virtue and popularity as Cicero in his large Sicily."[2] The zeal, indeed, with which he entered upon the discharge of his new military duties kept pace with the ardour with which he had fulfilled his previous and more important obligations to the State. In the mean time, in the month of October, 1775, early in the fatal war of American Independence, we find him, in a powerful speech in the House of Commons, charging Lord North and his political colleagues with the folly and wickedness of having involved their country in that memorable contest. "In the Commons," again writes Walpole, "Mr. Conway, in a hotter speech than ever was made, exposed all their

[1] Walpole's 'Reign of George III.,' vol. iv. p. 55.
[2] Walpole's 'Letters,' vol. vii. p. 266.

outrages and blunders; and Charles Fox told North, that not Alexander, nor Cæsar, had ever conquered so much as he had lost in one campaign."[1]

Up to this time the life of General Conway may be admitted to have been a singularly successful, prosperous, and even happy one. The next year, however, brought with it not only bodily disorder, but mental suffering and affliction. In the month of August, 1776, he was satisfactorily recovering from a seizure of a paralytic character which had occasioned great alarm to his friends, when the occurrence of a frightful tragedy in his domestic circle alike threatened him with a return of his formidable disorder, and brought misery and horror to his hearth. The person, it should be mentioned, who, next to Lady Aylesbury, was at this time dearest to him in the world, was their only child, Anne Seymour Conway, a young lady of many virtues and of great accomplishments, who, in the month of June, 1767, contracted an apparently highly desirable match by marrying the Honourable John Damer, eldest son of Joseph Lord Milton,[2] a young man already in possession of five thousand a year, and with a further fortune of twenty-two thousand a year in expectation. "Mrs. Damer, General Conway's daughter," writes Walpole on one occasion to Sir Horace Mann, "is going abroad to confirm a very delicate constitution. She

[1] Walpole's 'Letters,' vol. vi. p. 278.
[2] Created, in May, 1792, Viscount Milton and Earl of Dorchester.

has one of the most solid understandings I ever knew; astonishingly improved, but with so much reserve and modesty, that I have often told Mr. Conway he does not know the extent of her capacity and the solidity of her reason. We have, by accident, discovered that she writes Latin like Pliny, and is learning Greek. In Italy she will be a prodigy. She models like Bernini; has excelled the moderns in the similitudes of her busts, and has lately begun one in marble."[1] Unfortunately, Mr. Damer's resources, ample as they were, were outstripped by his extravagance; the debts in which they involved him increased to a ruinous amount; his father refused either to discharge them or to see his face. Whether, consequently, these circumstances preyed upon his mind, or whether insanity rendered him an irresponsible being, he formed the unhappy resolution of depriving himself of existence. "On Thursday," runs the remarkable account of Walpole, "Mr. Damer supped at the Bedford Arms in Covent Garden, with four common women, a blind fiddler, and no other man. At three in the morning he dismissed his seraglio, bidding each receive her guinea at the bar, and ordering Orpheus to come up again in half an hour. When he [the fiddler] returned, he found a dead silence, and smelt gunpowder. He called; the master of the house came up, and found Mr. Damer sitting in his chair, dead, with a pistol by him, and

[1] Walpole's 'Letters,' vol. viii. p. 76.

another in his pocket! The ball had not gone through his head, nor made any report. On the table lay a scrap of paper with these words: 'The people of the house are not to blame for what has happened, which was my own act.' This was the sole tribute he paid to justice and decency."[1] It was to Mr. Damer's widow—whom Walpole, to use his own words, loved as his "own child"—that he bequeathed Strawberry Hill for her lifetime. Mrs. Damer died in 1826, having survived her unhappy husband fifty years.

It was reserved to General Conway, in his place in the House of Commons, to render one more signal service to his country. The unpopularity, it should be mentioned, of Lord North and his colleagues had reached its height, and the people of England were becoming more and more convinced of the folly and madness of continuing the wretched war with America, when, on the 22nd of February, 1782, Conway, in a crowded and anxious House of Commons, rose and moved an Address to the Throne, praying "that the war on the continent of North America might no longer be pursued for the impracticable purpose of reducing the inhabitants of that country to obedience." For many reasons it may be questioned whether the task which he had undertaken could have been intrusted to a person better qualified to carry it into effect. He had not only

[1] Walpole's 'Letters,' vol. vi. p. 368.

been the first, in former years, to foretell the terrible mischief with which Grenville's fatal Stamp Act had been pregnant, but he was also the person who had moved for, and had carried, its repeal. Moreover, he had, in readiness for the present occasion, diligently investigated, and thoroughly mastered, the merits of the all-important question committed to his management; his patriotism and integrity were admitted to be of the very purest cast; and lastly, being unshackled by party connections, his arguments promised to carry with them all the weight emanating from strong sense, from mature experience, and from too holy and earnest intentions. Happily, the success which crowned his efforts was complete. "The effect of his speech," writes Walpole, " was incredible."[1] The truth and sincerity, indeed, which it breathed, combined with his manifest and affecting single-mindedness of purpose, and his intimate acquaintance with facts, rendered his speech, if not the most eloquent, at least one of the most convincing and effective of any in the memory of the oldest member of the House of Commons. To Lord North's Administration it may be said to have proved fatal. Such, in fact, was the effect which it produced, that when, amidst a scene of extraordinary excitement, a division took place, it was found that ministers were reduced to a majority of only one; the numbers being 194 to 193. Hearty congratulations

[1] Walpole's 'Last Journals,' vol. ii. p. 506.

greeted Conway on his noble success, of which the most eloquent was that of Charles Fox. Twice, he said, Conway had saved his country: this was his second triumph.

On the 20th of March, Lord North resigned the Premiership; and, on the 30th of that month, General Conway was appointed to succeed Lord Amherst as Commander-in-chief of the Forces. This appointment, the last he ever held under the State, he vacated in December the following year.

The old age of General Conway was, as may be readily anticipated, one of tranquillity and grace. His closing years were spent at his beautiful seat on the banks of the Thames—Park Place, near Henley; "happy," we are told, "in the resources of his own mind, and in the cultivation of useful science, in the bosom of domestic peace, unenriched by pensions or places, undistinguished by titles or ribands, unsophisticated by public life, unwearied by retirement,"[1] he not only enjoyed a literary taste, but was the writer of some light literary pieces, especially of a comedy entitled, 'False Appearances,' translated from 'L'Homme du Jour' of Boissy, which was privately performed before a patrician audience at Richmond House in 1788; Lord Derby, the future husband of Miss Farren, delivering the prologue, and Mrs. Damer, "with inimitable spirit and grace," the

[1] Earl Russell's 'Correspondence of John, fourth Duke of Bedford,' vol. iii. p. 384.

epilogue. The following year, 'False Appearances' was publicly acted at Drury Lane Theatre, where, as we learn from Walpole, who witnessed its performance from Mrs. Garrick's box, it met with considerable success.[1]

General Conway possessed not only a taste for literature, but also for science; the result of his chemical studies, it is said, proving very profitable to persons to whom he communicated his discoveries.[2] Having survived his advancement to the rank of Field-Marshal about a year and nine months, he died suddenly at Park Place on the 9th of July, 1795, at the age of seventy-five.

[1] Walpole's 'Letters,' vol. ix. pp. 128, 177; 'Auckland Correspondence,' vol. ii. p. 316.

[2] 'Bedford Correspondence,' vol. iii. p. 384, *note*.

LIEUTENANT-GENERAL JOHN MARQUIS OF GRANBY.

THERE was a time when the valour and virtues of John Marquis of Granby were not only household words on the lips of every Englishman, but when his popularity was such that his head was the distinguishing sign of half the taverns in the kingdom. The latter have probably severally passed away with the generations which lived contemporaneously with their favourite hero, and yet not on that account has the hero of Warburg and Philliphausen the less claim to the good word of the historian or of the biographer. Born on the 2nd of January, 1721, Lord Granby was the eldest son of John, third Duke of Rutland, by Bridget Sutton, daughter of Robert Sutton, last Baron Lexington. After quitting Eton— where, we may mention, he stood lower down in the school than Marshal Conway, but above another future eminent General, Sir William Draper—he

studied at Trinity College, Cambridge. His next,
and more welcome, call was to arms, on the breaking
out of the Scottish Rebellion of 1745, when, in
his twenty-sixth year, he alike afforded ample proof
of his loyalty to the reigning family, as well as of
his military ardour, by raising, at his own expense, a
regiment of infantry, with which he joined the
expedition of the Duke of Cumberland into Scotland,
and subsequently earned the special thanks of the
Duke on the field of Culloden. It was at this early
period, too, that probably commenced that complete
confidence and affectionate understanding between
Lord Granby and the soldiers who from time to time
served under his command; the instances of which,
when we sometimes meet with them in the biography
of distinguished military commanders, are usually
among its most pleasing episodes. Ever ready, not
only to share with them the dangers common to both,
but to dash with them into the thickest ranks of the
foe, Lord Granby was at the same time compassionate,
affable, and considerate to his men, prepared
at all times to listen to their grievances, to
administer to their comfort, and to alleviate their
sufferings when prostrated by sickness or wounds.
His heroism and humanity, in fact, rendered him the
idol of the military; while the nation was scarcely
behindhand with the army in dealing out to him
the credit which was ungrudgingly admitted to be
his due.

Needless it may be to point out to the reader, that by far the larger share of the high military reputations enjoyed by Lord Granby was achieved by him during the celebrated Seven Years' War, in which he served with the British forces employed under the general command of Prince Ferdinand of Brunswick. On the 4th of March, 1755, he had been promoted to be a Major-General, with which rank, in 1758, he proceeded to Germany as second in command of the British force serving in that country under the immediate orders of Lord George Sackville. On the 5th of February in the ensuing year, he was advanced to the rank of Lieutenant-General, and, on the 1st of August, the same year, was present at the battle of Minden, in which engagement the notable remissness of Lord George to lead the British cavalry to the charge, when expressly and urgently commanded to do so by Prince Ferdinand, alike deprived Lord Granby of an admirable opportunity of distinguishing himself, and robbed the Prince of half the fruits of his victory. The Prince, however, in his General Order dated after the battle, did all that lay in his power to heal the wounded feelings of his dashing companion-in-arms. Pointedly omitting all mention of Lord George Sackville, the Order runs— "His Serene Highness further orders it to be declared to Lieutenant-General the Marquis of Granby that he is persuaded that, if he had had the good fortune to have had him at the head of the cavalry of the right wing, his presence would have greatly contributed to make the decision of that day more complete and more brilliant."[1] Lord George's inexplicable conduct at all events made room for the advancement of Lord Granby. Before the close of the month, the latter was appointed to supersede Lord George as Commander-in-chief of the British forces serving in Germany.

At the celebrated court-martial which was subsequently held on Lord George, Lord Granby, though having little reason either to love or to screen his last commanding officer, gave his evidence against him with a compassionate forbearance and tenderness which were highly creditable to his heart. "So far," writes Walpole, "from exaggerating the minutest circumstance, he palliated or suppressed whatever might load the prisoner, and seemed to study nothing but how to avoid appearing a party against him, so inseparable in his bosom were valour and good-nature."[2]

On the return of Lord Granby to Germany, as well as during the remainder of the war, he continued, while in the active exercise of his military qualities, to justify the high opinion formed of them by his admirers and friends. At Warburg, in 1760, a spirited charge, led by him at the head of the

[1] Smollett's 'Hist. of England,' vol. iv. p. 269, *note*; 'Annual Register' for 1759, p. 233.
[2] Walpole's 'Reign of George II.,' vol. iii. pp. 271, 272.

British cavalry, proved mainly instrumental in deciding the fate of the battle; the following year, in the skirmishes before and in the action at Kirch-Denkern, he and Prince Ferdinand vied with each other in the display of personal bravery; and, lastly, at Lüttemberg, in 1762, Lord Granby commanded the right wing of the allied army.

With the termination of hostilities, Lord Granby, having returned to his own country, devoted himself to the more peaceful duties of a Member of Parliament and father of a family. At an early age he had sat in the House of Commons as Member for Grantham; but since 1754 had represented Cambridgeshire in Parliament. In the mean time, on the 15th of September, 1759, he had been appointed Lieutenant-General of the Ordnance; on the 2nd of May, the following year, he was nominated a Member of the Privy Council; on the 14th of May, 1763, he was constituted Master-General of the Ordnance; and, on the 13th of August, 1766, Commander-in-Chief of the Army, which latter high appointment he held till 1769.

The mother of Lord Granby's children was Lady Frances Seymour, eldest daughter of Charles, seventh Duke of Somerset, to whom he was married on the 3rd of September, 1750, and by which lady, besides other offspring, he was the father of Charles, fourth Duke of Rutland, and of Lord Robert Manners, who, when in command of the *Resolution* vessel of war, died, on the 23rd of January, 1782, of wounds received in action.

Of Lord Granby's personal appearance and peculiarities, his schoolfellow, Horace Walpole, has left us an interesting sketch. " His large and open countenance," writes the latter, " its manly and pure colours glowing with health, his robust and commanding person, and a proportion of florid beauty so great that the baldness of his head, which he carried totally bare, was rather an addition to its comely roundness than a defect, and a singularity more than an affectation; all distinguished him without any extrinsic ornament, and pointed out his rank when he walked without attendance, and was mixed with the lowest people who followed him to beg his charity, or to bless him for it. His mind was as rich in the qualities that became his elevated situation. Intrepidity, sincerity, humanity, and generosity were not only innate in his breast, but were never corrupted there. His courage and his tenderness were never disunited. He was dauntless on every occasion, but when it was necessary to surmount his bashfulness, his nerves trembled like a woman's; when it was requisite that he should speak in public, his modesty was incapable of ostentation. His rank, his services, and the idolatry of the people could inspire him with no pride—a sensation his nature knew not. Of money he seemed to conceive no use but in giving it away; but that profusion was so indiscriminate that compassion or solicitation, and consequently imposture, were equally the masters of his purse."[1]

"Granby stands without a flaw;
At least, each fault he did possess
Rose from some virtue in excess.
Pierced by the piteous tale of grief,
When wretches sought of him relief,
His eyes large drops of pearl distilling,
He'd give—till left without a shilling!
What most his manly heart-strings tore,
Was, when he felt, and found no more."[2]

Even Junius, unfriendly as are his comments on Lord Granby's civil administration of military affairs, is a panegyrist of his private virtues. "In private life," he writes, "he was unquestionably that good man who, for the interest of his country, ought to have been a great one."[3]

Lord Granby died suddenly at Scarborough on the 19th of October, 1770, in the fiftieth year of his age. His remains were interred in the burial-place of his ancestors, at Bottesford, in Leicestershire.

[1] Walpole's 'Reign of George III.,' vol. iv. pp. 176, 177.
[2] Poem by Major Henry Waller; 'Gentleman's Magazine' for September 1784, vol. liv. p. 688.
[3] Letter of February 21, 1769; note by Junius himself.

LIEUTENANT-GENERAL
SIR WILLIAM DRAPER, K.B.

PANEGYRIZED by the illustrious Chatham in one of his finest orations, as one "whose noble and generous spirit would do honour to the proudest grandee of the country," this accomplished soldier, the conqueror of Manilla and the controversial antagonist of Junius, could claim no higher birth than that of being the son of a Collector of the Customs at Bristol. He was born in 1721, the same year as his schoolfellow, fellow-soldier, and friend, Lord Granby,

From the foundation at Eton, to which he owed his education, William Draper was elected to King's College in 1740; took his degree of B.A. in 1744; of M.A. in 1749; and, apparently about the latter date, quitted King's College, of which he had become a Fellow, for a commission in the Guards. India, however, had in the mean time begun to present to the military aspirant the expectation of reaping a rich harvest of laurels and pagodas; and, accordingly, having betaken himself to that country, he there placed himself under the victorious banners of Clive and Lawrence; won for himself the good opinion and confidence of those distinguished officers; and especially signalized himself, in 1758, at the capture from the French of Fort St. George, as Madras was then designated.[1] Returning to England, in 1760, with the rank of Colonel, he was rewarded with the Governorship of Yarmouth, and, the following year, served in command of a brigade at the expedition against Belleisle. To these facts we should add that, on his return shortly afterwards to India, he carried with him no less flattering a testimonial than an especial recommendation from Lord Chatham to the East India Company for his active employment, this recommendation describing him as an officer "on whose intelligence and bravery Government could depend."

Happily, on the breaking out of the war with Spain, before the close of this year,[2] this timely recommendation of England's great War Minister had its due weight with the Indian Government. The important conquest of Manilla was the consequence. "An expedition against the Philippine Islands," writes Earl Stanhope, "had been sent out from Madras. It comprised only one King's regiment, and in all, including sepoys and marines, only 2300 men of land forces, commanded by Brigadier-

[1] According to contemporary authority, he retained his Fellowship at King's College all this time. "The King's men keep their Fellowships when Generals, as Sir W. Draper; or Ambassadors, as Hare to Warsaw."—'Gentleman's Magazine' for 1779, p. 641. [2] 1762.

General, afterwards Sir William, Draper. They landed near Manilla, the chief city, on the 24th of September, before the Spanish garrison had received any official tidings of the war. The Archbishop, however, who acted as General and Governor, maintained his walls with becoming resolution; nay, on one occasion he directed a sally of several hundred native islanders, who had been trained to arms in the Spanish service, and who came rushing on with savage ferocity; but they were soon repulsed, and many of them died gnawing like wild beasts the bayonets that pierced them. On the twelfth day after the landing, a practicable breach having been effected, the English carried the city by storm, and gave it up during several hours to all the horrors of pillage. The Archbishop and his officers, who had retired to the citadel, were admitted to a capitulation for the whole cluster of islands and the ships in harbour, by which they consented to pay as ransom for their property two millions of dollars in money, and the same sum in bills upon the Treasury at Madrid.[1] The colours captured by General Draper on this occasion he presented to the Provost and Fellows of King's College, in whose beautiful chapel they long remained suspended.

On General Draper's return to England, he obtained a seat in the House of Commons; was rewarded for his services at Manilla with the highest

[1] Earl Stanhope's 'Hist. of England,' vol. iv. pp. 400, 401.

grade of the Order of the Bath, that of K.B.; and on his regiment, the 79th, being reduced, was, unsolicited on his part, appointed by the King to the colonelcy of the 16th Foot. This latter command he exchanged with Colonel Gisburne for his half-pay of 200$l.$, Irish annuities, an arrangement which, though apparently of no uncommon occurrence at the time, was subsequently severely impugned by Junius. Of the Manilla ransom—his personal share of which was computed to amount to 25,000$l.$—neither he nor his brave followers ever received a farthing. It was to no purpose that, in an able pamphlet,[1] as well as in his place in Parliament, he indignantly inveighed against the false faith of which they had been made the victims: the bills drawn on the Treasury at Madrid were never honoured; the Spanish Government peremptorily refusing to abide by the treaty.

It was, as is well known, occasioned by his chivalrous defence of the conduct of his old schoolfellow and friend, Lord Granby, when Commander-in-Chief, that Sir William Draper first provoked the ire and affected scorn of Junius. Sir William's opening letter in vindication of his friend is dated the 26th of January, 1769; and, as that letter contained some strong condemnatory reflections on Junius as a cowardly stabber in the dark, it was only natural that the latter should be induced to divert his

[1] Entitled, 'An Answer to the Spanish Arguments for Refusing the Payment of the Ransom Bills.'

attention and spleen from Lord Granby to Lord Granby's defender. Junius accordingly retorted with great severity ; and Sir William, more to the credit of his heart than of his judgment, no less warmly reanswered Junius. The result of their famous altercation is well known. Sir William may have had truth and innocence on his side, on every point on which he was attacked, but, at all events, in the war of wit and recrimination in which he had involved himself, he was evidently no match for his merciless anonymous adversary. "I should justly," are the scornful words addressed to him by Junius, "be suspected of acting upon motives of more than common enmity to Lord Granby, if I continued to give you fresh materials or occasion for writing in his defence."[1]

Before the close of the year 1769, the state of Sir William Draper's health induced him to cross the Atlantic, when he paid a visit of some length to North America, in the course of which sojourn he married a Miss Delancy, daughter of the chief justice of New York. By this lady, who died in July, 1788, he had a daughter born on the 18th of August, 1773.

On the 29th of August, 1777, Sir William was advanced to the rank of Lieutenant-General, and, in 1779, was appointed Lieutenant-Governor of Minorca, in which double capacity, in 1781, he served as second in command under a tried and spirited officer, Lieutenant-General James Murray, at the

[1] Junius to Sir W. Draper, February 21, 1769.

heroic, though unsuccessful defence of that island, when attacked by the united military and naval forces of France and Spain. It was not till the devoted garrison of St. Philip's Castle had been reduced by disease and mortality to the lowest available numbers, that General Murray consented to capitulate, and then only on condition of his exhausted followers being accorded all the honours of war. "General Murray," writes Earl Stanhope, "had continued to maintain St. Philip's Castle with the greatest gallantry. Thus, on one occasion, by a sudden and well-directed sally, he had surprised and chased the Duke de Crillon from his head-quarters at Cape Mola. But, besides the havoc of war, our soldiers were laid low by diseases; not putrid fevers only, but scurvy and dysentery had set in among them. It was found that their zeal often rose superior to their strength. We are told of several soldiers who died on guard; their generous ardour to defend the place having made them hide their sickness to the last, and kept them from the hospitals.[1]

It was an unfortunate termination of the active military services of Sir William Draper that, after the loss of Minorca, he was induced to prefer charges—no fewer than twenty-nine in number—against his gallant superior officer, General Murray. Of these charges, twenty-seven were pronounced to be frivolous and groundless, and Sir William was adjudged to

[1] Earl Stanhope's 'Hist. of England,' vol. vii. p. 199.

make an apology to General Murray; a requisition with which, however unpalatable it may have been to him, he thought fit to comply.

From this period, Sir William Draper appears to have resided in retirement at Bath, where he died on the 8th of January, 1787.

SIR GEORGE BAKER, BART., M.D.

THIS eminent physician and accomplished classical scholar was the son of the Rev. George Baker, Archdeacon and Registrar of Totnes. He was born in 1722. In July, 1742, he passed from the foundation at Eton to King's College; in 1745, he took his degree of B.A.; in 1749, that of M.A.; and, in 1756, that of Doctor of Medicine. Commencing the practice of his profession at Stamford, he removed, after a few years, from that town to London, where, step by step, he raised himself to be physician in ordinary to George III., and physician to Queen Charlotte. On the 14th of August, 1776, he was created a baronet; and, in 1797, was chosen to fill the 'highest post in his profession, that of President of the College of Physicians. He was also a fellow of the Royal and Antiquarian Societies. He married Jane, daughter of Robert Morris, Esq., by whom he had two sons and a daughter, of whom the eldest son, George, died in June, 1802, in the lifetime of his father.

It was to Sir George Baker that Gray paid the

high compliment of dedicating his beautiful 'Elegy written in a Country Churchyard,' an honour which he not only merited on account of fine classical attainments, but from his practising all the virtues which embellish private life. "No man perhaps," writes Nichols, "ever followed the career of physic and the elegant paths of the Greek or Roman Muses for the space of several years with more success than Sir George Baker, the proofs of which may be seen in his published and unpublished works, the splendour of his fortune, the esteem, respect, and admiration of his contemporaries."[1]

When, in the autumn of 1788, the tranquillity of the Court at Windsor Castle was suddenly and painfully disturbed by the mysterious indisposition of George III., Sir George Baker seems to have been the first of the royal physicians to suspect, and the earliest to communicate to the King's ministers his suspicions, that insanity was creeping over the stricken monarch.[2] From this period, and for many months to come, Sir George's necessary share in the charge of the royal person appears to have afforded him neither a very enviable, nor, indeed, a very secure occupation. The population of London, incensed at the tardy advance made by their sick sovereign towards recovery, clamoured loudly against the Court physicians; the Queen had transferred her

---

[1] Nichols's 'Literary Anecdotes of the 18th Century,' vol. iii. pp. 70, 71.
[2] 'Journals of the House of Lords,' vol. xxxviii. pp. 272, 273.

former confidence in them to the shrewd, though irregular, practitioner, Dr. Francis Willis; while the King, in his hours of delirium, manifested an aversion towards the subject of the present memoir which disease alone could have originated. Of this last-mentioned fact, a remarkable example occurred on the night of the 6th of November, at a crisis in the King's malady, in which, in the opinion of the royal physicians in attendance, his Majesty's life was in imminent danger. On this night, then, the Prince of Wales, the Duke of York, and the physicians and equerries happened to be reposing, some on sofas, and others seated on chairs in an apartment close to that of the King, when, to their alarm and astonishment, the sick monarch suddenly appeared amongst them. His amazement at finding himself in the midst of so unusual an assemblage was as great as theirs, and accordingly he eagerly inquired of them what they were doing there. The Princes of the blood, owing to the stars which they wore on their breasts, ought to have been distinguishable from the rest, but, in consequence of the apartment being very dimly lighted, the King failed to recognize them, although from some touching words which escaped his lips, it was manifest that one of them, his favourite son, the Duke of York, was uppermost in his thoughts. In the mean time, no one present dared lay hands on, or remonstrate with their sovereign. "Sir George Baker was there," writes Madame D'Arblay, who was then at Windsor in attendance on the Queen, "and was privately exhorted by the gentlemen to lead the King back to his room; but he had not courage. He attempted only to speak, and the King penned him in a corner; told him he was a mere old woman; that he wondered he had ever followed his advice, for he knew nothing of his complaint, which was only nervous."[1] Nor is this the only occasion, at this period, on which we find Sir George suffering violence at the hands of his illustrious patient. "He" (the King), writes Lord Sheffield to Mr. Eden, on the 22nd of the month, "took Sir George Baker's wig, flung it in his face, threw him on his back, and told him he might star-gaze."[2]

In the mean time, so universally at this period was public sympathy excited in favour of the afflicted monarch, that the King's physicians not only began to receive anonymous letters threatening them with condign punishment in the event of his illness proving fatal, but Sir George Baker, having been stopped in his coach by the populace, would seem to have had a narrow escape from being subjected by his assaulters to personal violence. So high, indeed, ran at this time the altered tide of loyalty and affection, that another of the royal physicians, Sir Lucas Pepys, told Miss Burney that, in the event of the King dying, he believed that none of their lives would be safe."[3]

[1] Madame D'Arblay's 'Diary and Letters,' vol. iv. p. 299.
[2] 'Auckland Correspondence,' vol. ii. p. 244.
[3] Madame D'Arblay's 'Diary and Letters,' vol. iv. pp. 336, 337.

Sir George Baker, it may be mentioned, was the author of some occasional treatises on medical subjects, which in the present century are probably but seldom consulted. His Latin preface to a later edition of the Pharmacopœia of the Medical College affords, perhaps, the best example of that chaste Latinity for which his reputation stood so high among his classical contemporaries.

Exempted in a remarkable degree during a long existence from the infirmities incidental to human nature, Sir George Baker expired tranquilly in Jermyn Street, London, on the 15th of June, 1809, in the eighty-eighth year of his age.

CHRISTOPHER ANSTEY.

GENERALLY speaking, a life passed partly in academic seclusion as the Fellow of a College, and partly in following the pursuits of a country gentleman, can scarcely be expected to supply biography with any very important or very interesting materials ; nor does the uneventful career of the author of the celebrated humorous poem, the ' New Bath Guide,' present any exceptions to this remark. Christopher Anstey, the son of the Reverend Christopher Anstey, incumbent of the small living of Brinkley, in Cambridgeshire, by Mary, daughter of Anthony Thompson, Esq., of Trumpington, in that county, was born on the 31st of October, 1724. From Bury St. Edmunds, where he had been previously educated, he was transferred to the foundation at Eton, where he acquired a character for diligence and ability, and whence, in 1742, he was elected to King's College. Here his Tripos verses, composed by him when he was an undergraduate, in 1745, extended his reputation for classical scholarship, and of King's College he in due time became a Fellow

At Cambridge, Anstey continued occasionally to reside during the ensuing eight or nine years, when the death of his mother, in 1754, having put him in possession of the family estate of Trumpington, he resigned his Fellowship. He was now justified in indulging in the luxury of marriage ; and accordingly, in the year 1756, he married Ann, daughter of Felix Calvert, Esq., of Albury Hall, in Hertfordshire, and sister of John Calvert, Esq., who, during several successive Parliaments, represented the borough of Hertford in the House of Commons. With this lady—" who," to quote the words of her son, " was allowed to possess every endowment of person and qualification of mind and disposition which could render her interesting and attractive in domestic life, and whom he justly regarded as the pattern of every virtue and the source of all his happiness"—he passed nearly half a century of " uninterrupted and undiminished esteem and affection."[1] The first fourteen years of his married life were spent by him at his seat at Trumpington, in dispensing and receiving hospitality, and in occupying himself with country pursuits and pleasures. In the language of his own Muse—

"From wealth, from honours, and from courts removed,
I've kept the silent path my genius loved,
And pitied those whom Fortune oft beguiles
With flattering hopes from false Ambition's smiles ;

---

[1] Anstey's 'Poetical Works,' Memoir by his Son, prefixed, p. xii.

> Hence far from me the prostituted hour
> Of adulation based on pride or power;
> Hence, thanks to Heaven, I ne'er was doomed to know
> What bitter streams from disappointment flow;
>   Oh! bane of life's sweet cup!"[1]

"Habituated," writes his son, "to the charms of literary ease and retirement, passionately fond of the sports of the field and the amusements of a country life, he followed the bent of his natural genius and inclination without restraint; and, in the enjoyment of a competent and independent fortune, found leisure for the study of the Greek and Roman authors, and the poetry and polite literature of his own country."[2]

It was while Anstey was residing at Trumpington that he composed his 'New Bath Guide,' which was published in a quarto volume at Cambridge in 1766. The several facts of its author being as yet unknown to fame; of its prosaic title throwing out no hint whatever of its lively and original contents; and, lastly, the circumstance of its having been published by a country bookseller instead of in London or at Bath, could scarcely have failed to prove obstacles to its obtaining immediate popularity. It needed, however, but to become known in order to be appreciated by the severest judges of humour and verse. Coarse, indeed, it was in parts, but coarseness was a vice and a fashion of the days in which Anstey flourished, and in this case it would seem in no degree to have

[1] Anstey's 'Poetical Works,' *ut supra*, pp. xii. xiii.   [2] Ibid., p. xiii.

affected the success of the poem. "Have you read the 'New Bath Guide'?" writes Gray to Dr. Wharton. "It is the only thing in fashion, and is a new and original kind of humour."[1] Horace Walpole also writes to George Montagu: "What pleasure have you to come! There is a new thing published that will make you —— your cheeks with laughing. It is called the 'New Bath Guide.' It stole into the world, and for a fortnight no soul looked into it, concluding its name was its true name. No such thing. It is a set of letters in verse, in all kind of verses, describing the life at Bath, and, incidentally, everything else; but so much wit, so much humour, fun, and poetry, so much originality, never met together before.[2] The popularity and success, in fact, of the new poem proved to be almost unprecedented. Dodsley, who, after the publication of the second edition, purchased the copyright for two hundred pounds, candidly confessed, about ten years afterwards, that its sale had proved more profitable to him than that of any other work published by him during any period of corresponding length, and for this reason, in the year 1777, liberally gave back the copyright to the author.[3]

Besides the 'New Bath Guide,' Anstey was the author of an 'Elegy on the Death of the Marquis of

---

[1] Gray's 'Works,' vol. iv. p. 84; Aldine edition.
[2] Walpole's 'Letters,' vol. iv. pp. 504, 505.
[3] Anstey's 'Poetical Works,' ut supra, pp. xxiii. xxv.

Tavistock,' published in 1767; of 'The Patriot,' a poem published in 1768; 'An Election Ball,' in 1776; and other poems; none of which, however, approach in merit his first-published and celebrated effusion.

The last years of Anstey's long, cheerful, temperate, and prosperous existence seem. to have been principally passed by him in the bosom of his family at Bath. Tender-hearted and benevolent, a sincere and steadfast Christian, a devoted husband, a fond and judicious father, and a delightful and instructive companion, few men would seem to have had a larger claim on the affection and esteem of their family and friends. "His increasing years," writes his son, "stole imperceptibly on the even tenor of his life, and gradually lessened the distance of his journey through it without obscuring the serenity of the prospect. Unimpeded by sickness and unclouded by sorrow or any serious misfortune, his life was a life of temperance, of self-denial, and of moderation in all things; and of great regularity. He rose early in the morning, *ante diem poscens chartas*, and was constant on horseback at his usual hour, and in all seasons. His summers were uniformly passed at Cheltenham with his family during the latter part of his life, and, upon his return to Bath in the autumn, he fell habitually into the same unruffled scenes of domestic ease and tranquillity, rendered every day more joyous and interesting to him by the increase of his family circle and the enlargement of his hospitable table, and by many circumstances and occurrences connected with the welfare of his children which gave him infinite delight and satisfaction."[1] His end was a tranquil and apparently a painless one; the venerable poet expiring in the presence of his surrounding family, in 1805, in the eighty-first year of his age. His remains were interred in the parish church of Walcot, in the city of Bath; while a monument, erected by his eldest son, in Poets' Corner, Westminster Abbey, bears testimony to his intellectual endowments.

[1] Anstey's 'Poetical Works,' *ut supra*, pp. liii. liv.

ANTHONY CHAMPION.

THE little that is known of the life of this accomplished person appears to be derived from a biographical sketch of him, written by William Henry Lord Lyttelton, and prefixed by that nobleman to a posthumous collection which he published of his friend's poetical effusions. Far less, indeed, to his fame as a poet than to his virtues and accomplishments, to his benevolence, to his various and extensive scholarship, to his bright natural parts, and to his taste for what is beautiful in Art, Anthony Champion is indebted for the circumscribed niche which he fills in this our gallery of Etonian Worthies. The story of his life may, in fact, be narrated in a few lines. Descended from an ancient family residing at St. Columb, in Cornwall, of which his father, Peter Champion, an opulent Leghorn merchant, appears to have been the representative, he first saw the light at Croydon, in Surrey, on the 5th of February, 1725. Having previously received instruction in Greek and Latin at a school at Cheam, in that county, he was, in 1739, sent to Eton, whence, in February, 1742, he removed to St. Mary's Hall, Oxford, where he remained two years. He now entered himself as a student at law in the Middle Temple, of which corporation he was subsequently elected a Bencher, and for the society of which place he sufficiently testified his partiality, not only by continuing to fix his home there to the day of his decease, but also by bequeathing to it the sum of one thousand pounds. In the mean time, in 1754, while apparently still under thirty years of age, he had been returned to the House of Commons as Member for St. Germans, and, in 1761, sat in Parliament as member for Liskeard, in Cornwall. The same innate modesty and diffidence, however, which we find prevented him from submitting his poetry to the judgment of the world during his lifetime, is said to have also proved fatal to his achieving distinction as an orator. "Beloved and lamented," to use the words of his noble friend and biographer, Anthony Champion died on the 22nd of February, 1801, at the age of seventy-six.

ADMIRAL RICHARD EARL HOWE, K.G.

RICHARD EARL HOWE, to whose intrepidity and skill England is indebted for one of the, *par excellence*, four great naval victories of which she has the most reason to be proud, was the second son of Emanuel Scrope, Viscount Howe, by Mary Sophia Charlotte Kielmansegge, daughter of Sophia Charlotte Countess of Platen and Darlington, by her royal lover, King George I. Born in 1725, he had the misfortune, at the age of ten, to lose his father, who died as Governor of Barbadoes, in 1735. Inferring from the fact of his having entered the naval service at or about the age of fourteen, his continuance at Eton could scarcely have been of very long duration. "In my boyhood," was the reply of Provost Goodall to an inquiry of Sir John Barrow, "I understood that he left Eton in the Second or Third Form."[1]

The ship in which Richard Howe first encountered the perils of the sea was the *Severn*, of fifty guns,

[1] Barrow's 'Life of Earl Howe,' p. 4.

commanded by the Honourable Captain Edward Legge, and forming one of the squadron under the orders of Commodore Anson, intended to attack the Spanish settlements in the Pacific Ocean. A violent tempest, however, by which the *Severn* was overtaken after having rounded Cape Horn, compelled her to bear up for Rio de Janeiro to refit,and thus interposed an insurmountable obstacle to the young midshipman sharing the memorable adventures and fortunes of the gallant Anson. His career, however, from this period till his promotion to the rank of Captain, on the 10th of April, 1746, at the age of twenty-one, was not an undistinguished one. As midshipman of the *Burford*, he served in an attack, in 1742, on La Guayra, on the coast of the Caraccas; as a Lieutenant, he signalized himself by cutting out a captured English merchant-ship from under the guns of the Dutch settlement of St. Eustatias ; and, when Commander of the *Baltimore*, during the Scottish Rebellion of 1745–6, was severely wounded in the head in a successful engagement with two French frigates, laden with troops and ammunition for the service of the Pretender.

The next exploit performed by Captain Howe was in command of the *Dunkirk*, of sixty guns, in 1756, when he captured the *Alcide*, of sixty-four guns, off the coast of Newfoundland. In 1757-8, when in command of the *Magnanime*, and afterwards of the *Essex*, he performed valuable service at the attack and capture of the Isle d'Aix, in the operations against St. Malo, and at the capture of Cherbourg and the destruction of its strongly fortified basin. Under his command on board the *Essex*, in the last-named expedition, served Edward Augustus Duke of York, younger brother of George III., who had just joined the naval service as a midshipman, and who could scarcely have been committed to the care of an officer better qualified to take charge of a high-spirited young Prince of the Blood than was Captain Howe. Among the military officers, too, who were his associates in the expedition, were his former schoolfellow, General Conway, and General Wolfe. "Howe, brother of the lord of that name," writes Walpole in allusion to the chief leaders of the expedition, "was the third on the naval list. He was undaunted as a rock, and as silent; the characteristics of his whole race. He and Wolfe soon contracted a friendship like the union of a cannon and gunpowder."[1]

To Cherbourg succeeded the disastrous affair of St. Cas, in which Captain Howe's gallantry was surpassed only by his humanity. The British army, after the capture of Cherbourg, had again been successfully landed, about two leagues to the westward of St. Malo, but, in consequence of the rapid approach of a superior French force under the command of the Duc d'Aiguillon, found it advisable to re-embark as

[1] Walpole's 'Memoirs of the Reign of George II.,' vol. iii. p. 50.

soon as possible. While thus occupied, however, and while the beach was still crowded with retreating British soldiers, the enemy suddenly descended from the high grounds, and fell upon the rear-guard, most of whom, after the performance of acts of heroic gallantry, were cut to pieces. General Drury and ten other officers lost their lives. "On this trying occasion," writes Sir John Barrow, "the conduct of Howe was eminently conspicuous. The Grenadiers had nothing left for it but to escape with all speed to the boats or remain to be killed; they were ordered, therefore, to make to the shore as quickly as possible. A battery, thrown up on the hill, shattered several of the boats to pieces. As some of these approached the shore, many of the seamen were killed or wounded, which so intimidated the rowers that they hesitated to proceed, and lay upon their oars. Howe observing this, and suspecting the cause of their backwardness, jumped into his barge, rowed into the midst of the fire of shot and shells, and standing upright in the boat waved the seamen to follow him. His example animated their depressed spirits; no one now thought of shrinking, but all strived who could pick up the greatest number of poor fellows, some swimming, others wading into the sea."[1] To Howe, indeed, such a sensation as fear seems to have been almost a stranger. When subsequently, for instance, he was in command of the *Princess Amelia*, as Flag

[1] Barrow's 'Life of Earl Howe,' pp. 51, 52.

Captain to the Duke of York, then recently promoted to the rank of Rear-Admiral, he was one night roused from his sleep by the lieutenant of the watch, who, in much apparent agitation, informed him that the ship was on fire close to the magazine; at the same time, however, enjoining him not to be frightened, as the fire would soon be got under. "Frightened, sir," replied Howe; "what do you mean by that? I never was frightened in my life;" and, looking the lieutenant coolly and fixedly in the face, he added—"Pray, sir, how does a man *feel* when he is frightened? I need not ask how he *looks*. I will be with you immediately; but take care that his Royal Highness is not disturbed."[1]

Besides his share in the above-mentioned operations on the coast of France, there occurred other, though less stirring, events in 1758, which rendered that year an important one in Howe's existence. On the 10th of March, 1758, at the age of thirty-three, he married Mary, daughter of Chiverton Hartop, Esq., of Welby, in Leicestershire; four months after which he succeeded to the family title by the death of his elder brother, George Augustus, third Viscount Howe, whose intrepid and exemplary existence was brought to a close on the 5th of July by his receiving a musket-ball through his heart in a skirmish with the French in the expedition against Ticonderoga, in North America. The following year, in Sir Edward

---

[1] Barrow's 'Life of Earl Howe,' pp. 69, 70.

Hawke's action with the Brest fleet off Belleisle, Captain, now Viscount, Howe again bore a conspicuous part in his old ship, the *Magnanime*; bearing down with great effect upon the *Formidable*, the flag-ship of the French Admiral, de Conflans, and also attacking the *Thésée* so furiously as to compel her to strike. "Lord Howe, who attacked the *Formidable*," writes Walpole, "bore down on her with such violence, that her prow forced in her lower tier of guns."[1] On his return to England, his reception by his Sovereign seems to have been a most gracious one. "My Lord Howe," George II. is reported to have said to him on his being presented to him by Sir Edward Hawke, "your life has been a continued series of services to your country."[2]

In March, 1760, Lord Howe's recent services were rewarded by his being appointed Colonel of the Chatham Division of Royal Marines; in September the same year, he was sent on a detached, and as it proved, successful expedition to dispossess the French of the Island of Dumat; on the 23rd of August, 1763, he was appointed a Lord of the Admiralty, of which Board his old schoolfellow, Lord Sandwich, was at this time at the head; and in June, 1765, was transferred from the Admiralty to the Treasuryship of the Navy, an appointment which he continued to fill till August, 1770, when he was succeeded by Sir

---

[1] 'Reign of George II.,' vol. iii. p. 232.
[2] Barrow's 'Life of Earl Howe,' p. 66.

Gilbert Elliot. In the mean time, though an unfrequent speaker in Parliament, he had not only for several years represented Dartmouth in the House of Commons, but had so firmly established his influence in that borough as to secure his election for it till his elevation to an English peerage, on the 20th of April, 1782, by the title of Viscount Howe of Langar, in the county of Nottingham.

On the 15th of February, 1776, at the very critical period when not only had the American people risen in open and armed revolt, but when a war between France and England seemed to be inevitable, Lord Howe, having previously been promoted to be a Rear-Admiral in the month of October, 1770, and to be a Vice-Admiral on the 7th of December, 1775, was appointed Commander-in-Chief on the North American station. Disapproving, as he did on many points, the policy pursued by Great Britain towards her colonies, Lord Howe would probably have declined the appointment, but that, with his brother, General Sir William Howe, the then military Commander-in-Chief in America, he was associated in the further and far more pleasing commission of offering terms of reconciliation to the colonists, and of endeavouring to restore peace and unity between the two countries. Already, indeed, in his own country, Lord Howe, evidently with the knowledge and sanction of ministers, had laboured, in more than one interesting private interview with Benjamin Franklin, to bring about so desirable and holy a result, and had thus, at all events, prepared the way between them for future intimacy and for more momentary negotiations in the event of their remeeting across the Atlantic. A game of chess with Lord Howe's accomplished sister, Mrs. Howe, was the ostensible cause of Franklin's frequent visits to that lady's residence in Grafton Street; while, to confer in private with Lord Howe on American affairs was the real and important motive. "What," inquired Mrs. Howe of Franklin over their chess-board, "were the real and substantive grounds of quarrel between Great Britain and America?"—"There were no 'clashing interests,'" replied the other; "it was rather a matter of punctilio, which two or three sensible people might settle in half an hour."[1]

Nevertheless, notwithstanding all the philanthropic efforts of Lord Howe, this last hope of the illustrious Franklin to obtain redress for his suffering fellow-countrymen came to nothing; and accordingly, disappointed, mortified, and even threatened at this time with a prison, he prepared to return to his own country. One of the last visits which he paid on the eve of quitting London was to Edmund Burke.[2] Mournfully he predicted and bewailed to him the impending separation between the mother-country and her exasperated colonies. Under the rule of Great Britain, he admitted that America had enjoyed

---

[1] Franklin's 'Life and Writings,' vol. i. p. 441.
[2] Prior's 'Life of Burke,' vol. i. p. 306.

happier days than she might ever know again; he lamented, therefore, the separation, but he added, "it was inevitable."

Early in the year 1776, Lord Howe, having hoisted his flag on board the *Eagle*, sixty-four guns, sailed from Spithead for the coast of North America. In the mean time, the conciliatory powers with which he and his brother, Sir William Howe, were known to be invested, had, in combination with the high opinion formed by the public of the judgment and patriotism of the two brothers, gone far to raise sanguine expectations, in Great Britain at least, that the result of their mission would prove favourable to the cause of justice and reason. Furthermore, not only were these two high-minded men known to be opposed to the principles which had provoked the Americans to take up arms, as well as to be sensitively anxious to stop the further effusion of blood, but the additional fact of the name of Howe being at this time an especially cherished one in America, promised to improve their chances of success. In the late hostilities with the French in Canada, their brave elder brother, already spoken of, had not only fought side by side with many living Americans, to whose memories he was endeared by the sweetness of his disposition, his chivalrous courage, and untimely end, but the State of Massachusetts, in appreciation of his merits, had even honoured him with a monument. Neither was the name of Sir William Howe himself much less familiar to, or much less honoured among, the Americans; for, though now unhappily serving in arms against them, he, too, had formerly been their fellow-soldier when serving as a follower and favourite of the illustrious Wolfe. But the olive-branch from the British side of the Atlantic should have been despatched at an earlier date. The British fleet had scarcely appeared off Sandy Hook, on the 12th of July, when Lord Howe had the mortification of discovering that eight important days had elapsed since America had solemnly declared her independence; and, further, that the spell which had once attached itself to his family name had passed away for ever. Grieved they were, said the Americans, that men whom they had so sincerely revered, should have been induced to accept the command of an expedition which was clearly designed to complete the subjugation of their country. "America," said Congress, "is amazed to find the name of Howe in the catalogue of her enemies: she loved his brother."

Nevertheless, hopeless as obviously were now the prospects of success, the Commissioners proceeded to make every attempt to effect a reconciliation. Accordingly, being extremely anxious to open a direct communication with Washington, Lord Howe, under the convoy of a flag of truce, despatched a conciliatory letter to that great man; which letter, however, inasmuch as it indicated no acknowledgment of his military rank, but simply addressed him as "George Washington, Esq.," was returned unopened by the American general. A second letter, in which he was addressed as " George Washington, Esq., &c., &c., &c.," met with a similar fate. With quite as little respect also were treated certain circular letters, addressed by the Commissioners to the governors of the different provinces, one of which having fallen into the hands of Washington, and having been forwarded by him to the American Government, Congress turned it to good account by publishing it with comments of their own. By Washington the powers of the Commissioners were treated with profound contempt. It was tolerably evident, he said, that those powers extended no further than to grant pardons; whereas, the Americans, having been guilty of no offence, stood in need of no pardon. They were no longer the subjects of the King of England, but a free people, prepared to defend to the last what they believed to be their legitimate and indisputable rights.[1]

Lord Howe, however, was not yet entirely disheartened. Deeply anxious to prevent the further effusion of blood, he recalled to mind his old associate, Franklin, and the days when, at the cheerful tea-table of his sister, Mrs. Howe, in Grafton Street, he had seen tears of pleasure start into the eyes of the great philosopher, whenever the chances of returning peace and affection between Great Britain and

[1] Marshall's 'Life of Washington,' vol. ii. pp. 492-4.

America had worn an air of probability.¹ To Franklin, therefore, he appealed in a private letter; but Franklin's reply proved him to be as impracticable as Washington had previously shown himself to have been. It was not only cold and unsatisfactory, but was haughty almost to discourtesy. Speaking of Great Britain as your "proud and uninformed country," he argued that her persistent ill-treatment of America had put re-union utterly out of the question. It had extinguished every remaining spark of affection for that parent-country which Americans had once loved so well. "Before America," added Franklin, "could entertain any treaty of amity or peace, Great Britain must consent and agree to negotiate with her as a free and separate State, to punish the late Governors of Colonies who had caused and afterwards aggravated the mischief, and to rebuild the towns which British soldiers had destroyed." "I know," concluded Franklin, "your great motive in coming hither was the hope of being instrumental in [effecting] a reconciliation; and I believe when you find *that* impossible, on any terms given you to propose, you will relinquish so odious a command, and return to a more honourable private station."²

Franklin proved quite correct in his surmise. Convinced at last that the object which had principally induced him to accept the American

---

[1] Franklin's 'Life and Writings,' vol. ii. p. 27.   [2] Ibid. pp. 24-8.

command was a hopeless and unattainable one, Lord Howe, "tired and disgusted," to use his own words, was on the point of availing himself of the permission to return to England, which had been reluctantly granted him by the Admiralty, when the expected arrival in American waters of a powerful French fleet under the command of Count d'Estaing at once determined the British admiral to postpone his intentions. When subsequently the two fleets appeared in sight of each other off New York, the French fleet consisted of twelve sail of the line, while the naval force under the command of Lord Howe comprised only eleven, and these inferior in point of size and in weight of metal to the French ships. Nevertheless, when the attitude of d'Estaing seemed to threaten an immediate attempt to force the harbour of New York, Lord Howe manifested no unwillingness to meet his precursory attack. In the mean time, the people of New York, who were lookers-on from the shore, could scarcely fail to expect the result with the intensest interest. Should France succeed in achieving a victory over her ancient foe, the evacuation of New York by the British, the speedy termination of the terrible war which was devastating the American continent, and the recognition of American independence, not only by France, but by Great Britain, would in all probability be the consequences. In vain, however, the citizens of New York strained their eyes towards the waters, in the eager hope of beholding the banner of France floating over that renowned flag whose honour had, even in the memory of the young, been no less dear to an American's than to an Englishman's heart. D'Estaing, whether from want of spirit, or, as he himself pleaded, from there not being a sufficient depth of water to float his ships, not only neglected to make the most of his advantage, but, to the great grief and disappointment of the Americans, sailed with the first favourable wind for Rhode Island.

Happily, no very long period intervened before the arrival of reinforcements enabled Lord Howe, without any longer being deterred by superiority of force on the part of the French, to hand over the command of the American station to Vice-Admiral Byron. Sailing from Rhode Island in the *Eagle* on the 26th of September, 1778, he arrived at St. Helen's on the 25th of October, and on the 30th of that month was ordered to strike his flag and come on shore.

The relief of Gibraltar, in 1782, at the critical time when that renowned fortress was besieged by the combined forces of France and Spain, was the next eminent service rendered by Lord Howe to his country. In January, 1783, on Lord Rockingham's second accession to power, he succeeded Lord Keppel as First Lord of the Admiralty, an appointment which, with the exception of an interval of a few months, he continued to hold till July, 1788, when he was elevated to an earldom by the title of Earl Howe. His next and last employment afloat was at the breaking out of the French revolutionary war, in 1793, when he accepted the command of the Western Squadron, and from which time he continued on active service till April, 1797, when, two months after striking his flag, he was honoured with the Order of the Garter.

It was in the course of the foregoing interval of four years' active service that Lord Howe, on the 1st of June, 1794, achieved, in the Bay of Biscay, his memorable victory over the French fleet, commanded by Admiral Villaret Joyeuse. To the Earl's sister, Mrs. Howe, we find George III. writing on the 11th: " Mrs. Howe's zeal for the great cause in which this country is engaged, added to her becoming ardour for the glory of her family, must make her feel with redoubled joy the. glorious news brought by Sir Roger Curtis. She will, I hope, be satisfied now that *Earl Richard* has, with twenty-five sail of the line, attacked twenty-six of the enemy, taken six, and sunk two. Besides, it is not improbable that some of the disabled ships of the enemy may not be able to reach their own shore."[1] To Lady Howe, also, the King writes on the same day: " Lady Howe will, I trust, believe that, next to the signal advantage to the great cause in which this

[1] Barrow's 'Life of Earl Howe,' p. 263.

country is engaged, nothing can give me more satisfaction than that it has been obtained by the skill and bravery of Earl Howe, and, I sincerely return thanks to the Almighty, without any personal loss to himself. The 1st of June must be reckoned as a proud day for him, as it will carry down his name to the latest posterity."[1] There was at this time, it should here be mentioned, no private family in England with whom the King associated and corresponded on more affectionate terms than with the house of Howe. For the Earl especially, and for his accomplished sister, Mrs. Howe, he ever retained the strongest respect and regard. The intimacy appears to be easily accounted for; since not only, in past days, had their mother been a lady of the bedchamber to the King's mother, but by the marriage of their father with George I.'s natural daughter, Sophia Kielmansegge, the Earl and his sister were first cousins once removed to George III.

In the mean time, the tidings of the great battle which had been fought and won had created the liveliest sensation throughout England. London was illuminated for three nights; the thanks of both Houses of Parliament were voted to Lord Howe and his brave companions; and, lastly, the King and Queen expressed their intention of visiting the victorious fleet on its return to British shores. That

[1] Original MS.

event occurred on the 13th of June, on which day Portsmouth witnessed the heart-stirring spectacle of six of the enemy's line-of-battle ships entering its harbour in tow of their captors. On the 26th, George III., accompanied by the Queen, the three youngest Princesses, and Prince Earnest, afterwards King of Hanover, arrived at Portsmouth to do honour to his favourite admiral. The King's visit to the Earl's flag-ship, the *Queen Charlotte*, accompanied by his officers of state as well as by the officers of the fleet, must have afforded a most interesting sight; more especially when, on the quarter-deck, the King presented Lord Howe with a valuable diamond-hilted sword and a gold chain, to which a medal, struck for the occasion, was afterwards appended. "Sir Roger Curtis,"[1] writes the second daughter, Lady Mary Howe, to her sister Lady Altamont, "received the King, and led him immediately upon deck. Our attendance on the Queen and Princesses prevented Mama and I from seeing the first meeting of the King and my glorious father, which I am told was the most affecting thing possible. My father's knees trembled with emotion when he kissed the King's hands, who presented him with a most magnificent sword set with diamonds, and afterwards with a gold chain, to which is to be hung a gold medal struck for the occasion, which is also

---

[1] Sir Roger Curtis, Bart., Earl Howe's flag-captain in the great battle of the 1st of June, died an Admiral of the Red in November, 1816.

given to the other admirals and captains who have contributed to this victory, considered as the greatest ever obtained on the sea. My father afterwards kissed the Queen's hands, and then his flag was lowered, and the royal standard raised to the main-top-mast's head and saluted by the whole fleet. The royal family then went into the cabin, and appeared happy and comfortable to the highest degree, giving us a thousand proofs of the kindest interest. About three o'clock they went to dinner, after which the King gave a toast, drank by all at the table, the Princesses, the Prince, Lady Courtown, Lady Caroline Waldegrave, Lady Frances Howard, Mama, and I; my father waiting on the King and Queen; and this toast was pronounced in the most solemn manner—' May her great Admiral long command the *Queen Charlotte*, and may she long be an example to future fleets!' A short time after this, the whole royal family walked through the ship's company, drawn up in line, when my father told the King aloud that their diligence and propriety of conduct, in all respects, since the victory, was not less commendable than their resolution and bravery during the action. Nothing, during the day, was more pleasing to me than this walk through these brave fellows, every one of whom, I am certain, would attend my father to a cannon's mouth, and all of whom have exposed their lives for him."[1] The

---

[1] Barrow's 'Life of Earl Howe,' pp. 281, 282.

King and royal party remained at Portsmouth for four days. On quitting the *Queen Charlotte*, they were rowed up Portsmouth Harbour, with Lord Howe leading the way in his barge, to inspect the French prizes; on Sunday they attended Divine service in Portsmouth Church; and on Monday embarked on board the *Aquilon* frigate, which carried them to Southampton, from which town they proceeded to Windsor.

One more eminent service was yet reserved for Lord Howe to perform for his country. When, in 1797, the alarming mutiny of the fleet at Portsmouth threatened the most deplorable calamities to the State, it was from Lord Howe's sound judgment, from his high sense of justice and honour, his thorough knowledge of the character of British seamen, and especially as the "sailors' friend," by which title they delighted to designate him, that Government mainly trusted to bring back the refractory to a proper sense of allegiance and duty. He was urged, accordingly, to repair to Portsmouth, to play the part of negotiator with the mutinous delegates from the fleet; nor, though now advanced in years and debilitated in constitution, was this naturally distasteful and most responsible mission declined. Happily, the appearance in the midst of the mutineers of one who had so often led them to victory, of one who had not only ever advocated their just rights and claims, but whose wont it had been, during the period they had recently served under him as their Commander-in-Chief, to sit by the pillow of the wounded, and to minister to the sufferings of the sick, produced the most satisfactory results. Having pledged his word to the seamen, as justified by his instructions, that every promise made them by the Government should be faithfully kept, they paid him the high compliment of declaring their complete confidence in his personal assurance, and relying implicitly upon it, returned to their respective duties.

Of Lord Howe, writes an eminent historian of the revolutionary era, "perhaps, more truly than of any other of England's illustrious chiefs may it be said, as of the Chevalier Bayard, that he was without fear and without reproach. He had the enterprise and gallant bearing so general in all officers in the naval service of Great Britain; but these qualities were in him combined with coolness, firmness, and systematic arrangement, with a habitual self-control and humanity to others, almost unrivalled in those intrusted with supreme command."[1] In private life, Lord Howe's conduct seems to have been no less irreproachable than it was in his public capacity. His moral character was stainless; his habits of living were temperate; his temper mild and equable; his nature singularly generous, compassionate, and forgiving. Moreover, he was a warm friend, a generous enemy, an affectionate husband and father, and not

[1] Alison's 'Hist. of Europe,' vol. v. p. 352; 7th edition.

only an indulgent, but a gratefully munificent master to servants who had served him faithfully and long.

Lord Howe survived his retirement from the command of the Western Squadron rather more than two years, during which period he seems to have chiefly resided at his seat, Porter's Lodge, in Hertfordshire, or at his house in Grafton Street. The chief enemies to the serenity of his declining years were severe and frequent attacks of gout; the visits of which were, however, assuaged by the affectionate care of a devoted wife, and of his interesting and accomplished daughter, Lady Mary Howe, by both of whom he was watched over with anxious solicitude. "The Countess," writes Sir John Barrow, "was a most affectionate wife, watching over her lord in all his illnesses, accompanying him wherever he went; and, when employed afloat, it was her special care that everything was provided for his convenience and comfort."[1] According also to his old Flag Captain, Sir Roger Curtis, whose home when in London was under the Earl's roof in Grafton Street,—" his [Lord Howe's] domestic circle was blessed with the happiest state of harmony ; his Countess and daughter looked on him with the most affectionate regard ; and although to a stranger he appeared to present a rough outside and a coldness of manner, it contained a warm heart; he was kind and attentive to all around him,

[1] Barrow's 'Life of Earl Howe,' p. 360.

and possessed an evenness and suavity of temper that put every one at his ease in his company."[1]

The disorder by which this great and good man had been so constantly afflicted eventually occasioned his death. He died in Grafton Street, of gout in the head, on the 5th of August, 1799, at the age of seventy-three. How truly George III. appreciated the pure and noble qualities of his favourite and distinguished admiral, is manifested by the following beautiful letter addressed by the King to his old friend, Mrs. Howe, the late Earl's gifted and venerable sister:

"Weymouth, September 2nd, 1799.

"I trust Mrs. Howe knows me better than to suppose my long silence on the great loss the public has sustained, as well as her family, by the unexpected death of her excellent brother, has been occasioned by any other motive than the desire not to intrude while she was so fully employed in acts of attentive kindness to her relations, who must have found much comfort from such attention. I trust the example he has set to the navy will long continue to stimulate, not only the matchless bravery of the officers, but convince them of the necessity to view the profession in a scientific light, by which alone those improvements are to be acquired which will retain that superiority over other nations which every Englishman must desire.

[1] Barrow's 'Life of Earl Howe,' pp. 424, 425.

"His exemplary conduct in private life must, on the present melancholy occasion, be the only true comfort to those who loved him, as it gives that hope of his having quitted this transient world for eternal happiness, through the mediation of our Blessed Redeemer. If I did not feel the propriety of not adding more on so glorious a theme, my pen would but too willingly continue.

"The family, I find, are removed to Porter's Lodge. The first moments there were of fresh sorrow, but I trust that the quietness of the place, and the good air, will be of use. I fear Mrs. Howe does not now render that justice to air she formerly did; but if she was here, and saw how well it agrees with her *little* friend, and how much she *hops* about, I think she could not deny it has some efficacy.

"GEORGE R."[1]

This interesting letter, it may be mentioned, was but the precursor of other proofs of kindness and sympathy accorded at this time to the Howe family by George III. "You will like to know," writes the widowed Countess to Sir Roger Curtis, on the 14th of January following, "that nothing can have been more strongly *marked* than the King's affection and regrets. The Queen came over to me as soon as she returned from Weymouth, and the King ordered my daughters to see him first in private, as less pain-

---

[1] Barrow's 'Life of Earl Howe,' pp. 387, 388.

ful to them and to himself. But I must stop writing. This is a subject I could for ever dwell upon, but it will be painful to you and hurtful to me."[1]

Besides Lady Mary Howe, who died unmarried, Lord Howe was the father of two other daughters, of whom the eldest, Lady Charlotte Sophia, her father's successor in the barony, married, first, the eldest son of Assheton, first Viscount Curzon, and, secondly, Sir Jonathan Wathen Waller, Baronet. Her younger sister, Lady Louisa Katherine, married, first, John Dennis, Lord Altamont, afterwards first Marquis of Sligo, and, secondly, William Scott, Lord Stowell.

The monument by Flaxman to the memory of Lord Howe in St. Paul's Cathedral was erected by a parliamentary vote at the expense of the nation. His remains were, however, interred in the family vault in Nottinghamshire.

[1] Barrow's 'Life of Earl Howe,' p. 391.

DAVID DALRYMPLE, LORD HAILES.

COMBINING, with the endowments of a profound lawyer, of an upright judge, and of a steadfast Christian, the accomplishments of a fine classical taste, of ready wit, and a keen perception of the ridiculous, this learned and excellent person seems to have been born to attract general admiration and esteem. "The erudition of Lord Hailes," writes his friend, Lord Woodhouselee, " was not of a dry and scholastic nature. He felt the beauty of the composition of the ancients. He entered with taste and discernment into the merits of the Latin poets, and that peculiar vein of delicate and ingenious thought which characterizes the Greek epigrammatists; and a few specimens which he has left us of his own composition in that style evince the head of a master."[1]

David, or rather Sir David, Dalrymple was the eldest son of Sir James Dalrymple, Baronet, of Hailes, in the county of Haddington, by Lady Christian Hamilton, daughter of Thomas, sixth Earl of

[1] 'Encyclopædia Britannica,' note; Art. Dalrymple.

Haddington. He was born at Edinburgh on the 28th of October, 1726. After having obtained at Eton a character for diligent scholarship and steady conduct, he passed through a further course of instruction at the University of his native city, and from there repaired to the University of Utrecht, where he remained studying the civil law till 1746. In 1748, he was called to the Scottish bar; in 1751, occurred the death of his father, an event which, though it put him in possession of an ample fortune, apparently in no degree prejudiced his devotion to the study of the dry profession which he had adopted; in March, 1766, he was appointed a Judge of the Court of Session, when he assumed the title of Lord Hailes; and in May, 1776, on the resignation of his father-in-law, Lord Coalston, was made a Lord Commissioner of the Justiciary.

Lord Hailes was twice married. His first wife was Anne Brown, only daughter of Lord Coalston, a lady whose untimely death in giving birth to twins drew from him the following admired and touching lines—

"Vidi gemellos, et superbivi parens,
　　Fausti decus puerperi;
At mox sub uno flebilis vidi parens
　　Condi gemellos cespite.
Te, dulcis uxor! Ut mihi sol occidit,
　　Radiante dejectus polo!
Obscura vitæ nunc ego per avia,
　　Heu, solus, ac dubius feror!"[1]

[1] Chalmers' 'Biog. Dictionary,' *note*; Art. Dalrymple.

His second wife was Helen Fergusson, youngest daughter of Lord Kilkerran, who survived him. By each of his wives he was the father of an only daughter, of whom the issue of the first marriage inherited the family estate; the baronetcy, however, on Lord Hailes' decease, descending to a nephew.

To most readers, perhaps, the name of Lord Hailes has been principally rendered familiar by the frequent mention of him in Boswell's 'Life of Johnson.' It was not, however, till a rather late period of the great lexicographer's life that they became personally acquainted; Dr. Johnson, it should be added, having by this time been taught by Boswell to appreciate the virtues and talents of his friend and countryman, the learned Scottish judge. "He" (Johnson), writes Boswell in 1763, "this evening drank a bumper to Sir David Dalrymple, as a man of worth, a scholar, and a wit. 'I have,' said he, 'never heard of him, except from you; but let him know my opinion of him; for, as he does not show himself much in the world, he should have the praise of the few who hear of him.'"[1]

To introduce even a very summary account of the numerous publications which from time to time emanated from Lord Hailes' pen, would in these compressed annals be a work of supererogation. Of his lordship's literary labours, in fact, it seems to be sufficient to observe that his most important work is

[1] Croker's 'Boswell's Life of Johnson,' pp. 153, 154; ed. 1848.

his 'Annals of Scotland, from the Accession of Malcolm Canmore to the Accession of the House of Stuart,' a work, a great part of which was submitted in manuscript to the inspection of Dr. Johnson, and of which that severe critic observed, that it contained "such a stability of dates, such a certainty of facts, and such a punctuality of citation, that it must always sell." Of his lighter literary efforts, his papers in the 'World' and 'Mirror' afford perhaps the most favourable evidence of his ability.

Although enabled by the state of his health to discharge his duties on the judicial bench till within three days before his death, Lord Hailes had nevertheless been long sinking under an enfeebled constitution. His decease took place on the 29th of November, 1792, in his sixty-seventh year.

THE REVEREND GEORGE GRAHAM.

OF this neglected votary of the drama we have little more to relate than that he was the younger son of a clergyman; that he was born about the year 1727; that, in 1746, he was elected from Eton to King's College, Cambridge; and that from King's College he subsequently returned to Eton as an assistant master. He had, it may be mentioned, an elder brother, David, who was also a Fellow of King's College, an epigram by whom, on Richardson's 'Clarissa Harlowe,' Nichols has thought worthy of being inserted in the notes to his 'Life of Bowyer.'[1]

George Graham, besides having written an unnamed and unprinted tragedy, known to have been rejected by Garrick, was also the author of 'Telemachus,' a masque, published in 1763, a production so far honoured in its day as to be pronounced by Boswell a "beautiful poem," and to have been reviewed by Dr. Johnson in the 'Critical Review.'[2]

[1] Page 348.
[2] Croker's 'Boswell's Life of Johnson,' p. 139; ed. 1848.

With Dr. Goldsmith, as well as with Dr. Johnson, he seems to have associated on terms of intimacy. These three men of letters, for instance, were on one occasion dining together, when the amount of wine in which the Eton master had indulged betrayed him into unconsciously giving way to an awkward habit which he seems to have contracted, of looking one of his friends in the face while he was addressing his conversation to the other. "Doctor," he said, meaning the invitation for Johnson, "I should be happy to see you at Eton."—"I shall be glad to wait on you," answered Goldsmith. "No," said Graham, "'tis not you I mean, Dr. *Minor*; 't is Dr. *Major*, there." "What effect," added Johnson, in relating this story, "this had on Goldsmith, who was as irascible as a hornet, may be easily conceived." " Graham," was once an observation of Goldsmith, in recalling this *contretemps*, "is a fellow to make one commit suicide."[1] The author of 'Telemachus,' it remains but to add, died on the 3rd of February, 1767, about the age of forty.

[1] Croker's 'Boswell's Life of Johnson,' p. 294, and *note;* ed. 1848.

GENERAL VISCOUNT HOWE, K.B.

WILLIAM HOWE, who in his youth had not only been a chosen follower in arms of the illustrious Wolfe, but who had led the detachment which first planted the British colours on the Heights of Abraham, was a younger brother alike of the gallant and lamented George Viscount Howe, who fell in the expedition against Ticonderoga, and of the celebrated admiral, Earl Howe. Born on the 10th of August, 1729, he quitted Eton at an early age to accept a commission presented him by William Duke of Cumberland in his own regiment of Light Dragoons, in which regiment he probably fought under the Duke at the battle of Culloden. His next active military service was during the Seven Years' War, when he served under the memorable command of General Wolfe against the French in Canada. In 1764, he was appointed to the command of the 4th Regiment of Foot; on the 22nd of May, 1772, he was promoted to be a Major-General; and, on the 7th of August, 1777, to be a Lieutenant-General.

In the mean time, on the death of his gallant elder brother, in 1758, he had been elected Member of Parliament for Nottingham, for which town he continued, during many years, to sit in the House of Commons. Nor did he neglect to provide himself with a sharer of his advancing fortunes. The lady on whom he conferred his hand, but by whom, by-the-by, he left no children, was Frances, daughter of the Right Hon. William Conolly, of Castletown, in the county of Kildare, by Lady Anne Wentworth, daughter of Thomas, third Earl of Strafford.

To the prominent part played by General Howe in the great struggle of the Americans for independence, he owes the transmission of his name to posterity. It was at a very early and at a very critical period of that memorable contest, that, on the 25th of May, 1775, he arrived at Boston, Massachusetts, bringing with him reinforcements for the small British army then serving in America under the chief command of General Thomas Gage. Unhappily, he had scarcely landed before the most disheartening news reached his ears. Not only had British and American blood been recently shed and intermingled at Lexington and Concord, but the most exaggerated accounts of the behaviour of the British forces on those occasions had flown rapidly over the great American continent, spreading everywhere the profoundest indignation and alarm. America, as it too soon appeared, was resolved to do battle for independence. "With one impulse," writes one of her historians, "the colonies sprang to arms. With one spirit they pledged themselves to each other to be ready for the extreme event. With one heart, the continent cried—'Liberty or Death.'"[1] Within an incredibly short space of time, the British army in Boston was invested by 20,000 armed men; in addition to which number, it was calculated that, in the middle of June, between Nova Scotia and Georgia, no fewer than 100,000 men were in daily military training.[2]

It was at this crisis, at all events, that the arrival of General Howe had the effect of breathing a more hopeful spirit into the British army blockaded in Boston. The military force under General Gage now amounted to 10,000 men; a force which, supported as it was by the powerful squadron of ships of war that floated despotically in Boston harbour, seemed to render the British at least equal in strength, if inferior in numbers, to the Provincialists. Now, then, while the latter were still only half disciplined, and while their line was weakened by its extension over an area of no fewer than ten miles, the opportunity seemed to offer itself to Gage of striking a blow with sure and terrible effect. For some reason, however, he contented himself with proclaiming martial law in the

---

[1] Bancroft's 'Hist. of the United States,' vol. vii. p. 312.
[2] 'Rockingham Papers,' vol. ii. p. 278.

province, with issuing puny promises of pardon to some, and hurling idle threats of condign punishment against others. Such inaction, combined with such pretensions, naturally evoked ridicule, as well in England as in America. "When," writes Walpole to Mason, " did you ever read before of a besieged army threatening military execution on the country of the besiegers?" "I have heard of ships," said Burke, "but never of armies, securing a port."[1]

Moreover, Gage at this time committed another act of neglect or oversight, which, but for the distinguished gallantry displayed by his newly-arrived companion-in-arms, might have proved almost equally productive of evil consequences. Opposite, for instance, to Boston, on the other side of the river Charles, stands the town or suburb of Charlestown, at the rear of which rises some high ground, the possession of which was, for obvious reasons, of no less importance to the insurgents than to the British. Gage, it is said, had been "repeatedly advised to occupy and fortify this commanding post,"[2] but not thinking proper to do so, it was only natural that the Americans, at the risk of some loss of life, should attempt to take advantage of his remissness. Accordingly, about eleven o'clock on the night of the 16th of June, a detachment of about one thousand intrepid Provincialists,

[1] Walpole's 'Letters,' vol. vi. pp. 238, 160; ed. 1857.
[2] Stedman's 'Hist. of the American War,' vol. i. p. 125, *note*.

who had previously joined together in a solemn prayer, commenced their march in silence and stealth up a part of the heights known as Bunker's Hill, situated within cannon-range of Boston, and commanding a view of every part of that town. This brigade was composed chiefly of husbandmen, who not only wore no uniform, but whose only weapons, their fowling-pieces, were unprovided with bayonets. Their leader, distinguished by his tall and commanding figure, though no otherwise attired than in his ordinary calico frock, was William Prescott of Pepperell, who had formerly served at the overthrow of the French in Nova Scotia, but who was now colonel of a Middlesex regiment of militia. For himself, he told his men, he was resolved never to be taken alive.

In the mean time, the insurgent engineers had succeeded in drawing the lines of a redoubt, and the first sod was being upturned when the clocks of Boston struck twelve. During the short remaining period of darkness, Colonel Prescott from time to time crept down towards the river bank, where the sound of the tread of the British sentries as they walked their rounds, and their intimations of "All's well," as they relieved guard, gave him constant assurance that the enemy entertained no suspicion of what was taking place on the heights above.

The dismay therefore of General Gage, when at daybreak he discovered that an intrenchment, extending from the Mystic River to a redoubt on the American left, had been thrown up during the night, may be readily imagined. Of course no time was to be lost in attempting to dislodge the Provincialists, and accordingly a large detachment, under the command of General Howe, was ordered on this critical service. Colonel Prescott and his brave peasants watched them as they crossed the Charles River, and watched them undismayed.

It was past three o'clock in the afternoon when, protected by a cannonade from the *Lively* sloop of war, as well as by the fire from a battery of heavy guns on Copp's Hill, in Boston, General Howe landed his detachment at Charlestown, and formed it for the attack. Prescott's instructions to his men, as he watched the British steadily advancing up the hill, were sufficiently laconic. "The redcoats," he said, "will never reach the redoubt if you will but withhold your fire till I give the order, and be careful not to shoot over their heads." Accordingly, it was not till the British infantry had advanced unmolested to within a few yards of the enemy's works, that Prescott gave the word—" Fire!" when so destructive proved to be the discharge that nearly the whole front rank of the British fell. Volley after volley was now poured in upon them from behind the intrenchments, till at length even the bravest began to waver and fall back; some of them, in spite of the threats and passionate entreaties of their officers, retreating even as far as to the boats. To rally his men, and then to renew the deadly contest, was of course the unswerving resolve of General Howe; yet intrepid as were the spirits who followed him, he could not but have felt how critical was his situation. Exposed, as his men had been, to the scorching rays of the sun, encumbered with heavy knapsacks containing provisions for three days, compelled, as they had been, to toil up very disadvantageous ground with the grass reaching to their knees—clambering over rails and hedges, and not only led against men who were fighting behind intrenchments, but who were continually receiving reinforcements even by hundreds—few soldiers perhaps but British infantry would have been prevailed upon to renew the conflict. General Howe, at all events, was not the man to falter even in such an hour. Again, then, he led his men to the charge; again, when within five or six rods of the redoubt, the same tremendous discharge of musketry was opened upon them; and again, in spite of many heroic examples of gallantry set them by their officers, they retreated in no less disorder than before. The Grenadiers and light infantry had by this time lost three-fourths of their men; some companies had only eight or nine men left; one or two had even fewer. For a few moments General Howe was left almost alone; nearly every officer of his staff had been either killed or wounded. It was remarked by the Americans, who had done honourable justice to his gallantry, that, conspicuous as he stood in his general officer's uniform, it was a marvel that he escaped unhurt. He retired, indeed; but it was with the stern resolve of a hero—to return and vanquish.

A much longer interval than the former one appears to have preceded General Howe's last and effective attack upon the enemy's intrenchments. That interval, however, having been employed by him in disencumbering his men of their knapsacks, and in bringing the British artillery to play so as to rake the interior of the American breastworks, had greatly improved his chances of success. Once more, then, in steady unbroken line, the British infantry advanced to the deadly struggle. Once more the cheerful voice of Colonel Prescott was heard exhorting his men to reserve their fire till their enemies were close to them; once more the same galling fire was poured down upon the advancing royalists. Again, on their part, there was a stagger—a pause—an indication of wavering—but on this occasion it was only momentary. Onward and headlong, against breastworks and against vastly superior numbers, dashed the British infantry with an heroic devotedness never surpassed in the annals of chivalry. Almost in a moment of time, in spite of a second volley as destructive as the first, the ditch was leaped and the parapet mounted. In that final charge fell many of the bravest of the brave. Still the British continued to pour forward, flinging themselves among the American militiamen, who met them with gallantry equal to their own. The powder of the latter having by this time become nearly exhausted, they endeavoured to force back their assailants with the butt-ends of their muskets. The British bayonets, however, carried all before them. Then only it was, when further resistance was evidently fruitless, that the heroic Prescott gave the order to retire. From the nature of the ground, a flight, rather than a retreat, almost necessarily followed. Many of the Americans, leaping over the walls of the parapet, attempted to fight their way through the British troops; while the majority endeavoured to escape by the narrow entrance to the redoubt. In consequence of the fugitives being thus huddled together, the slaughter became terrific. Colonel Prescott was one of the last to quit the redoubt. Happily, although more than one British bayonet had pierced his clothes, he escaped without a wound.

The recall of General Gage to England in the month of October, 1775, was followed by the appointment of General Howe to the chief command of the British land forces in North America. For a time he contented himself with maintaining a defensive position at Boston, till having eventually been compelled, from the want of provisions, to evacuate that city, he withdrew his troops in the first instance by sea to Halifax, and subsequently to Staten Island, in the province of New York, where, in the month of June, 1776, he succeeded in landing them without meeting with opposition. Here, on the 12th of July, he was joined by a large reinforcement of men which he had been long and anxiously expecting; a force which increased the British military strength in America to nearly thirty thousand soldiers. It was about this time, as should be borne in mind, that he was associated with his brother, Earl Howe, in their well-intentioned, but futile, commission for restoring peace and amity between Great Britain and her colonies.

It was not, however, till after the commission had proved to be a failure—not till all hope of reconciliation was, for the present, at least, evidently at an end, that, on the 22nd of August, General Howe, under the protection of the guns of the fleet commanded by the Earl, his brother, landed his forces on Long Island, a fertile tract of land in view of the Island and City of New York. Of the degree of credit to which he is entitled for his military conduct during the ensuing two years and a half that he held the chief command in America, little more need be said than that, though his management of the war met on the whole with much disapprobation, his generalship was very far from being unattended by frequent and signal successes in the field. Five days, for example, after the landing on Long Island, was fought the battle of Brooklyn, in which the defeated Americans lost about two thousand men in killed and wounded, and nearly eleven hundred prisoners. This timely success obtained for General Howe the Order of the Bath, as well as the warm approbation of those high in authority in England. "Those," wrote Lord George Germaine to him, "who, in the earlier part of your life—from an observation of the inborn courage and active spirit which you manifested in inferior stations—were led to form favourable conjectures relative to your future exploits, will, with me, be happy to find their expectations answered, and will be agreeably surprised to see you making such hasty advances towards military excellence, by thus uniting to the fire of youth all the wisdom and conduct of the most experienced commander."[1]

The next signal success achieved by General, now Sir William, Howe, was the capture, in the middle of September, of New York; a blow to the Americans which seems to have been regarded by their great leader, Washington, as the heaviest which had yet befallen their newly-declared independence. That illustrious patriot happened to be at his head-quarters at Haarlem, about nine miles from New York, when the distant roar of artillery from that quarter gave him notice that the British were pressing closely

[1] American MS. in the Library of the Royal Institution.

upon his troops. Instantly mounting his horse, he rode impetuously towards the battle-ground, where a heart-rending scene of rout and slaughter met his eyes. "We made," writes General Greene, "a miserable, disorderly retreat from New York, owing to the dastardly conduct of the militia, who ran at the appearance of the enemy's advanced guard."[1] Washington himself describes his troops as "retreating with the utmost precipitation."[2] In the intensity of his vexation and wrath, he is said to have thrown himself in front of the panic-struck fugitives, threatening to run them through the body unless they came to a stand-still, and even snapping his pistol at those who persisted in continuing their ignominious flight. In the agony, indeed, of the hour, so lost is Washington said to have been to every consideration of personal safety, that his staff were compelled to seize hold of the bridle of his horse and forcibly withdraw him from the field.[3] That day Sir William Howe entered New York in triumph.

Other successes now rapidly attended the British arms. The capture of New York was followed by the battle of White Plains, in which, on the 28th of October, Sir William Howe, at the head of thirteen thousand British, defeated eighteen thousand three hundred Americans. Less than three weeks afterwards, Fort Washington, with its valuable magazine

[1] Washington's 'Writings,' by Sparks, vol. iv. pp. 94, 95.
[2] Ibid., p. 94.   [3] Sparks' 'Life of Washington,' vol. i. pp. 198, 199.

of stores, was gallantly stormed and captured by the British troops; no fewer than three thousand Americans being either killed, wounded, or taken prisoners. Washington, as he beheld the slaughter of his troops, is said to have "cried with the tenderness of a child." "This is a most unfortunate affair," he writes to his brother, "and has given me great mortification."[1] Nor was this the only territory on which the Americans found themselves worsted. Before the close of the year, General Clinton had compelled the Americans to abandon Rhode Island; Lord Cornwallis, having effected a landing in New Jersey, had driven the enemy beyond the Hakensack River, and overrun the entire province; the American Congress had been forced to transfer its sittings from Philadelphia to Baltimore; and lastly, Sir William Howe had advanced his troops to the banks of the Delaware, where he withdrew them into winter quarters.

In the mean time, despite the severities of an American winter, Washington, in the hope of some event occurring to favour the American cause, had determined to prolong hostilities till an indefinitely later period in the season. Thus, Sir William Howe having, on his withdrawing his troops into winter quarters, extended his cantonments to too impolitic a length, the error naturally suggested to the American general the feasibility of dealing a crushing blow at

Gordon's 'Hist. of the American Revolution,' vol. ii. p. 351.

his too confident enemy. "Now," said Washington, "that their wings are so spread, is the time to clip them." In the face, accordingly of a violent storm of hail and snow, and with a mass of floating ice clogging the Delaware, Washington, on the night of Christmas Day, 1776, succeeded in transporting two thousand five hundred men across the river to Trenton, where he surprised a body of fifteen hundred Hessians, nearly a thousand of whom he took prisoners. This success he followed up, a few days afterwards, by a well-conceived and well-executed attack on a British brigade at Princeton. "We found Princeton," writes Washington, "with only three regiments, and three troops of light horse in it, two of which were on their march to Trenton. These three regiments, especially the two first, made a gallant resistance, and in killed, wounded, and prisoners, must have lost five hundred men. Upwards of a hundred of them were left dead on the field."[1] For a time, indeed, the tide of success had turned against the British. By a series of masterly manœuvres on the part of Washington, New Jersey was delivered from the dominion of Great Britain; the Congress was again enabled to hold its sittings in safety in Philadelphia.

In the mean time Sir William Howe, having failed to force a general engagement upon Washington, had crossed with his army from New Jersey to

[1] Washington's 'Writings,' by Sparks, vol. iv. p. 259.

Staten Island, where, however, he remained but a short time during the month of June, when he re-embarked his troops, and on the 24th of August, after a tedious voyage, landed them on the banks of the Chesapeake. Washington rightly conjecturing that the object of the British general was the capture of Philadelphia, immediately followed him to the banks of the Brandywine, where, on the 11th of September following, was fought the important battle to which that river has given its name. The Americans suffered a signal defeat, of which the capture of Philadelphia was one of the consequences; the Congress, at the approach of the British forces, flying in the first instance to Lancaster, and subsequently to York Town. On the 26th of September, the British entered Philadelphia in triumph; the band of the advanced guard, as it marched along the streets, playing 'God save the King.' Eight days afterwards, on the 4th of October, took place the not less decisive engagement at German Town, about six miles from Philadelphia, in which the Americans were again unsuccessful. "It was a bloody day," wrote Washington to his brother; "would to Heaven I could add that it had been a more fortunate one for us."[1] Not long afterwards Sir William Howe established himself in comfortable winter quarters in Philadelphia.

In the mean time, the Government and people of

[1] Washington's 'Writings,' vol. v. p. 108.

England had not only expected a series of victories from Sir William Howe, but had confidently hoped that by this time, either by conciliation or by force of arms, the colonists would have been reduced to their former dependence upon the mother-country. That the successes which we have seen the English general achieving would, by a younger and more enterprising general, have been turned to a more serviceable account, is very far from improbable; but, on the other hand, considering the vastness and difficult features of the country which he was expected to subdue, as well as the inadequacy of the military force under his command, we not only incline to the opinion that at no period of the late hostilities was it in his power to effect the permanent subjugation of the American colonies, but, finding such to be the opinion of Lord Cornwallis, and of other competent military men, as pronounced by them in evidence on a parliamentary investigation which took place into Sir William Howe's conduct in 1779, our complete exoneration of so brave and devoted a soldier naturally follows.

At all events, Sir William had not long emerged from his pleasant winter quarters in Philadelphia when the resignation which he had recently tendered of his appointment as commander-in-chief in America was met by the appointment of General Sir Henry Clinton as his successor. As evidence of his popularity at this time with the army may be mentioned the gorgeous, but silly and ill-timed, ovation—the "Mischianya," as it was named—which was given him by the British officers at Philadelphia on the eve of his sailing for Europe, and which was long remembered in America. "The entertainment," writes Sir John Barrow, "is described as not only to have far exceeded anything that had ever been seen in America, but as rivalling the magnificent exhibition of that vain-glorious monarch, Louis XIV. of France. All the colours of the army were placed in a grand avenue, three hundred feet in length, lined with the King's troops, between two triumphal arches, for the two brothers, the Admiral and General to march along in pompous procession, followed by a numerous train of attendants, with seven silken knights of the *Blended Rose*, and seven more of the *Burning Mountain*, and fourteen damsels dressed in the Turkish fashion, each knight bearing an appropriate motto to the damsel of his choice. From this avenue they marched into an open area, one hundred and fifty yards square, lined also with the King's troops, for the exhibition of a tilt and tournament, or mock fight of old chivalry, in honour of those two heroes. On the top of each triumphal arch was a figure of Fame, bespangled with stars, blowing from her trumpet, in letters of light, '*Tes lauriers sont Immortels?*' Lord Cathcart acted the character of chief of the knights."[1] The entertainment lasted

[1] Barrow's 'Life of Earl Howe,' pp. 114, 115.

from four o'clock in the afternoon, till four o'clock the following morning. The fireworks are described as having been magnificent.

On the 24th of May, 1778, Sir William Howe, amidst the tears of the brave men whom he had so often led to battle, bade farewell to the shores of America. "I am just returned," writes a spectator of his departure, "from conducting our beloved General to the water-side, and have seen him receive a more flattering testimony of the love and attachment of his army than all the pomp and splendour of the 'Mischianya' could convey to him. I have seen the most gallant of our officers, and those whom I least suspected of giving such instances of their affection, shed tears while they bade him farewell. The gallant and affectionate General of the Hessians, Knyphausen, was so moved, that he could not finish a compliment he begun to pay him in his own name, and that of the officers who attended him. Sir Henry Clinton accompanied him to the wharf, where Lord Howe received him into his barge, and they are both gone down to Billingsport. On my return I saw nothing but dejected countenances."[1]

From this time, but little interest is to be found either in the personal or professional career of Sir William Howe. From 1782 to 1804, he held the appointment of Lieutenant-General of the Ordnance; on the 25th of October, 1793, he was promoted to be

[1] 'Annual Register,' vol. xxi.; 1778.

a General; in 1795 he was appointed Governor of Berwick; on the death of his brother, Earl Howe, on the 5th of August, 1799, he succeeded him in the Irish Viscountcy of Howe; and, lastly, in 1805, he was removed from the Governorship of Berwick to that of Plymouth, which latter appointment he continued to hold till his decease.

Sir William Howe lived to a very advanced age; displaying, on the bed of sickness and death, and under the agonies of a long and excruciating disorder, the same courage and equanimity which, in his youth, had distinguished him on the Heights of Abraham, and which, in middle age, had rendered him conspicuous in the midst of the galling fire of Bunker's Hill. His death took place on the 12th of July, 1814, in the eighty-fifth year of his age.

CHARLES WATSON-WENTWORTH,
MARQUIS OF ROCKINGHAM, K.G.

THIS straightforward and high-minded statesman—the third Etonian who, in the first five years of the reign of George III., filled the high post of Prime Minister of England—was born on the 19th of March, 1730. His father, Thomas Watson, a country gentleman, having succeeded a kinsman in the Barony of Rockingham, was thereupon rapidly advanced by Sir Robert Walpole to be a Knight of the Bath, Lord-Lieutenant of the County of York, Baron of Waith, Viscount Higham, Earl of Malton, and Marquis of Rockingham. "I suppose," was a playful remark of Sir Robert's, "that we shall soon see our friend Malton in Opposition, for he has had no promotion in the peerage for the last fortnight." To this record of titles it should be added, that the new Marquis was, on the female side, lineally descended from the celebrated Thomas Wentworth, Earl of Strafford, whose noble estates and ancient family seat had passed into his possession, and whose more aristocratic surname he assumed.

The mother of the future Prime Minister was Lady Mary Finch, daughter of Daniel Earl of Winchilsea and Nottingham. Of the five sons of which she was the mother, he was the youngest, and the only one who survived his childhood. Whether it was to Eton solely that he was indebted for such amount of classical erudition as he may have succeeded in acquiring, there seems to be no means of ascertaining. He was still, however, a boy at Eton, with the title of Lord Higham, when, on the breaking out of the Scottish rebellion, an incident occurred which occasioned great temporary distress to his parents. "Little is known of him till the winter of 1745," writes Lord Albemarle, "when, at the age of fifteen, he went to Wentworth to pass the Christmas holidays. One morning he went out hunting, attended by a confidential groom, named Stephen Lobb. Night came on, and neither master nor groom made their appearance. The next day it was reported that Lord Higham and Stephen were seen riding in a northerly direction. A short time afterwards a letter arrived from the truant himself, dated Carlisle, the headquarters of the Duke of Cumberland, who had just taken the field against the Pretender. Zeal for the Whig cause had impelled him to join the royal army."[1] The transgression, considering that he was

[1] 'Rockingham Papers,' edited by the Earl of Albemarle, vol. i. p. 138.

an only son and surviving hope of his family, did not probably long remain unforgiven. "Dear Madam," he writes to his mother, "when I think of the concern I have given you by my wild expedition, and how my whole life, quite from my infancy, has afforded you only a continued series of afflictions, it grieves me excessively that I did not think of the concern I was going to give you and my father before such an undertaking; but the desire I had of serving my King and country, as much as lay in my power, did not give me time to think of the undutifulness of the action. As my father has been so kind as entirely to forgive my breach of duty, I hope I may, and shall, have your forgiveness, which will render me quite happy."[1] Five years after this penitent letter was written, the Eton boy, on the death of his father, in 1750, succeeded, at the age of twenty, to the titles, estates, and powerful Whig influence of his house.

The young Whig Marquis, on his coming of age, was naturally regarded as no improper object for Court favour to shine upon. George II. accordingly appointed him a lord of his bed-chamber; he was nominated Lord-Lieutenant of the North and West Ridings of Yorkshire; and, in 1760, was honoured with the Order of the Garter. The following year, at the coronation of George III., by whom he was continued as a lord of his bed-

[1] 'Rockingham Papers,' vol. i. p. 139.

chamber, we find him, as deputy to the Duke of Norfolk in his Grace's capacity of Lord of the Manor of Worksop, holding the sceptre with the cross during the ceremony of the Lords Spiritual and Temporal paying their homage to their Sovereign. Hitherto, no yearning to high State employment seems to have entered the mind of the future Premier.

George III. had on no occasion since his accession found himself in a more disagreeable, and, at the same time in a more humiliating, political strait than when, in the month of May, 1765, after having summarily got rid of George Grenville and his obnoxious fellow-ministers, he found himself in the dilemma of being unable to fill up their places, and was consequently reduced to sue to them to remain in office. "His Majesty," writes Mr. Stuart Mackenzie to Sir Andrew Mitchell, "offended in the highest degree with the insolence of his present ministers, would have put any mortal in their place that could have carried on business."[1] Nor need this state of the King's feelings be a matter of surprise. Again, as he was only too well aware, he would find himself subjected in the royal closet to the tedious lectures of Grenville, and the haughty invectives of the Duke of Bedford; again, in all probability, his good faith would be called in question; his wishes persistently thwarted, his motives misunderstood. It was under these circumstances that the King, by

[1] Ellis's 'Original Letters,' vol. iv. p. 481; 2nd series.

the advice of his uncle, the Duke of Cumberland,
conjointly with that of the veteran head of the
Whig party, the Duke of Newcastle, was induced to
invite Lord Rockingham to attempt the construction
of an Administration, of which it was intended that
the Marquis should himself be the leader. Whether
this advice of the two Dukes to the King was a
matter of the greatest surprise to the King, to the
Marquis, or to the public, seems to be somewhat
questionable. "I thought," said the King on one
occasion, "that I had not two men in my bedchamber of less parts than Lord Rockingham;"[1]
while so diffident was Lord Rockingham himself
of his own capacity for high office, that it was
with difficulty that the arguments and entreaties
of the Duke of Cumberland overcame his aversion
to accept the proffered honour. It was his conviction, he told the Duke, that he should be enabled to
render much more effectual service to his Sovereign
if allowed to remain in a private and independent
station; but, he added, if his friends thought otherwise, he was willing to sacrifice his inclinations
to his duty, and to serve the State in any capacity
which might be deemed most for its advantage.[2]
Neither had the public much more reason for
feeling confidence in the wisdom of the selection
than had the Marquis himself. Utterly unaccus-
tomed, as he was known to be, to official business,

[1] Walpole's 'Reign of George III.,' vol. i. p. 291.
[2] 'Rockingham Papers,' vol. i. pp. 192, 197.

he had not only entered on his thirty-sixth year without having filled any post more responsible than that of a lord of the bed-chamber, but, devoted to the pursuits and pleasures of a private life, he was as yet chiefly known to the world as a wagerer of large sums on race-horses, and as a munificent patron of the turf. "Like Godolphin," writes Earl Russell, "he loved gaming; and his singular wager with Lord Orford on a race between two geese at Newmarket has been recorded by Horace Walpole; but he overcame this propensity on entering public life."[1]

Another drawback to Lord Rockingham's success as a minister, was a timid and embarrassed manner, which he was unable to shake off when addressing Parliament. Even after he had become a second time Prime Minister, he never rose to speak in the House of Lords without a feeling of nervous distress. "How could you worry the poor dumb thing so?" is said to have been a question asked by Lord Gower of Lord Sandwich, while the meek Premier was still wincing under the merciless raillery of the latter nobleman.[2] "I am much pleased," writes the King to him on one occasion, "that Opposition has forced you to hear your own voice, which I hope will encourage you to stand forth in other debates."[3]

If Lord Rockingham, however, as first Minister of

---

[1] 'Bedford Correspondence,' vol. iii. p. 307, *note*.
[2] Walpole's 'Reign of George III.,' vol. i. p. 291.
[3] Earl Stanhope's 'Hist. of England,' vol. v. p. 167.

the Crown, had to contend against many deficiencies and many difficulties, he was, on the other hand, endowed with the no despicable advantages derivable from high birth, from a princely fortune, from strong sound sense, and a high reputation for probity and virtue. Burke, indeed, seems to have done him no more than justice when he descants on the "sound principles, enlarged mind, clear and sagacious sense, and unbroken fortitude" of his early patron and steadfast friend.[1] "Surely," writes Philip Thicknesse, who knew him well, "if there ever lived a truly good man, the Marquis of Rockingham was such."[2] His political as well as private integrity were, indeed, beyond all suspicion; the sincerity of his devotion to his country was undisputed even by his enemies; and, lastly, he was gifted with that happy art of acquiring the confidence and affection of others, which subsequently, during long years of adverse fortune, enabled him to secure the devoted adhesion of his political followers as well as of his personal friends. Neither did the conduct and character of his followers reflect any discredit on their chief. Like him, indeed, they were deficient in official experience and luminous abilities; but, on the other hand, like him, they possessed the advantages of birth, fortune, and clear judgment. They were united, moreover, by the bonds of mutual esteem;

[1] Prior's 'Life of Burke,' vol. i. p. 134.
[2] Thicknesse's 'Memoirs,' p. 105.

they were agreed on the capital political questions of the day; their intentions were pure, and their reputation stainless.[1]

Brief as was the duration of the Rockingham Administration, it lasted long enough for Lord Rockingham and his colleagues to merit for themselves the gratitude of their King and country. To use the words of Burke, they at least "treated their Sovereign with decency;" they discountenanced the dangerous and unconstitutional practice of removing military officers for their votes in Parliament; in addition to carrying into law their great measure, the repeal of Grenville's unfortunate Stamp Act, they prevailed upon the House of Commons to condemn the use of General Warrants and the seizure of papers in cases of libel; and, lastly, in an age of great political profligacy, they were the first to set the example of that purity and disinterestedness which have since become the distinguishing characteristics of British statesmen.

Nevertheless, the Rockingham Administration, after having with difficulty lasted for twelve months, succumbed to its own weakness. Charles Townshend and Lord Chesterfield had severally and early

[1] The chief appointments to the new Administration were Lord Rockingham as First Lord of the Treasury; the Duke of Grafton and General Conway as Secretaries of State; William Dowdeswell as Chancellor of the Exchequer; Lord Egmont as First Lord of the Admiralty; the Earl of Winchilsea as President of the Council; the Duke of Newcastle as Lord Privy Seal; and the retention of Lord Northington as Lord Chancellor.

predicted the brevity of its existence. "It was a mere lute-string administration," were the former's well-known words, "pretty summer wear, but it would never stand the winter." "It is an heterogeneous jumble of youth and caducity," writes Lord Chesterfield to his son, "which cannot be efficient."[1] Very early, indeed, after its birth, the death of the Duke of Cumberland had deprived it of its most sagacious and powerful supporter; less than six months after that event, a still severer blow was dealt it by the Duke of Grafton's resignation of the seals as Secretary of State; and, finally, the defection of another colleague, Lord Chancellor Northington, completed its overthrow. It was at this crisis that the retiring Chancellor advised the King in the royal closet to send for Mr. Pitt, and that advice being followed, quickly led to the upsetting of the Rockingham Administration. Little loth, however, as the King had shown himself to part with his Whig ministers, his farewell words to them in the royal closet were, especially as far as their chief was concerned, not ungracious : "I wish you all well," he said, "particularly Lord Rockingham."[2]

It was nearly sixteen years after the fall of the Rockingham Ministry that, on Lord North's resignation of the Premiership, in March, 1782, George III. proposed to Lord Rockingham, through the

[1] Chesterfield's 'Letters,' vol. iv. p. 403; edited by Earl Stanhope.
[2] Walpole's 'Reign of George III.,' vol. ii. pp. 337, 338.

medium of the then Lord Chancellor, Thurlow, to
return to his former post of First Lord of the
Treasury. The result proved, if it proved nothing
else, that, long as the Whigs had been exiled from
Downing Street, they were inclined to abate but
little from the pretensions which they had never
been very slow in arrogating to themselves. Thus,
in the opinion of the King, the terms proposed to
him by the Marquis were too hard, and the changes
demanded by him in the Government too sweeping
to be carried out with safety to the State; and,
accordingly, in the hope of obtaining easier conditions from Lord Shelburne, the King sent for that
efficient though unpopular statesman, and proposed
to him to attempt to form an administration. Lord
Shelburne, however, aware of his own shortcomings,
not only declined acceding to the proposition, but
very properly and judiciously advised his Sovereign
to repeat his overtures to Lord Rockingham; his
own party, he added, not only being the weaker
of the two, but it being his misfortune to have made
many personal enemies, whereas Lord Rockingham
had none. " My Lord," subsequently remarked Lord
Shelburne to Lord Rockingham, "you can stand
without me, but I cannot without you."[1]

At all events, when Lord Shelburne quitted the
royal closet, it was with the distinct understanding,

[1] Walpole's 'Letters,' vol. viii. p. 183; Walpole's 'Last Journals,'
vol. ii. pp. 522, 523.

however reluctantly consented to by the King, that Lord Rockingham was to resume his former seat at the head of the Treasury Board, with ample powers for constructing an administration. Nor does any time appear to have been lost by the Marquis in making his necessary arrangements. When, for instance, a day or two afterwards, Dr. Watson, the Whig Bishop of Llandaff, dined with the new Premier at his residence in Grosvenor Square, he found his host's mind already made up with regard to the principal measures which it was his intention to press upon the consideration of the King and Parliament. Those measures, for the most part, consisted, as the Marquis confided to his guest, ot the concession of independence to the American colonists, of the diminution of the influence of the Crown, the disqualifying contractors from becoming members of the House of Commons, the exclusion of revenue officers from the privilege of voting at parliamentary elections, the abolition of sinecure offices, and, lastly, of the introduction of a general and stringent system of economy into the several departments of the State.[1]

These essential measures, however, it was not the will of Providence that Lord Rockingham should live to carry into effect. Leaving his enlightened projects to be worked out by others, he survived his second elevation to the Premiership only fifteen

[1] Bishop Watson's 'Anecdotes of his Life,' vol. i. pp. 144, 145.

weeks. He had for some time past regarded his end as approaching; giving, it is said, as his only motive for wishing to live, the desire he felt to see his country emancipated from the perils and troubles with which she was at this time afflicted. On the 1st of July, 1782, a violent spasmodic seizure suddenly terminated his existence in the fifty-third year of his age. His remains were interred in the vault of the Earls of Stafford, in York Minster.

By his wife, Mary, daughter and heiress of Thomas Bright, Esq., of Badsworth, in Yorkshire, Lord Rockingham left no children. With regard to such of his surviving relatives as were benefited by the disposition of his large fortune, he bequeathed to his widow, on the condition of her never remarrying, the sum of 5000*l*. a year, in addition to the jointure already settled on her; to his nephew, William, second Earl Fitzwilliam, he demised the great bulk of his property; while to a second nephew, the son of his sister, Lady Henrietta Alicia Wentworth, by her husband and former footman, William Sturgeon, he bequeathed 300*l*. a year.

THE REVEREND JOHN FOSTER, D.D.

JOHN FOSTER, the learned successor of Dr. Barnard in the Head Mastership of Eton, was the son of an alderman of Windsor, who afterwards filled the office of mayor of the corporation of that borough. He was born at Windsor in 1731. At Eton, his uncommon abilities and attention to his studies attracted the observation and won for him the flattering encouragement of more than one of the learned authorities of the school. From Eton he was elected, in 1748, to King's College, where, while still an undergraduate, he increased his reputation for scholarship by composing a copy of admired Latin hexameters on the death of Frederick Prince of Wales, which were printed in the 'Academiæ Cantabrigiensis Luctus' in 1751. In 1753 he took his degree as B.A.; in 1756, as M.A.; and in 1766, as D.D. He had not long obtained his fellowship when he returned to Eton as an assistant master, in which subordinate capacity he must be presumed to have displayed qualifications of no mean order, inasmuch as, on the removal of Dr. Barnard to the Provostship, in October, 1765, he was elected to the Head Mastership in the room of that prince of aristocratic schoolmasters. Unfortunately, however, the result of his advancement, so far as the prosperity of the school was concerned, sadly disappointed the expectations of his friends and supporters. True it is that, were scholarship the sole qualification required in the head master of a great public school, it might have been difficult to select a person better fitted for the post than Dr. Foster; but, on the other hand, unfortunately he stood in need of that tact, judgment, and command of temper, that knowledge of the world and of human nature, that happy combination of the *suaviter in modo* with the *fortiter in re*, which had so eminently characterized his predecessor. Accordingly, not only under his ministration did Eton fall off from its late flourishing condition, but his health giving way under the harassing effects of disappointment and failure, he was constrained, in the summer or autumn of 1773, to repair to Spa in the hope of recovering it, the result however being that, in July of that year, he resigned his Head Mastership. Happily for him the loss of academical position and of its emoluments which he thus suffered was in some degree counterbalanced by the fact of his Sovereign having recently conferred upon him a canonry of Windsor, vacant by the death of Dr. John Sumner, Provost of King's College. His enjoyment, however, of this honourable preferment was of no long duration, his decease occurring at Spa, in the month of September, 1773, at the comparatively early age of forty-two. His remains were, in the first instance, interred at that place, but were afterwards removed to England and placed by those of his father in Windsor churchyard. On his tomb, which was erected on the spot, his epitaph, in graceful Latin, was composed by himself.[1]

It may be mentioned that, of Dr. Foster's occasional literary productions, the most valuable, especially to the Greek student, is admittedly his 'Essay on the Different Nature of Accents and Quantity, with their Use and Application in the Pronunciation of the English, Latin, and Greek Languages, with a Defence of the present System of Greek Accentual Marks, &c.;' published in octavo, in 1762.

[1] It may be read in Nichols's 'Lit. Anecdotes of the 18th Century,' vol. iii. p. 25.

FREDERICK LORD NORTH, K.G.,
EARL OF GUILFORD.

It may possibly be remembered that, in our memoir of Lord Rockingham, we alluded to that nobleman as having been the third Etonian who, during the first five years of the reign of George III., filled the high post of Prime Minister of England. To far more than Lord Rockingham's power, if not to the actual office held by him as First Lord of the Treasury, succeeded a fourth Etonian, Lord Chatham; and, lastly, before the completion of the first decade of the reign of George III., we have to add to the list the name of Lord North as the fifth Etonian on whom, during that period, devolved the Premiership.

Frederick Lord North—"Blubbery North," as he was, somewhat irreverently, nicknamed in his earlier years—was born on the 13th of April, 1732. He was the son of Francis, seventh Lord North and first Earl of Guilford, a lord of the bedchamber to Frederick Prince of Wales, and subsequently Governor to Prince George, afterwards George III. The mother of the future Premier was Lady Lucy Montagu, daughter of George Earl of Halifax. It may be mentioned that, as early as the days of old Lord Guilford's domestication at Prince Frederick's court, commenced in boyhood the long and memorable intimacy between the subject of this memoir and his future Sovereign. When, be it pointed out, on the 4th of January, 1749, on the occasion of the performance of Addison's play of 'Cato' by the Prince's children at Leicester House, "Master North" played Syphax to Prince George's Portius,[1] how little could either of the two boys have anticipated the far more perilous parts which, in process of time, they were destined to perform together in the real drama of life!

That Lord North's career at Eton was not an undistinguished one is manifested by his having been the author of the first copy of verses in the 'Musæ Etonenses,' as well as of several others in that classical miscellany. If not a profound, he was at least an elegant and enthusiastic scholar. From Eton he passed to Trinity College, Oxford, whence, after having taken his degree of M.A., in March, 1750, he proceeded to make what was then called the grand tour of Europe; settling for some time at Leipsic to study the Germanic constitution under the

[1] Lady Hervey's 'Letters,' p. 139.

once celebrated Professor Mascove, and eventually returning to England, not only with the continued reputation of being a good classical scholar, but an adept in the French, German, and Italian languages.

At the general election in 1754, not very long after Lord North had come of age, he was returned to the House of Commons as member for the family borough of Banbury, in Oxfordshire. Young, however, as he was, his youth seems to have proved no obstacle to his rising rapidly in the estimation of the House, since, before the close of the year, notwithstanding the ungainliness of his gait and utterance, he had achieved for himself a parliamentary position. "I hear of nothing," writes Horace Walpole to George Montagu on the 16th of November, 1754, "but the parts and merit of Lord North."[1] Yet, by those who were only superficially acquainted with him, the superiority of his parts seems to have been still questioned. It was probably, for instance, about this period that George Grenville, while walking in the park with a friend, happened to encounter Lord North, apparently rehearsing a speech: "Here comes Blubbery North," said the latter to Grenville; "I wonder what he is getting by heart, for I am sure it can be nothing of his own."—"You are mistaken," replied Grenville; "North is a man of great promise and high qualifications, and if he does not relax in his political pursuits, is very likely to be

[1] Walpole's 'Letters,' vol. ii. p. 405.

Prime Minister."[1] A similar prediction of Lord North's impending rise to a high office was, as we shall presently perceive, pronounced by the celebrated Charles Townshend.

From June, 1759, till the formation of the Rockingham Administration in 1765, Lord North held the appointment of a Lord of the Treasury; in 1766, the joint Paymaster-Generalship of the Forces was conferred upon him by Lord Chatham; and, on the 1st of December, 1767, he succeeded, on the death of Charles Townshend, to the Chancellorship of the Exchequer. "If anything should happen to him," said the latter, speaking of himself, "that 'great, heavy, booby-looking' Lord North would succeed to his place, and very shortly afterwards would become First Lord of the Treasury."[2]

From a modest apprehension of entering the lists against one so thoroughly conversant with financial questions as George Grenville, Lord North for a time shrank from the idea of filling the responsible post of Chancellor of the Exchequer, which he, nevertheless, eventually accepted. Creditable to him, however, as was this self-distrust, so little occasion was there for entertaining it, that it was, in fact, in opening a budget, and in his lucid expositions of the public finances, that, during many subsequent years, he achieved his completest triumphs in the House of Commons. "Yesterday,"

[1] 'Rockingham Papers,' vol. i. p. 314.   [2] Ibid.

writes Richard Rigby to the Duke of Bedford on the 11th of April, 1769, "Lord North opened his budget in the Committee of Ways and Means; and in the four and twenty years that I have sat in Parliament, in very few of which I have missed that famous day of the sessions, I verily think I have never known any of his predecessors acquit themselves so much to the satisfaction of the House." And, again, Rigby writes to the Duke on the 25th of April the following year : " I am just come from the House of Commons, where Lord North has to-day opened his budget in a most masterly manner. He has given the House and the public the satisfaction of knowing that he has paid off a million and a half of the National Debt in the course of the year. Nobody spoke but Grenville, who had much better have held his tongue, for he never made so bad a figure upon a day of finance in his life."[1]

In the great political embarrassment in which, by the Duke of Grafton's resignation of the Premiership, in January, 1770, George III. found himself involved, it was not unnatural that, as the most desirable successor to the Duke, all the King's personal preferences should point to a statesman of so yielding a disposition, and therefore so likely to be easily induced to shape his ministerial policy according to the royal wishes, as Lord North. There were, moreover, other circumstances which were calculated

[1] 'Bedford Correspondence,' vol. iii. pp. 408, 411, 412.

to render Lord North an acceptable minister to George III. His morals and reputation were untainted by the libertinism of the age; he was unconnected by blood or marriage with the objects of the King's paramount dread and dislike, the great Whig lords; he had shown himself a staunch and unflinching enemy of Wilkes and the ultra-democratic party; and, lastly, unlike more than one member of the amiable Rockingham party, he had shown himself loftily indifferent to popular applause. " In all my memory," he had lately exclaimed in the House of Commons, " I do not recollect a single popular measure I ever voted for; no, not even for the Nullum Tempus Bill, nor the declaring the law in the case of General Warrants. I state this to prove that I am not an ambitious man. Men may be popular without being ambitious, but there is rarely an ambitious man who does not try to be popular."[1] Such was the statesman to whom George III. now turned, if not with unmixed confidence, at least with hope. " Lord Weymouth and Lord Gower," writes the King to him on the 23rd of January, 1770, "will wait upon you this morning to press you in the strongest manner to accept the office of First Lord Commissioner of the Treasury. My mind is more and more strengthened in the rightness of the measure, which will prevent every other desertion."[2]

[1] Speech, March 2, 1769, 'Cavendish's Debates,' vol. i. pp. 299, 300.
[2] Brougham's 'Statesmen of the Time of George III.,' vol. i. pp. 68, 69; ed. 1858.

To this call from his Sovereign, Lord North, notwithstanding the responsibilities and peril which he was entailing upon himself, chivalrously and unhesitatingly responded. In Walpole's words, he "plunged into the danger at once." On the 5th of February he was gazetted as First Lord of the Treasury; the Chancellorship of the Exchequer being retained by him, agreeably with former precedents.

The new Premier, as may be readily imagined, had no sooner assumed the lead of public affairs than he found himself involved in a vortex of political antipathy and contention. The acrimony with which the Grenville and Rockingham parties had lately assailed the Duke of Grafton was now turned upon Lord North; Lord Chatham bore down upon him with his fiercest invectives; abuse and ridicule were heaped upon him in both Houses of Parliament. Much, indeed, of his chance of maintaining his ground had depended on the result of an impending division in the House of Commons, and happily that result had proved favourable to the Court. "Wednesday, the very critical day," writes Walpole to Sir Horace Mann on the 2nd of February, "is over, and the Administration stands. The Opposition flattered themselves with victory, and the warmest friends of the Court expected little better than a drawn battle, yet the majority for the latter was forty. Few enough in conscience for triumph, but sufficient to make a stand with. Lord North pleased all that could bring themselves to be pleased. He not only spoke with firmness and dignity, but with good humour, and fairly got the better of Colonel Barré, who attacked him with rudeness and brutality."[1] Nevertheless, the danger to the Ministry had not yet passed away : before spring had set in the Opposition had nearly recovered its ground ; the Government, according to Lord Temple, lived only upon moments. " The alarm at Court," writes Calcraft in March, " is beyond imagination ; if our friends stand firm, they own all is over with them."[2] " Now is the crisis," writes Junius to Woodfall; " I have no doubt we shall conquer them at last."

Still, unpromising as was this aspect of affairs, Lord North's protracted administrative career was very far from being near its termination. Many months afterwards, indeed, its existence was threatened by the effects of the popular tumults which sprang out of the famous dissensions fomented by Wilkes between the city of London and the House of Commons, but happily he weathered the peril. To Lord North, the situation would seem to have been fraught with imminent personal danger. It was, for example, on the day on which the Lord Mayor had been cited before the Commons and committed to the Tower that Lord North, when on his way to the House, found himself suddenly exposed to a cowardly

[1] Walpole's ' Letters,' vol. v. p. 225.
[2] ' Chatham Correspondence,' vol. iii. p. 426.

and apparently preconcerted attack from an infuriated mob. Happily, at the window of a neighbouring house, happened to be standing Sir William Meredith, who, though the political enemy of the Premier, generously rushed down into the street with a friend, a Mr. La Roche, and by rescuing him from the hands of his assailants, probably saved him from being torn to pieces. As it was, the rabble wounded him in the hand, "punched a constable's staff in his face," utterly demolished his carriage, and, having obtained possession of his hat, divided it into pieces, which they sold as memorials of the day's violence. In the mean time a cruel rumour that the Premier was on the eve of forsaking his now hazardous post, had gained credence within the walls of Parliament; and, inasmuch as such an imputation, if founded on fact, would fairly have exposed him to the charge of abandoning his Sovereign in his hour of difficulty and danger, it not unnaturally aggravated his already painful sense of the ill-usage to which he had been subjected. Accordingly, though, in addressing the House of Commons on entering its walls after his escape from the rabble, he spoke of himself in tones of manly firmness, it was not without tears in his eyes that he alluded to the reflections which had been indirectly cast on his courage and honour. "I certainly," he said, "did not come into office at my own desire. Had I my own wish I would have quitted it a hundred times. My love of ease and

retirement urged me to it; but as to my resigning
now, look at the situation of the country; look
at the transactions of this day—and then say
whether it would be possible for any man with
a grain of spirit, with a grain of sense, with the
least love for his country, to think of withdrawing
at such a moment from the service of his King
and his country!"[1]

Fortunately, from this time till the breaking out
of the war of American Independence, in 1775, Lord
North and his Sovereign were permitted by their
political adversaries to enjoy a state of comparative
repose. There had been several circumstances
which had tended to produce this grateful lull. In
the words of Lord Barrington, "the Ministry,
though not highly rated, was not disliked;"[2] Junius
had laid down his pen; the great Whig lords had at
last discovered that the royal closet was not to be
carried quite so easily by storm as they had once
imagined; the death of George Grenville had sadly
weakened the party of which he was the chief;
Lord Rockingham and his friends, dispirited by
repeated defeats, contented themselves, till the
arrival of more propitious times, with watching
over and guarding the integrity of the constitution;
and, lastly, difficult as it may be to conceive, Lord

---

[1] Walpole's 'Reign of George III.,' vol. iv. pp. 302, 303; Earl Stanhope's 'Hist. of England,' vol. v. pp. 435, 436.
[2] Ellis's 'Original Letters,' vol. iv. p. 530; 2nd series.

Chatham would almost seem to have reconciled himself to the Tory Administration of Lord North. "I have long held one opinion," he writes to Lord Shelburne on the 6th of March, 1774, "as to the stability of Lord North's situation. He serves the Crown more successfully and more efficiently upon the whole than any other man to be found could do."[1]

In the mean time, unsought for, and little prized by him, as had been Lord North's elevation to the Premiership, he had since found his acceptance of it followed by advantages and distinctions which he could scarcely have failed to appreciate. On the 14th of June, 1771, for instance, he was appointed Ranger of Bushy Park, with the use and enjoyment of its pleasant Lodge; on the 3rd of October, 1772, he was unanimously chosen Chancellor of the University of Oxford; and the same year was honoured with the Order of the Garter; "the only one except my father's," writes Walpole, "that has shone in the House of Commons since Queen Elizabeth's day;" but to which we may remark, the Garters of two other Commoners, Lords Castlereagh and Palmerston, have since been added.[2] Neither was the grant of the Lord Wardenship of the Cinque Ports—the bestowal of which on Lord North was the spontaneous act of his Sovereign—a boon to be

[1] Chatham 'Correspondence,' vol. iv. pp. 332, 333.
[2] Walpole's 'Letters,' vol. v. p. 379, and *note*.

despised by a minister whose private means were not only, comparatively speaking, slender, but who, without the help of the emoluments appertaining to that sinecure post, would probably have retired from the Premiership a poorer man than when he entered upon its duties: How willingly George III. would have relieved the apparent necessities of his favourite minister, how grateful the King felt to him for having come to his succour on the resignation of the Duke of Grafton, may be read in the following interesting communication from the King to Lord North, dated the 19th of September, 1777. "I have now signed," he writes, "the last warrant for paying up the arrears due on my Civil List, and therefore seize with pleasure this instant to insist on doing the same for you, my dear Lord. You have at times dropped to me that you have been in debt ever since your first settling in life, and that you had never been able to get out of that difficulty; I therefore must insist that you will now state to me whether twelve or fifteen thousand pounds will not set your affairs in order; if it will, nay, if twenty thousand pounds is necessary, I am resolved you shall have no other person concerned in freeing them but myself. Knowing now my determination, it is easy for you to make a proper arrangement, and at proper times for to take by degrees that sum. You know me very ill if you do not think that of all the letters I have ever written to you, this one gives me the most pleasure, and I want no other return, but you being convinced that I love you as well as a man of worth as I esteem you as a minister. Your conduct at a critical moment I never can forget, and am glad that, by your ability and the kindness of Parliament, I am enabled to give you this mark of my affection, which is the only one I have ever yet been able to perform, but trust some of the employments for life will in time become vacant that I may reward your family."[1]

At the time when Lord North was elevated to the Premiership, he was in the thirty-eighth year of his age. He had married, on the 10th of March, 1756, shortly before the completion of his twenty-fourth year, Anne, daughter and co-heir of George Speke, Esq., of White Lackington, in Somersetshire, a young lady of only sixteen. " Whether they had been in love with each other when they married," writes their daughter, Lady Charlotte Lindsay,[2] " I don't know, but I am sure there never was a more happy union than theirs during the thirty-six years that it lasted. I never saw an unkind look or heard an unkind word pass between them ; his affectionate attachment to her was as unabated as her love and admiration of him." By this gentle and accomplished lady, Lord North became the father of three sons, of whom the

[1] 'Correspondence of George III. with Lord North,' vol. ii. pp. 82, 83.
[2] Letter to Lord Brougham, ' Brougham's Statesmen of the Time of George III.,' first series, p. 244; edition 1845.

two eldest, George Augustus and Francis, respectively succeeded as third and fourth Earls of Guilford; and of three daughters, of whom the youngest, Lady Charlotte Lindsay, survived to be loved and admired in our own time for her genial nature and playful wit. Such was the amiable circle of which Lord North was not only the central figure, but the idol and delight. Whatever may have been his political errors, in private life it would be difficult to discover a more charming person. Generous, open-hearted, and hospitable, beloved by his private friends as well as idolized by his family; delighting in the society of the young, and never so happy as when sharing the mirth and frolics of his children, and diffusing gaiety and happiness around him—such in domestic life was the well-intentioned statesman to whose many amiable qualities we have endeavoured to do justice.

Nor were these Lord North's only claims on the admiration and love of his family and friends. Gifted with conversational powers of no mean order, he had the happy art of accommodating those powers to every society in which he found himself. He enjoyed a temperament completely free from irascibility; a thorough appreciation and almost childlike love of the ridiculous; an ever-ready, playful, and genial wit; an utter absence of all pride and ostentation; powers of raillery which he never suffered to wound the feelings of others; and lastly, a sweetness of temper which not all the prosings of the dull, nor the flippancies of the pert, could ever ruffle. "I never," writes his daughter, Lady Charlotte Lindsay, to Lord Brougham, "*saw my father really out of humour*. He had a drunken, stupid groom, who used to provoke him, and who, from this uncommon circumstance was called by the children the 'man who puts papa in a passion;' yet," adds Lady Charlotte, "I think he continued all his life putting papa in a passion and being forgiven, for I believe he died in his service." [1]

In the House of Commons, Lord North's wit, combined with the sweetness of his temper, displayed itself in a scarcely more delightful manner than in private life. No one could more frequently, nor with better effect, carry out the axiom of his favourite Horace—

"Ridiculum acri
Fortius et melius magnas plerumque secat res."

Of his sense of the ridiculous and powers of raillery he availed himself with the most consummate skill. If his adversaries pressed too closely upon him, his good-humoured banter and jest were often more than a match for their bitterest invectives. Not inappositely, he might over and over again have

[1] Lord Brougham's 'Statesmen of the Time of George III.,' first series, p. 295; ed. 1815.

applied to himself a couplet which he had composed when a boy at Eton—

> "Non te jam expectant laurus, non præmia palmæ,
> Victori post tot prælia risus adest."[1]

The almost boyish gaiety and triumph which he displayed whenever he had discomfited a political adversary, was only matched by the unruffled good humour with which he had borne that adversary's attack. Sometimes, indeed, it suited his purpose or his humour to turn the joke against himself. On an occasion, for instance, of a member of the House of Commons speaking contemptuously of him as "that thing called a minister"—"Well," he said, patting his capacious sides, "to be sure, I am a thing: the honourable member, therefore, when he called me 'a thing,' said what was true, and I could not be angry with him. But when he added 'that thing called a minister,' he called me that thing which of all things he himself most wished to be, and therefore I took it as a compliment."[2] So equable was his temperament, so indifferent was he to the bitter personal attacks which are commonly gall and wormwood to a minister, that, even during the stormiest debates, he might be seen sleeping calmly and soundly on the Treasury Bench. While

---

[1] "―――――――― Peccare docentes
    Historias.
NORTH.   A.D. 1748."

[2] Butler's 'Reminiscences,' p. 159.

snatching these *sollicitæ jucunda oblivia vitæ*, it was to little purpose that the powerful eloquence of Charles Fox or of Barré denounced him as an enemy to his country, or that Burke thundered impassioned threats of impeachment in his ears. "Even now," once exclaimed a political opponent, "the noble lord is slumbering over the ruin of his country."—"I wish to Heaven," muttered Lord North, as he slowly opened his eyes, "that I was."[1] "The cause of Government," writes Gibbon, then a member of the House of Commons, "was ably vindicated by Lord North, a statesman of spotless integrity, a consummate master of debate, who could wield with equal dexterity the arms of reason and of ridicule. He was seated on the Treasury Bench, between his Attorney- and Solicitor-General, the two pillars of the Law and State, *magis pares quam similes;* and the minister might indulge in a short slumber, whilst he was upholden on either hand by the majestic sense of Thurlow, and the skilful eloquence of Wedderburn."[2]

As a parliamentary speaker, in the general sense of the term, no great praise can be awarded to Lord North. His utterance was disagreeable, his delivery inelegant, his manner awkward. "Nothing," writes Walpole, "could be more coarse or clumsy or ungracious than his outside. Two large prominent

---

[1] Earl Russell's 'Memorials of Fox,' vol. i. p. 121.
[2] Gibbon's 'Miscellaneous Works,' p. 93; edition 1837.

eyes that rolled about to no purpose, for he was utterly short-sighted, a wide mouth, thick lips, and inflated visage, gave him the air of a blind trumpeter."[1] Burke, in the House of Commons, once hit off Lord North's infirmities, apparently to his very face. "The noble lord," he said, "after extending his right leg a full yard before his left, rolling his flaming eyes, and moving his ponderous frame, has at length opened his mouth."[2] Notwithstanding these defects, however, Lord North's extraordinary command of language, and a memory so retentive that it enabled him to carry in his mind every argument that had been urged in the course of a debate, his extensive knowledge of books and men, his abundance of shrewd common sense, his perfect presence of mind and complete mastery over his temper, and lastly, his thorough knowledge of the rules, constitution, and character of the House of Commons, unquestionably qualified him to figure, if not as a great orator, at least as a debater of no mean order.

Lord North, to repeat the words of Gibbon, was "a statesman of spotless integrity." When, on some occasion in the House of Commons, he was accused of clinging to office and prolonging the American War from pecuniary inducements, the charge was repudiated by him with so calm and solemn a dignity as to make a deep and lasting impression upon his

[1] Walpole's 'Reign of George III.' vol. iv. p. 78.
[2] 'Parl. Hist.' vol. xvi. p. 720.

hearers. "I do not desire," he said, "to make any affected display of my personal purity and disinterestedness. I will, however, declare, with respect to my income, that most cheerfully would I give it all—not only the part which I derive from the public purse, but my own private fortune—if I could only thereby accelerate an honourable, speedy, and advantageous peace." In the opinion of Sir Nathaniel Wraxall, who was present, there was not a member in the House, not one even of his bitterest enemies, but believed in the sincerity of that asseveration.[1] "Curse on his virtues!" exclaimed Alderman Sawbridge on one occasion from Addison's 'Cato,' "they've undone his country."[2]

Lord North had held the Premiership for a little more than five years, when, in the month of April, 1775, the occurrence of the memorable hostile collisions at Lexington and Concord, between British troops and bodies of American citizens, produced the immediate and disastrous effect of plunging the two countries into civil war. Happy would it have been, alike for Lord North and for his country, had his tenure of power ceased at this period; but, unfortunately, seven more years of official existence were in store for him; those years being pregnant with greater disaster and disgrace than during any past period of corresponding duration in the annals

[1] Wraxall's 'Hist. Memoirs,' vol. ii. p. 140.
[2] Act iv., scene 1; Wraxall, *ut supra*, p. 141.

of Great Britain. " Year after year," writes an historian of those times,[1] "our blood and treasure were expended to no purpose; myriads of men were killed; hundreds of millions were lavished without obtaining any valuable object; temporary gleams of partial success were followed by the permanent gloom of general disaster." That, at the commencement of the American War, the majority of the upper and middle classes in England not only, like the King, took a harsh view of the conduct of the American people, but that they were prepared to approve the coercive policy pursued towards them by Lord North and his colleagues, seems to be sufficiently manifested by the number of loyal addresses favourable to the prosecution of hostilities, which, to the agreeable surprise of ministers, poured in from all parts of the kingdom to the foot of the Throne.[2] As yet the little likelihood, or rather the impossibility, of England conquering, and keeping in subjection a continent so distant and so vast as America, and a people so high-spirited and so united as the Americans, had, on this side of the Atlantic, impressed itself upon the convictions only of the far-sighted and of the few; and, accordingly, so long as there had remained a prospect of relieving the pecuniary

[1] Dr. Bisset.
[2] See the 'London Gazette' from the 12th of September, 1775, to the 9th of March, 1776, inclusive; and letter from Gibbon, the historian, to Mr. Holroyd, dated the 14th of October, 1775; Gibbon's 'Miscellaneous Works,' p. 271; edition 1837.

burdens of Great Britain by the taxation of America, the war had been a popular one in the mother-country. No sooner, however, did the tide of disaster and financial distress set in, than the public began to raise its voice against the further prosecution of hostilities; nor was Lord North by any means one of the latest persons to discover the increasing probability of the conflict terminating unfavourably and calamitously for England. Long since, indeed, tired of the worry, the fatigues, and the responsibilities of office, the object of his heart had been to bring the dispute with America to an honourable close, and, having accomplished this philanthropic purpose, to be allowed to retire into private life with the consolatory reflection that he had done his utmost to serve his King and country. As it was, nothing but his unwillingness to forsake his Sovereign in his hour of difficulty, combined with the King's earnest entreaties to him to remain at the head of the Treasury, had, over and over again, prevented his resigning his post. "I should have been greatly surprised," writes the King to him on the 31st of January, 1778, "at the inclination expressed by you to retire, had I not known that, however you may now and then be inclined to despond, yet that you have too much personal affection for me and sense of honour to allow such a thought to take any hold on your mind."[1] Thus,

[1] 'Correspondence of George III. with Lord North,' vol. ii. p. 125.

also, on the 22nd of March following, the King again writes to his harassed Minister: "My dear Lord,—Your now always recurring to a total change of the Administration obliges me to ask you one clear question, which in my own mind I am almost certain cannot be your intention: If I will not by your advice take the step I look on as disgraceful to myself and destruction to my country and family, are you resolved, agreeably to the example of the Duke of Grafton, at the hour of danger to desert me?"[1] Such an appeal as this, addressed to him by his Sovereign, it was not in the generous nature of Lord North to withstand. His reply, indeed, is not forthcoming, but, at all events, it seems to have satisfied the apprehensions of the King. "I cannot," replies his Majesty, "return the messenger without expressing my satisfaction at your determination not to desert at this hour, which indeed I always thought your sense of honour must prevent."[2]

It may be mentioned that, towards the close of the year 1779, the King, affected by Lord North's renewed and earnest entreaties to be released from the cares and toils of office, at length reluctantly consented to his opening a negotiation with Lords Camden and Shelburne, with a view to their collectively endeavouring to construct a strong Coalition Ministry. "I can state my sentiments in three

[1] 'Correspondence of George III. with Lord North,' vol. ii. p. 159.
[2] Ibid., vol. ii. p. 160.

words," writes the King to Lord North; " I wish Lord North to continue ; but if he is resolved to retire, he must understand the step, though thought necessary by him, is very unpleasant to me."[1] The overtures, however, to the two Whig lords were not only scouted by them as utterly inadmissible, but the language in which their refusal was couched, however unintentionally irritating, seems to have given deep offence to the King. " From the cold disdain with which I am thus treated," he writes to Lord Chancellor Thurlow, " it is evident to me what treatment I am to expect from Opposition if I was to call them now to my service. Nothing less will satisfy them than a total change of measures and men : to obtain their support I must deliver up my person, my principles, my dominions, into their hands."[2]

At length, the surrender at York Town, in the month of October, 1781, of the fine British army under the command of Lord Cornwallis, may be said to have brought to a close the unnatural and sanguinary war which had so long been raging on the other side of the Atlantic ; while, at the same time, it established the unity of the Americans as a free, sovereign, and independent people. It was on Sunday, the 25th of November, that the despatch, containing the news of the terrible calamity which

---

[1] ' Correspondence of George III. with Lord North,' vol. ii. p. 290.
[2] Ibid., vol. ii. p. 208.

had befallen the British arms on the York River, arrived at the private residence of the Secretary of State for American affairs, Lord George Germaine, in Pall Mall. Lord George, having in the first instance forwarded the despatch to the King at Kew, proceeded to Downing Street in order personally to communicate the distressing intelligence to Lord North. It was received by that usually stoical minister, not only with every appearance of dismay, but with a manifestation of mental agony the poignancy of which was doubtless increased by the bitter reflection that he had for some time past carried on the war in opposition to his own conscientious convictions. "I asked Lord George afterwards," writes Sir Nathaniel Wraxall, "how he [Lord North] took the communication when made to him?—' As he would have taken a bullet through his breast,' replied Lord George, 'for he opened his arms, exclaiming wildly, as he paced up and down the apartment a few minutes—"Oh, God! it is all over!"—words which he repeated many times under emotions of the greatest consternation and distress.'"[1]

The disaster at York Town went far, as may be supposed, to complete the unpopularity, not only of the American War, but also of Lord North and his Tory colleagues. True it is that, on the reassembling of Parliament, which took place two days after the arrival of the painful tidings, ministers, in

[1] 'Wraxall's 'Hist. Memoirs,' vol. ii. pp. 434, 435; 3rd edition.

both Houses, carried their Address to the Throne by
considerable majorities; but not on that account was
it the less manifest, even to the less far-sighted,
that the beginning of the end was fast approaching.
Not only, for example, were public meetings condemnatory of the further prosecution of the war
convened with triumphant effect by the corporation
of London, by the counties of Middlesex and Surrey,
by the electors of Westminster, and by the West
India merchants, but, within the walls of Parliament, several independent members of the House
of Commons, who had till now been staunch supporters of Lord North, proved themselves more
than waverers in their allegiance. Two such notable
defections were those of the not less wealthy and
powerful commoners, Sir James Lowther, member
for Cumberland, and Mr. Thomas Powys, member
for Northamptonshire, who, on the 12th of December,
went so far as to move and second a resolution to
the effect that any attempt to reduce America to
obedience by force of arms was impolitic, and ought
to be abandoned. Ministers, indeed, succeeded in
defeating the resolution, but it was only by a
reduced majority of forty-one. " I was rather disappointed," writes the King on the following day
to Lord North, " at the majority not being greater,
particularly when I read the question moved by Sir
James Lowther."[1] But, if the King was thus

[1] 'Correspondence of George III. with Lord North,' vol. ii. p. 395.

disappointed, how far greater must have been his dissatisfaction when, on the 22nd of February following, on General Conway's famous motion to the same effect, he found his favourite minister left in a majority of only *one!*

In the mean time, owing to the fierce party struggle which was raging in Parliament, the House of Commons had for some time past been daily the scene of the most lively excitement. Not only was attack after attack made upon ministers, but by both parties every available opportunity was seized of securing the attendance and votes of the sick, the halt, and the lukewarm. It was on Lord North, of course, that Opposition levelled its fiercest attacks— attacks, however, which were repelled by him with a complacent dignity, and in language so unmistakably sincere, as to win for him the admiration even of his enemies. Whatever amount of humiliation and disaster his Tory principles may have inflicted on his country, his behaviour to his Sovereign had, at all events, been indisputably and eminently chivalrous and unselfish. Unpalatable, he declared in the House of Commons on the 5th of March, as was his present post to him, and great as were the vexations and anxiety which he had to contend against, he was resolved not to quit that post until he should either have received his Sovereign's command to leave it, or till the will of the House of Commons, expressed in the most unequivocal terms, should point out to him the propriety of retiring. And in similar language he expressed himself in the House on the 15th. His wish, he said, was not only for peace, but to see an adminstration established that would act unanimously, unselfishly, and effectually for the public welfare. He would offer no obstacle to a coalition, in which he should have no share of power or place. There were persons, he continued, who well knew that for years past he had been ready to make way for such an adminstration, nor had it been from any desire of his own that he had so long remained in his present post. "I declare to God," he exclaimed, "that no love of office or of emolument should detain me for a moment in place if I could with honour leave it, and if certain circumstances, which I cannot now explain, did not prevent my resignation. A time may come, I flatter myself, when I can better speak upon this point; I act in obedience to a sense of duty, which neither persuasions nor menaces can influence me to abandon."[1]

At length, notwithstanding a strongly-expressed resolution on the part of the King, that under no circumstances would "he throw himself into the hands of the Opposition,"[2] the famous North Administration succumbed to popular condemnation and to repeated defeats in the House of Commons. On the 8th of March, a string of resolutions in that House,

[1] 'Parl. Hist.,' vol. xxii. cols. 1108, 1193, 1194.
[2] 'Correspondence of George III. with Lord North,' vol. ii. p. 414.

to the effect that to the incapacity of the present ministers of the Crown were attributable all the calamities which afflicted the country, was brought forward by Lord John Cavendish, and defeated only by a majority of ten; on the 15th a motion for a direct vote of want of confidence in ministers was proposed by Sir John Rous, a county Tory member, and lost by the still smaller majority of nine; while, pending over ministers' heads for debate on the 20th, was a second vote of want of confidence, moved for by the Earl of Surrey. On this latter day, the House of Commons presented a scene of extraordinary excitement, resembling, if it did not parallel, the famous debate which, forty years previously, had preceded the downfall of Sir Robert Walpole from power. At four o'clock it was computed that no fewer than four hundred members were already assembled. In the mean time, Lord North, after a long conference the same day with the King in the royal closet at St. James's, had at length wrung from his Sovereign the reluctant admission that it would be hopeless for his present servants to attempt to carry on the Government any longer, and consequently that he regarded the Administration as at an end. "Then, sir," inquired the overjoyed minister, "had I not better state the fact at once?" To this the King no longer offering any objection, Lord North hurried off in his court dress and blue riband to the House of Commons, on the doors of which, in anxious expectation of his arrival, every eye in the crowded assembly had for some time been fixed. The loud cries of "Order, order! Places, places!" which had greeted him as he passed up the House to the Treasury benches, had no sooner ceased than, simultaneously with Lord Surrey, who had a prior right to address the House, he rose to speak. A scene of great confusion was the result, in the midst of which Charles Fox, having with difficulty secured a moment's hearing, formally put the question that "The Earl of Surrey do now speak." " I rise to speak to that motion," was the adroit rejoinder of Lord North, who, having thus succeeded in gaining the ear of the House, at once communicated to it the exciting intelligence that the Administration was at an end. As for himself, he said, in touching yet manly language, his Sovereign would probably find it easy enough to supply his place with a minister of sounder judgment and more brilliant abilities; but one more jealous of the honour of his country, one more anxious to advance its interests, and to maintain the Constitution inviolate, or one animated by more devoted feelings of loyalty towards his Sovereign, his Majesty would find it difficult to enlist in his service. Whoever, he continued, might be the individuals appointed to succeed him and his colleagues in the Ministry, he trusted their measures might be such as to extricate their common country from its present critical situation, to render her happy and prosperous at home, and honoured and glorious abroad. As regarded his past conduct as a minister, he was aware, he said, that he was responsible for whatever measures he might have adopted; he had often been threatened with an investigation into his public conduct, but so far was he from shrinking from such an inquiry, that he would ever be ready to encounter it, let the ordeal prove what it might.

The feelings of Lord North, now that he was at length released by his Sovereign from his political engagements, would seem to have partaken rather of the exhilaration of a schoolboy when emancipated for his holidays, than of the despondency natural to a discomfited minister in his hour of fallen greatness. Happily, moreover, his satisfaction was shared to the full by Lady North and their amiable and sympathizing daughters. "This," writes the youngest, Lady Charlotte, "was a great relief to his mind; for though I do not believe that my father ever entertained any doubt as to the justice of the American war, yet I am sure that he wished to have made peace three years before its termination. I perfectly recollect the satisfaction expressed by my mother and elder sisters upon this occasion, and my own astonishment at it, being at that time a girl of eleven years old; and hearing in the nursery the lamentations of the women, about 'my Lord's going out of power'— viz., the power of making their husbands tidewaiters—I thought going out of power must be a sad thing, and that all the family were crazy to rejoice at it."[1] "No man," writes his friend, Mr. Adam, "ever showed more calmness, cheerfulness, and serenity. The temper of his whole family was the same. I dined with them that day, and was witness to it."[2] A few days afterwards, on the occasion of another friend intimating to him the surprise which he had felt at his fall from power, "What!" exclaimed the ex-minister in the words placed by Shakespeare in the mouth of Cardinal Wolsey—

> "amazed
> At my misfortunes? can thy spirit wonder
> A great man should decline?"
> *King Henry VIII.*, act iii. sc. 2.

Of the genial humour and cheerfulness displayed by Lord North at this crisis, more than one other instance has been recorded. Of these, not the least pleasing happened on the night of the unexpected hindrance of Lord Surrey's motion for the dismissal of ministers and the consequent early adjournment of the House of Commons. "Snow was falling," writes Lord Holland, "and the night tremendous. All the members' carriages were dismissed, and Mrs. Bennet's room at the door was crowded. But Lord North's carriage was waiting. He put into it one or two of his friends whom he had invited to go

[1] Lord Brougham's 'Statesmen of the Time of George III.,' first series, pp. 214, 215; edition 1845.
[2] Earl Russell's 'Memorials of Fox,' vol. i. p. 295.

home with him, and turning to the crowd, chiefly composed of his bitter enemies, in the midst of their triumph, exclaimed, in this hour of defeat and supposed mortification, with admirable good humour and pleasantry, '*I have* my carriage; you see, gentlemen, the advantage of being in *the secret*. Good night.'"[1] No less unfavourable was the weather on the day that Lord North was admitted to his parting interview with the King; the rain, as he entered the royal closet, falling in torrents. "Have you been out to-day—have you been out to-day?" inquired the King with that nervous rapidity of utterance which was habitual to him in moments of excitement or mental distress. "Sire," replied the fallen minister, "I was turned out yesterday; I would not turn a dog out on such a day as this." Lastly, the King's notorious aversion to the new Whig ministers, by whom his late Tory advisers were about to be replaced, afforded Lord North a favourable opportunity of raising a harmless laugh at their expense, of which he did not fail to avail himself. Their appointments having been announced in the 'London Gazette' of the 30th of March with the usual phraseology—"The King has been pleased to constitute and appoint the Most Honourable Charles Marquis of Rockingham, Lord John Cavendish," &c. "*Pleased!*" is said to have been Lord North's exclamation on reading the Gazette, "why,

[1] Earl Russell's 'Memorials of Fox,' vol. i. p. 296.

I have often been abused for lying Gazettes, yet there are more lies in this single Gazette than in all of mine put together."[1]

According to Walpole, the King's manner to Lord North at their farewell interview was not only cold, but ungracious almost to rudeness. "Remember, my Lord," are stated to have been his parting words, "it is you that desert me, not I you."[2] Whether, however, these words were in reality ever spoken, or rather whether, at this rather unlikely period, the King's regard for his old servant and friend had undergone so radical a change as to provoke them from his lips, seems to be very questionable. All the evidence, indeed, points to an opposite conclusion. "The effusion of my sorrows," writes the King to Lord North on the 27th of March, " has made me say more than I had intended; but I ever did, and ever shall, look on you as a friend as well as a faithful servant."[3] Again, one of the few conditions for which the King stipulated with his new minister, Lord Rockingham, was his sanction to Lord North's retiring with a pension of 4000*l*. a year.[4] Nor is this all. During the twelve last years, be it remembered, they had fought the same battles, shared the same unpopularity, and incurred the same hazards. Neither is it likely that the King should

[1] Walpole's 'Letters,' vol. viii. p. 211.
[2] Walpole's 'Last Journals,' vol. ii. p. 521.
[3] 'Correspondence of George III. with Lord North,' vol. ii. p. 420.
[4] Walpole's 'Last Journals,' vol. ii. p. 536.

have altogether forgotten the boyish days when they had disported among the lilacs and seringas at Kew, or performed their several parts in Addison's classical drama in the saloons of Leicester House. At that period, words had been enunciated by both in the course of delivering those allotted parts which, however inapplicable to the future of each those words may then have appeared, were probably afterwards called to mind by them as having been almost prophetic in their character:

> *Portius* [Prince George].—" The friendships of the world are oft
> Confederacies in vice, or leagues of pleasure;
> Ours has severest virtue for its basis,
> And such a friendship ends not but with life."
> *Cato*, act iii. sc. 1.

And again—

> *Syphax* [Master North].—"Our first design, my friend, has proved abortive,
> Still there remains an after-game to play."
> *Cato*, act iii. sc. 1.

Undoubtedly George III.'s long friendship for Lord North was destined to be eventually brought to an untoward close; but this it is needless, perhaps, to remark, was part of an "after-game" which remained to be played by them at a later period of their lives. "If I was asked," writes the late King of Hanover, "which minister the King during my life gave the preference to, I should say Lord North; but the Coalition broke up that connection, and he never forgave him."[1]

[1] MS. letter to the late Right Hon. J. W. Croker.

The subsequent and almost inexplicable devotion of Lord North to the ranks of the Whig party, which took place early in the spring of 1783, unquestionably fell a heavy blow upon George III. If one, for instance, on whom he had delighted to heap favours and honours—one with whom, for years past, he had associated on terms of the most affectionate intimacy—could thus prove faithless, in what other living statesman could the King hope to meet with gratitude and fidelity? So cruelly, indeed, in the King's opinion, had he been abandoned by his former minister and friend, that, happening to encounter Lord North's father, the venerable Earl of Guilford, in the Queen's apartments, the sight of the Earl flung him into a state of agitation which he found it impossible to suppress. "My Lord Guilford," he exclaimed, as he wrung the Earl's hands, "did I ever think that Lord North would have delivered me up in this manner to Mr. Fox?"[1]

To the world in general, Lord North's defection from his party seems to have been scarcely less a matter of astonishment than to the King. Seldom in England, indeed, have political circles been more completely taken by surprise than when, towards the close of Lord Shelburne's brief administration, it became, in the first instance, suspected, and afterwards manifest, not only that an understanding of the most friendly nature had been established between

[1] Earl Russell's 'Memorials of Fox,' vol. ii. p. 41.

Lord North and his late political arch-enemy, Charles Fox, but that they had actually united their parliamentary forces in the hope of ejecting the present ministers from power, and installing themselves conjointly in their stead. Certainly, a much more unnatural alliance it would not be easy to imagine. Not only for years past had Fox systematically opposed every measure proposed, and every political principle advocated by Lord North; but, over and over again, in language too eloquent and too impassioned not to have made a lasting impression upon the House of Commons, he had charged him and his late colleagues with incapacity, corruption, treachery, and falsehood. Over and over again he had laid to their charge all the miseries and calamities of the American war, and had even threatened them with impeachment and the scaffold. Lord North he had denounced as a man "void of honesty and honour." Should he (Fox), the latter had solemnly asseverated, ever make terms with any one member of the late Ministry, he would "rest satisfied to be called the most infamous of mankind." In the hands of such men, he exclaimed, he would not trust his honour even for a moment.[1]

The ground selected by Fox and Lord North to be their common point of attack upon the Shelburne Ministry, was the alleged incompleteness and inadequacy of the recent Treaty of Peace between Great

[1] Fox's 'Speeches,' vol. ii. p. 39.

Britain and France and Spain, the preliminary articles of which had been signed at Versailles on the 20th of January. " That nothing," writes Lord Macaulay, "might be wanting to the scandal, the great orators who had during seven years thundered against the war, determined to join with the authors of that war in passing a vote of censure on the peace."[1] The first skirmish in the House of Commons between the newly organized parties took place on the 17th of February, on the vote of an address to the Throne, on which occasion, though Fox and Lord North severally abstained from any open admission of their recently cemented alliance, the fact of its existence became only too startlingly manifest. Fox, for instance, when taxed by Dundas with tenderness for his political adversaries, rather seemed to glory in than to take umbrage at the charge. The state of things, he said, which had formerly bred hostility between himself and the noble lord lately at the head of the Government no longer existed. The American war, and with it the rancour and feuds which it had engendered, were at an end. Happy he was at all times to bury his animosities in oblivion, but his friendships he hoped would never die. He had found the noble lord, he added, an honourable adversary, and he entertained no doubt of his openness and sincerity as a friend. That, coming from the lips of Fox, such equivocal

[2] Life of Pitt, ' Macaulay's Biographies,' p. 160.

words as these should have excited indignation and disgust in the minds of many members present was no more, perhaps, than was to have been expected. "It was an age· of great conspiracies," said Powys, member for Northamptonshire; "a *monstrous coalition* had taken place between a noble lord and an illustrious commoner; the lofty assertor of the prerogative had joined in alliance with the worshippers of the majesty of the people."[1] The effect which this state of things produced on the issue of the debate was in due time made manifest. "Some of the staunchest friends of Fox and the Cavendishes," writes Walpole, "left them, because they had joined Lord North; and some of Lord North's friends deserted him because he had united with Fox."[2] "There are great numbers of members," writes Lord Bulkeley to Lord Temple, "who are outrageous at the junction of Fox with Lord North.[3] Nevertheless, so considerable was the support for which Fox was indebted to his new Tory allies, that when, at seven o'clock in the morning, a division took place, the ministers were found to have been defeated by a majority of sixteen.

The exciting scene presented on this occasion in the House of Commons was repeated four days afterwards, when, on the 21st of February, Lord

[1] 'Parl. Hist.,' vol. xxiii. col. 487.
[2] Walpole's 'Last Journals,' vol. ii. p. 583.
[3] 'Buckingham Papers,' vol. i. p. 156.

John Cavendish moved in explicit terms a condemnation of the conditions of the peace. Again, the Opposition violently inveighed against those conditions, and again the ministerial party as violently denounced the profligacy of the alliance between the Fox and North factions. "If," exclaimed young William Pitt, then on the threshold of his greatness, "this baneful alliance is not already formed, if this ill-omened marriage is not already solemnized, I know a just and lawful impediment, and in the name of the public safety I here forbid the bans."[1] On Lord North personally the weight of Pitt's indignant eloquence chiefly fell. If, he said, there was anything amiss in the proposed articles of peace, it was attributable, not to the present Government, but to the noble lord in the blue riband, whose profligate expenditure of the public money, whose obstinacy in protracting a pernicious and oppressive war, and whose utter unfitness to fill the high station which he had recently quitted, rendered a peace, of some description or other, absolutely indispensable for the preservation of the State. Magnificent, however, as was Pitt's speech on this occasion, a majority of 207 to 190 declared against ministers; and accordingly, three days afterwards, Lord Shelburne and his colleagues, having been thus a second time signally defeated, resigned their seals of office into the King's hands.

[1] 'Parl. Hist.,' vol. xxiii. cols. 543, 552.

In the mean time, so satisfied had Lord North and Fox felt that their own elevation to power would be the inevitable result of Lord Shelburne's fall, that already they had had the presumption to settle between themselves the ministerial arrangements which they were resolved to force upon the King. Even the constitutional right of the Sovereign to nominate his own first minister was to be denied him; the Duke of Portland, a cipher in all respects but as regarded his ducal rank and ducal fortune, was to be nominally at the head of the Government, while Lord North and Fox, as Secretaries of State, were to be the real dispensers of place and power. Neither did Fox's presumption, in which Lord North must be admitted to have gone all lengths with him, end here. Two days, for instance, previously to Lord Shelburne's resignation, Lord Temple was, in the most unauthorized manner, entreated to remain as Lord Lieutenant of Ireland,[1] while, only two days afterwards, the Duke of Richmond was urged to remain in office as Master-General of the Ordnance. By both noblemen were these proffers declined, and by the Duke apparently with something like scorn. He had seen his name, he said, attached to so many protests against Lord North, that it was impossible he could act in concert with that nobleman.[2] But, though Lord North and Fox eventually triumphed over their Sovereign,

---

[1] 'Buckingham Papers,' vol. i. p. 162.
[2] Walpole's 'Last Journals,' vol. ii. pp. 588, 589.

their success was not so easily achieved as they had anticipated. It was not, in fact, till after a spirited resistance, which lasted for five weeks—not till the King had earnestly, but in vain, pressed the Premiership upon William Pitt, then only in his twenty-fourth year—not till he had urged Lord Shelburne to make a second attempt to carry on the Government—not till he had ineffectually sounded Lord Gower—and, lastly, not till, in repeated interviews in the royal closet, he had entreated Lord North to break off his connection with Fox and to resume his seat at the Treasury Board—that his Majesty could be induced to succumb to what he designated " the most unprincipled coalition the annals of this or any other country can equal."[1] Great, as the King intimated to William Grenville, was his aversion both to Fox and Lord North, but of the two he should prefer the latter for his minister.[2] It was to Lord North, accordingly, that, at their final interview on the 1st of April, the King addressed his last appeal for succour in this his hour of pressing difficulty and humiliation. Would he, or would he not, he asked him, relieve the mind of his Sovereign by consenting to return to his former post? " I have told your Majesty," replied Lord North, " that I cannot."—" Then," said the King, " you may tell the Duke of Portland he may kiss my hand

---

[1] 'Buckingham Papers,' vol. i. p. 219.
[2] Ibid., vol. i. p. 192.

to-morrow."[1] That Lord North's refusal greatly distressed the King, little doubt can exist. To Lord Temple he writes in the course of the day : " I trust the eyes of the nation will soon be opened, or my sorrow may prove fatal to my health if I remain long in this thraldom."[2] Thus harassed, then, it was only natural that, when on the following day the Duke of Portland kissed his hand as First Lord of the Treasury, and Lord North and Fox as Secretaries of State, the King should have found some difficulty in concealing his feelings. To the Duke and Fox, indeed, he behaved graciously ; but not so to Lord North, to whom his manner, very different from that of former days, was that of marked coldness, if not of aversion.[3]

On the fate of Fox's famous India Bill, or rather, on what was consequent on it—on the fate of the short-lived Coalition Ministry, we have no occasion to dilate. Fox, it should be observed, had succeeded in carrying his favourite measure triumphantly through the House of Commons, but, inasmuch as defeat might still be its fate in the House of Lords, and as such defeat would obviously justify the King in getting rid alike of his present ministers and of their obnoxious measure, the further progress of the Bill through the Upper House was naturally watched by

[1] Walpole's 'Last Journals,' vol. ii. p. 612.
[2] 'Buckingham Papers,' vol. i. p. 219.
[3] Walpole's 'Last Journals,' vol. ii. p. 612.

him with the most lively anxiety. Eventually, to his great relief, it was defeated on its second reading, on the 17th of December, by a majority of ninety-five peers against seventy-six.

On the following morning, at a "meet" of the royal stag-hounds, the King, notwithstanding the hounds had thrown off, was observed to linger behind in an abstracted manner, when suddenly the approach of a horseman, bringing him a sealed packet, worked an entire change in his aspect. Eagerly breaking open the seal, his hurried glance no sooner mastered the contents of the packet, than, throwing his arms wide open, he emphatically exclaimed, "Thank heaven! it is all over; the House has thrown out the Bill, so that there is an end of Mr. Fox."[1] Thus certified of his approaching emancipation from what he regarded as a state of dependency, so impatient became the King to get rid at once of the services of his two obnoxious advisers, that being disappointed at night setting in without his having received their resignations, he despatched messengers, late as was the hour, to Lord North and Fox, commanding them to send their seals of office to the palace forthwith, through their respective Under Secretaries. In the case of Lord North, he was in bed with Lady North, when, at one o'clock in the morning, Sir Evan Nepean, the Under Secretary of State for the Home Department

[1] 'Quarterly Review,' vol. cv. p. 482.

knocked at his bedchamber door, and desired to see him on most important business. "Then," said the easy minister, obstinately refusing to rise, "you must see Lady North too." Sir Evan having accordingly been admitted, Lord North delivered to him the key of the closet in which the seals of office were kept, and then, quietly turning round in his bed, composed himself for further sleep.[1] It may be mentioned that from this time Lord North never again held office in the State.

From Lord North as a minister we now willingly return to Lord North in his private capacity. Delighting, as he did, in literary ease and in the entertainment to be derived from books, it became a source of aggravated distress to his devoted family, no less than to himself, that, during the four or five last years of his life, he became afflicted by perhaps the heaviest calamity to which human nature is subject, loss of vision. "In the year 1787," writes his youngest daughter, "Lord North's sight began rapidly to fail him, and in a few months he became totally blind in consequence of a palsy on the optic nerve. His nerves had always been very excitable, and it is probable that the anxiety of mind, which he suffered during the unsuccessful contest with America, still more than his necessary application to writing, brought on this calamity, which he bore with the most admirable patience and resignation;

[1] Massey's 'Reign of George III.,' vol. iii. p. 209, *note*.

nor did it affect his general cheerfulness in society."[1] Such was the condition in which, in the month of April, 1787, he was unhappily found by his friend Storer; being, writes the latter to Lord Auckland, "all but blind, and unable to discover the colour of one wine from that of another." "He has no hopes," writes Lord Sheffield, who visited him the following month; "he says he has no expectations but of darkness. He held up his hand and said he could not see it. He was, however, pleasant, and with his usual ability took up the subjects of the day."[2]

No less "pleasant" appears to have been the afflicted statesman when, in the course of the autumn, Horace Walpole dined with him at Bushy Park. "Never," says Walpole, "had he seen a more interesting scene. Lord North's spirits, good-humour, wit, sense, drollery," he writes, "are as perfect as ever; the unremitting attention of Lady North and his children, most touching. Mr. North leads him about, Miss North sits constantly by him, carves meat, watches his every motion, scarce puts a bit into her own lips; and if one cannot help commending her, she colours with modesty and sorrow till the tears gush into her eyes. If ever loss of sight could be compensated, it is by so affectionate a

[1] Lord Brougham's 'Statesmen of the Time of George III.,' first series, p. 247; edition 1845.
[2] 'Auckland Correspondence,' vol. i. pp. 400, 418.

family."[1] Nor should it be left unrecorded that, of the many persons who were affected by Lord North's misfortune, not one seems to have more deeply sympathized with him than his lately offended Sovereign, George III. More than once, for instance, during the terrible mental and bodily illness which prostrated the King in 1788, we find the thought of his old servant, blind and helpless, affecting him even to tears.[2]

The further brief notices of Lord North's condition at this period, as we meet with from time to time in the familiar correspondence of the day, are invariably interesting. Such, for instance, may be said of a visit paid by Gibbon, the historian, in company with Lord and Lady Sheffield, to Lord North at his favourite watering-place, Tunbridge Wells, in the month of July, 1788. "My Lady and I," writes Lord Sheffield, "accompanied him [Gibbon] to Tunbridge Wells, where we passed three days with Lord North, who appears in better health than he has had for several years. He can walk a great deal, and has no longer a bloated look; but at times he is low. While we were with him he had the best spirits. He delights in the Pantiles. He has a very good society at present; several agreeable personages, besides three Dukes and three Knights of the Garter."[3] Gibbon,

---

[1] Walpole's 'Letters,' vol. ix. p. 114.
[2] 'Memoirs of Hannah More,' vol. ii. p. 145.
[3] 'Auckland Correspondence,' vol. ii. p. 220.

it may here be mentioned, not only held Lord
North's private virtues and public integrity alike in
high estimation, but, in his great work, 'The Decline
and Fall of the Roman Empire,' has perpetuated his
warm sense of the rare qualities of his friend.
"Were I ambitious," runs his famous compliment
to the retired minister, "of any other patron than
the public, I would inscribe this work to a statesman,
who, in a long, a stormy, and at length an unfortunate administration, had many political opponents,
almost without a personal enemy; who has retained,
in his fall from power, many faithful and disinterested friends; and who, under the pressure of
severe infirmity, enjoys the lively vigour of his mind,
and the felicity of his incomparable temper. Lord
North will permit me to express the feelings of
friendship in the language of truth; but even truth
and friendship should be silent, if he still dispensed
the favours of the Crown."[1] This passage, it should
be further remarked, bears the author's date of the
1st of May, 1788, a few weeks before Gibbon's visit
to Lord North at Tunbridge Wells. Before the end
of July, Gibbon had reached his home at Lausanne,
nor did he again visit England during the lifetime
of Lord North.

With the grievous calamity which darkened Lord
North's closing years we find Tunbridge Wells on

[1] Preface to the fourth volume of Gibbon's 'Decline and Fall of the
Roman Empire.'

more than one other occasion associated. He was one day, for instance, walking on the Pantiles, led by an attendant, when he encountered the celebrated Colonel Barré, formerly his bitter political antagonist, but now unhappily afflicted with blindness like himself. After some compliments had been interchanged between them, the conversation took a turn in which the latter happened to make some allusion to their parliamentary warfare of former days. "Ah, Colonel," gaily exclaimed Lord North, "whatever may have been our former animosities, I am persuaded there are no two men who would now be more glad to *see* each other than you and I."[1]

Another eminent person, into whose society Lord North was thrown at his favourite watering-place, was Richard Cumberland, the dramatic writer. "When I call to mind," writes Cumberland, "the hours I passed with Lord North in the darkness of his latter days, there was such a charm in his genius, such a claim upon my pity in the contemplation of his sufferings, that I could not help saying within myself, 'The minister, indeed, has wronged me, but the man atones.' His house at Tunbridge Wells was in the Grove. One day he took my arm and asked me to conduct him to the parade upon the Pantiles. 'I have a general recollection of the way,' he said, ' and if you will make me understand the posts upon the footpath and the steps about the chapel,

[1] Wraxall's 'Hist. Memoirs,' vol. ii. pp. 136, 137.

I shall remember them in future.' 'I could not lead blind Gloster to the cliff.' I executed my affecting trust, and brought him safely to his family. The ministering and mild daughter of Tiresias received her father from my hands."[1]

> "There is a cliff, whose high and bending head
> Looks fearfully in the confined deep:
> Bring me but to the very brim of it,
> And I'll repair the misery thou dost bear,
> With something rich about me: from that place
> I shall no leading need."
>
> *King Lear*, act iv. sc. 1.

It should here be mentioned, as coming within order of date, that it was not till the 4th of August, 1790, when Lord North had entered his fifty-ninth year, that he succeeded his venerable father as Earl of Guilford. Another year had nearly rolled on, when, in the ensuing month of June, 1791, he received an interesting visit, of some days' duration, at Bushy Park from Dr. Beattie, the author of 'The Minstrel.' "I was happy," writes the poet, "to find that Lord Guilford, though he has entirely lost his sight, is in perfect health and spirits, and retains all his wonted vivacity and good humour, of which he indeed possesses a very uncommon share. He wears no fillet on his eyes, nor needs any, as their outward appearance is not altered in the least."[2] Society had always had its attractions for Lord

[1] Cumberland's 'Memoirs,' by himself, vol. ii. p. 349.
[2] Sir William Forbes's 'Life and Writings of Dr. Beattie,' vol. iii. p. 112; 2nd edition.

North, and, accordingly, on finding himself bereaved of the priceless resources which are dependent upon the preservation of sight, it was only natural that his love of society should increase. Happily, his distinguished social position afforded him the opportunity of indulging it to the full. "In the evenings," writes Lady Charlotte Lindsay, " Grosvenor Square was the resort of the best company that London afforded at that time." Among the guests on these occasions were not unfrequently Fox, Burke, Sheridan, Lord Stormont, Lord John Townshend, and Mr. Windham. "These," continues Lady Charlotte, " with various young men and women, his children's friends, and whist-playing ladies for my mother, completed the society. My father always liked the company of young people, especially of young women who were sensible and lively; and we used to accuse him of often rejoicing when his old political friends left his side and were succeeded by some lively young female."[1]

Unhappily, with the summer of 1792, altogether passed away that "perfect health" of which Dr. Beattie had found Lord North in the enjoyment on his visiting him at Bushy Park in the summer of 1791. He slept indifferently; his appetite failed him; symptoms of dropsy manifested themselves. At last, after an unusually uneasy night, as Lady

[1] Lord Brougham's 'Statesmen of the Time of George III.,' first series, pp. 247, 248; edition 1845.

Charlotte Lindsay informs us, he questioned his friend and physician, Dr. Warren, begging him not to conceal the truth; the result was, that Dr. Warren owned that water had formed upon the chest, that he could not live many days, and that a few hours might put a period to his existence."[1] The intimation was not only received by Lord North with pious resignation, but from this time a depression of spirits, to which he had been previously subject, no more visited him. "I saw him and conversed with him last Thursday night, *i.e.* preceding his death," writes Storer to Lord Auckland, "and the last words he said to me were, 'God bless you!' uttered in such a tone as if he never expected to see me again. The benediction still sounds in my ears; one's heart must have been of steel not to have been touched with his situation."[2] Cheered by the tender attentions of the beloved beings who surrounded him, Lord North, to the last, took a pleasure in listening to his favourite passages in Shakespeare's plays, from the lips of his eldest and accomplished daughter, Lady Glenberrie. He continued also to take a lively interest in the more important passing political events of the day. One of the latest sentiments which he breathed was an expression of gratitude to Heaven at the prospect of his quitting

---

[1] Lord Brougham's 'Statesmen of the Time of George III.,' first series, p. 218; edition 1845.
[2] 'Auckland Correspondence,' vol. ii. pp. 428, 429.

the world previously to the breaking out of the horrors which he foretold would be the effects of the French Revolution. "I am going," he said; "and thankful I am that I shall not witness the anarchy and bloodshed which will soon overwhelm that unhappy country." Lord North expired on the 5th of August, 1792, in the sixty-first year of his age.

SHUTE BARRINGTON, BISHOP OF DURHAM.

Pious, learned, amiable, charitable even to munificence, and withal dignified in his manners and majestic in his person, it would be difficult apparently to point out on the episcopal bench of modern times a more graceful union of the high-bred English gentleman with the Christian divine, than was manifested in the instance of this distinguished prelate.

Shute Barrington, sixth and youngest son of John, first Viscount Barrington, was born at Beckett, in Berkshire, on the 26th of May, 1734. Of his academical career we have only to record that he passed from Eton to Merton College, Oxford, as a Gentleman Commoner in 1752; that he became a Fellow of that College in 1755; and that he took his degree of M.A. on the 10th of October, 1757. Having entered into holy orders in 1756, he was in due time appointed one of the chaplains of King George II., and at the commencement of the succeeding reign, in October, 1760, became a chaplain to King George III. In 1761 he was appointed a canon of Christ Church, Oxford; and on the 2nd of February in that year, married Lady Diana Beauclerk, only daughter of Charles, second Duke of St. Albans. Lady Diana survived their union not much more than five years, dying in child-bed on the 28th of May, 1766, and bequeathing her husband no surviving issue.

The future prelate may be said to have been still young, when his zeal and piety led to his being rewarded with some of the higher prizes of his profession. In 1768, he was nominated Canon Residentiary of St. Paul's, which he subsequently exchanged for a canonry of Windsor; in 1769, he was consecrated Bishop of Llandaff; in 1782, he was translated to the bishopric of Salisbury, and, in 1791, succeeded Dr. Thurlow in the princely see of Durham, a preferment which he continued to hold during the long period of thirty-five years. In the mean time, on the 20th of June, 1770, he had married his second wife, Jane, daughter of Sir John Guise, Bart., of Rendcombe, in Gloucestershire, and sister of Sir William, the last baronet of his family. By this lady, whom he also survived many years, he had likewise no children.

In the absence of any passages of lively interest in the career of Bishop Barrington, we propose to introduce into this memoir, from the pen of one who not only professes to have enjoyed the bishop's society, but who was evidently familiar with his habits as well as with the chief occurrences of his exemplary life, three or four pleasing extracts drawn from a brief biographical sketch of the bishop, published shortly after his decease.[1] "The qualities of this distinguished prelate," proceeds the writer, "were such as will ever cause his name to be venerated in the history of the English Church. His learning was various, and extended through all the branches of knowledge connected with his profession. As a preacher, he was in his day of no mean order; and, as a speaker in the House of Lords, he was always heard with attention and respect."

"His manners were dignified, courteous, bland, and engaging; his compositions were elegant, chaste, and classical; his piety fervent, devout, charitable, and pure. The son of a nobleman who had been among the firmest supporters of the Protestant establishment at a time when the Church was considered in danger, he never departed from his hereditary attachment to the same sacred institution;" nor, it should be added, though recoiling from the eventuality of the return of the Roman Catholics to either temporal or spiritual power, was there any intolerance in the bishop's hostility to the Church of Rome. "His house," continues his biographer, "was

[1] 'Gentleman's Magazine' for April, 1826; vol. xcvi. pp. 299-302, passim.

open to the French emigrant bishops and clergy. He supplied their wants by his bounty; he admitted the most distinguished among them to his table, and introduced them to his friends. Though he strictly adhered to every article of the established faith himself, his personal kindnesses and beneficences to those who conscientiously and openly dissented from the same hallowed code were dictated by the purest sentiments of toleration. We have seen at his table Presbyterian divines and respectable Quakers; nor," adds the writer, "did his confidential conveyancer, Mr. Charles Butler, the author of the 'Reminiscences,' though not only an earnest Roman Catholic, and even engaged in an antagonistic controversy with the bishop's own chaplains, Dr. Phillpotts and Mr. Townshend, ever forfeit his lordship's friendship."

The bishop's exemplary dispensation of the rich archdeaconries, prebends, and livings in the gift of the see of Durham, forms another subject of his biographer's warm encomiums. "One anecdote," he writes, "of his lordship, which does high honour to his liberality and his piety, but for the authenticity of which we cannot vouch, was published many years ago. A relation of Mrs. Barrington, it is said, having experienced some embarrassments and disappointments in life, wished to amend his situation (being a military officer) by entering into the Church, thinking that the bishop would provide handsomely for him. On making the necessary application to his kinsman, he was asked what preferment would satisfy him. To this home question he readily answered, that five hundred a year would make him a happy man. 'You shall have it,' said his lordship, 'but not out of the patrimony of the Church. I will not deprive a regular and worthy divine to provide for a necessitous relation. You shall have the sum you mention yearly out of my own pocket.'"

"There was no scheme of useful charity which had not his name among the foremost contributors; and there were even few institutions for the advancement of any object of public utility, particularly for the cultivation of the fine arts, of which he was not a generous supporter. But large as were his acts of public munificence, they bore but a small proportion to the deeds of private, unobtrusive charity which were the daily occupation of his life. Unnumbered are the objects who were blessed by his bounty, and whose tears are now flowing in vain regret for the benefactor whom they have lost. His bounties, indeed, were of no ordinary kind. They were dispensed on suitable occasions, with a liberality which not even his ample means would have enabled him to indulge, had it not been sustained by a just and exact economy. No one, perhaps, ever better understood the true value of money, or employed it more judiciously as the instrument of virtue."

Bishop Barrington's conversational powers are

described as not only having been eminently entertaining and instructive, but, even after he had reached the almost patriarchal age of ninety, are said to have formed the peculiar charm of the little dinner-parties, rarely consisting of more than eight guests at a time, at which he took a pleasure in assembling his friends. According to the same authority from which we have already so freely quoted, "Those who have been of his parties, and among them are included many of the most eminent in literature and science, have never failed to come away impressed with admiration of the singular talents of their venerable host in leading the conversation of the day. Without effort, and without artifice, he had recourse to such topics as interested all, and yet drew forth in turn the peculiar talents of each. His own talk was cheerful, lively, and even humorous; but at the same time ever assuming a tone of manly indignation at the mention of a deed of wickedness, and of the warmest sympathy for unmerited distress. A religious spirit pervaded the whole, and he rarely omitted a fit occasion of quietly exciting similar feelings in the minds of those around him. Religion, indeed, was the great presiding principle of his mind."

In the fields of literature, during his protracted tenure of the episcopal dignity, Bishop Barrington was far from idle. In addition to various sermons, charges, and tracts, which were afterwards collected into one volume, he contributed some valuable notes to the third edition of Bowyer's 'Critical Conjectures on the New Testament;' engaged in a literary controversy with the Calvinists in 1783, and with the Roman Catholics in 1806. He also published a new and improved edition of his father's 'Miscellanea Sacra,' and gave to the world a sketch of the political life of his brother, William Viscount Barrington.

During the last year of the bishop's life, several months were passed by him in a mansion situated near the Steyne at Worthing, in Sussex, interesting as having been formerly the residence of the lamented Princess Charlotte of Wales. Standing, though almost close to the sea-shore, in a garden sheltered by trees and shrubs of luxuriant growth, the abode proved so agreeable to the venerable prelate as to induce him to become its purchaser. Happily, during the short period that he lived to occupy it, including his last illness, he was subjected to little or no bodily suffering, while his mind remained unclouded almost to the last. His strength, indeed, so far continued to support him, that on the Sunday preceding his decease he was able to read the appointed lessons to his family; the occasion, however, being saddened to those near and dear to him, by the melancholy intimation from him that they were listening to them from his lips for the last time.

Bishop Barrington expired at his house in Cavendish Square on the 25th of March, 1826, in the ninety-second year of his age, and in the fifty-seventh year of the discharge of his episcopal functions. "In his person," writes his biographer, " Bishop Barrington was tall and majestic; yet in his youth he was supposed to be far from possessing a vigorous constitution, and he underwent an operation for the stone at a very early age."[1] This terrible disorder, as the author has been credibly informed, was occasioned by his exposure to the elements, when very young, at the execution of the Scottish lords on Tower Hill in 1746 : a remarkable fact, if true, since, in that case, he must have survived the operation for a period verging on eighty years.

[1] 'Gentleman's Magazine' for April, 1826, vol. xcvi. pp. 301, 302.

GEORGE STEEVENS.

This celebrated Shakespearian commentator and cynical man of letters was the son of a director of the East India Company, from whom it may be presumed that he inherited that easy fortune which, happily, through life enabled him to indulge his insatiable love of literature unshackled by the duties and interruptions of a profession. Born at Stepney on the 10th of May, 1736, he received instruction for a time at the grammar school of Kingston-upon-Thames; was removed thence to Eton, and from Eton, in 1754, to King's College, Cambridge, where he was admitted as a Gentleman Commoner. From the fact of a proficiency in classical scholarship having been one of the attainments for which he became most distinguished in after-life, the time he passed at Eton and at the University may be presumed to have been turned by him to good account. Nevertheless, he quitted the University without having taken a degree; having, as it would seem, in the mean time settled himself in chambers in the Temple.

"Not only," to quote the language of James
Boswell,[1] "deeply skilled in ancient learning, and of
very extensive reading in English literature, but at
the same time of acute discernment and elegant
taste," Steevens's chief, if not whole, object in life
now became centred in the acquisition of a thorough
knowledge, not merely of the literature, but of the
manners, laws, obsolete publications, and provincial
peculiarities, whether of language or custom, which
prevailed in the Elizabethan age in England, with
the view of illustrating and giving to the world an
edition of the works of Shakespeare worthy of the
genius of the great dramatist. The earliest fruits of
his labours appeared in 1766, when, at the age of
thirty, he published twenty of Shakespeare's plays in
four volumes octavo. In 1770, he became associated
with Dr. Johnson in the elucidation of the immortal
writings of his favourite poet; the result being that,
in 1773, under their joint editorship, appeared a
complete edition of Shakespeare's works, in ten
volumes octavo, known as 'Johnson and Steevens's
Edition.' A second edition made its appearance in
1778; and a third, the editorship of which was
intrusted to an eminent brother Shakespearian critic,
Isaac Reed, of Staple Inn, in 1785. But it is to
the fourth and last edition, the sole editorship of
which Steevens reserved for himself, that by far the
greatest credit is due. The labour, in fact, which he

[1] Croker's 'Boswell's Life of Johnson,' p. 216; edition 1847.

expended upon it seems to have been almost unprecedented of its kind. "To this work," states a writer who signs himself Etonensis, "he devoted, solely and exclusively of all other attentions, a period of eighteen months; and, during that time he left his house every morning at one o'clock with the Hampstead patrol, and proceeding, without any consideration of the weather or the season, called up the compositor. and woke all his devils—

> 'Him late from Hampstead journeying to his book,
> Aurora oft for Cephalus mistook;
> What time he brush'd the dews with hasty pace,
> To meet the printer's dev'let face to face.'

At the chambers of his friend, Mr. Reed—where he was allowed to admit himself, with a sheet of the Shakespeare letter-press ready for correction, and found a room prepared to receive him—there was every book which he might wish to consult, and on Mr. Reed's pillow he could apply, on any doubt or sudden suggestion, to a knowledge of English literature perhaps equal to his own. This nocturnal zeal greatly accelerated the printing of the work, as, while the printers slept, the editor was awake; and thus, in less than twenty months, he completed his last splendid edition of Shakespeare, in fifteen large octavo volumes; an almost incredible labour, which proved the astonishing energy and persevering powers of his mind."[1]

[1] 'Gentleman's Magazine' for February, 1800, vol. lxx. p. 179.

On the apparent causes which led to George Steevens becoming, as he did, an object of fear and dislike, not only to his brother literati, but occasionally to the domestic circles into which he was admitted, we have happily no occasion for dwelling at length. "Sir," said Dr. Johnson of him, "he lives the life of an outlaw;"[1] and yet Johnson, well aware as he could scarcely fail to have been of Steevens's unpopular qualities, advocated, and advocated successfully, his admission to the celebrated Literary Club, to which exclusive society Steevens was elected in March, 1774, at the same time with Charles James Fox, Sir Charles Bunbury, Dr. Fordyce, and, apparently, Gibbon.[2] "Last night," writes Johnson to him on the 5th of that month, "you became a member of the club. If you call on me on Friday, I will introduce you. A gentleman, proposed after you, was rejected."[3]

Another man of letters, on whom Steevens seems to have made a favourable impression, was William Cole, the antiquary. "I met him," writes the latter, "at dinner, with Dr. Farmer, &c., at Dr. Lort's chambers in Trinity College, August 9th, 1780. He is much of a gentleman, well-bred, civil, and obliging; editor of Shakespeare. He told me he was admitted in King's College, 1754, the year after I had quitted it. He is an Essex gentleman; in the

---

[1] Croker's 'Boswell's Life of Johnson,' p. 456; edition 1847.
[2] Ibid., 411, 412, and *note*.   [3] Ibid. p. 411.

militia; well-made, black, and tall."[1] Nor, among
Steevens's better qualities, must we omit to mention
his occasional generosity, which at times amounted
almost to munificence; nor his charming conversational powers, which, when he laid himself out to
please, rendered him a most delightful companion.
Even Miss Hawkins, notwithstanding the "abhor-
rence" in which she tells us that she held his moral
character, hastens to do justice to his powers of
pleasing. "Such conversation," she writes, "could
not be heard without interest, and much do I now
regret that I did not then commit to paper some of
its leading features."[2] But, unfortunately, the unfavourable verdict on his character as pronounced by
more than one of his contemporaries, goes far to
bear out that of Miss Hawkins. "Mr. Steevens,"
writes Dr. Dibdin, "lived in a retired and eligibly
situated house just on the rise of Hampstead Heath.
It was paled in; and had immediately before it a
verdant lawn skirted with a variety of picturesque
trees. Formerly, this house had been a tavern,
which was known by the name of the *Upper Flash*;
and which my fair readers (if a single female can
have the courage to peruse these bibliomaniacal
pages) will recollect to have been the scene to which
Richardson sends Clarissa in one of her escapes from

---

[1] Nichols's 'Lit. Anecdotes of the 18th Century,' vol. ix. p. 803.
[2] Miss Hawkins's 'Memoirs, Anecdotes, Facts,' &c., vol. i. pp. 273, 274; 1824.

Lovelace. Here Steevens lived, embosomed in books, shrubs, and trees, being either too coy, or too unsociable to mingle with his neighbours. His habits were, indeed, peculiar; not much to be envied or imitated, as they sometimes betrayed the flights of a madman, and sometimes the asperities of a cynic. His attachments were warm, but fickle both in choice and duration. He would frequently part from one, with whom he had lived on terms of close intimacy, without any assignable cause; and his enmities, once fixed, were immovable. There was, indeed, a kind of venom in his antipathies; nor would he suffer his ears to be assailed or his heart to relent in favour of those against whom he entertained animosities, however capricious and unfounded; in *one* pursuit only was he consistent—*one* object only did he woo with an inflexible attachment—and that object was *Dame* DRAMA."[1]

That, however incongruous it may appear, the intellectual organization of this admittedly fine scholar was imbued with a taste for the frivolous quite as much as for the classical and the sublime, is shown by the double testimony of Miss Hawkins and Dr. Dibdin. " But can it be credited," writes the former,[2] " that a mind so fraught, as was that of this elegant scholar, with classic recollections—that a man of such incessant industry and occupation, and who seemed

---

[1] Dibdin's ' Bibliomania,' p. 437; edition 1812.
[2] ' Memoirs,' &c., vol. i. pp. 262, 263.

to have no moment for thought that did not forward his great undertaking—should be guilty of all the petty faults of the scandal-mongers of a village, and the gossips of a card-table? Yet so it was; and he would talk of the interior of families and the trifles of economy till his conversation was disgusting and contemptible. With the most manly sense of the sublime and beautiful—enraptured when repeating passages from the finest poets—regardless of all personal inconvenience, and superior to all the common modes of passing time, he yet could panegyrize the delicacy of furniture, make nonsense of indispensable importance, and affect to be a follower of fashionable folly." Another of his eccentricities is recorded by Dr. Dibdin. "I have sat behind him," he writes, "within a few years of his death, and watched his sedulous attention to the performances of strolling players who used to hire a public room in Hampstead, and towards whom his gallantry was something more substantial than mere admiration and applause, for he would make liberal presents of gloves, shoes, and stockings—especially to the female part of the company. His attention, and even delight, during some of the most wretched exhibitions of the dramatic art, was truly surprising; but he was then drooping under the pressure of age, and what passed before him might serve to remind him of former days, when his discernment was quick and his judgment matured."[1]

[1] Dibdin's 'Bibliomania.'

During his latter years, Steevens, neither seeking nor sought by others, lived the life of a recluse at his villa at Hampstead, where, on the 22nd of January, 1800, he died, unmarried, in his sixty-fourth year. His remains were interred in the chapel at Poplar, where he had been baptized, and where a fine monument by Flaxman, bearing an inscription by Hayley, was erected in the north aisle to his memory.

JOHN HORNE TOOKE.

A SCHOLAR of no mean order, and withal of polished manners and distinguished appearance, there was probably not one of the passing acquaintances of this remarkable man who would have guessed him to have been the offspring of plebeian parents, and still less that he had been born and brought up on the verge of the shambles of a butcher's market. John Horne—his assumption of the name of Tooke being of much later date—was the son of John Horne, a poulterer, who carried on business in Newport Market, Long Acre, where, at his father's residence in Newport Street, adjoining the market, the future philologist, on the 25th of June, 1736, first saw the light. In later days, when questioned by some of his aristocratic Eton schoolfellows touching his father's profession, his reply was that his father was a " Turkey merchant."

The father of as many as seven children, and consequently burdened with the heavy expenses incidental to the maintenance of a large family, it was probably owing to the remarkable abilities displayed by his third son, John, that the elder Horne was induced to accord him an education so little in unison with his condition in life, and apparently so much superior to that which fell to the share of his elder brothers. Benjamin, the eldest son, was, for instance, brought up to be a market-gardener, and Thomas, the second son, to be a fishmonger. Not impossibly, too, a mother's tenderness may have been brought to bear in the uncommon preference shown to the third son; this partial parent, we are told, " always treating him with unvarying kindness and affection; while her gifted son, on his part, is said, to the last moment of his existence, to have tenderly cherished his mother's memory.[1] At all events, no pains seem to have been neglected, and no cost spared, in disciplining him with a view to his achieving distinction in after-life. At the age of six he was sent to an academy in Soho Square; in 1744, he was removed to Westminster School, where, however, he remained but for a short time, and two years afterwards, at the age of ten, was placed at Eton.

At Eton, the boy's progress in learning probably fell far short of the expectations of his sanguine parents. The superiority, indeed, of his abilities was acknowledged; but, as he himself candidly admitted to his biographer, Stephens, he had been " but little addicted to study while a youth."[2] For the ordinary sports of the school, too, the inference is that he entertained no very strong predilection. An

[1] Stephens's 'Memoirs of John Horne Tooke,' vol. i. pp. 13, 14.
[2] Ibid., vol. i. p. 17.

old lady, for instance, whose recollections of him were of long date, being asked by his biographer whether she remembered him when he was a boy, "No!" was her reply; "he never was a boy; with him there was no interval between childhood and age—he became a man all at once upon us."[1]

After all, if his exceptional training failed on some points, it may have been to Eton, as much as to Nature, that he was indebted for that "grace, vivacity, frankness, dignity," that courtesy of the *vielle cour*, which, notwithstanding his long subsequent intercourse with vulgar and uneducated men, rendered him, in the valuable judgment of one of his contemporaries, "one of the best bred gentlemen of the age," one in whom "courts and high stations have seldom produced a better example of polite and elegant behaviour."[2]

After having quitted Eton, young Horne's next academical remove was to St. John's College, Cambridge, where he was admitted in 1755, at the age of nineteen, and where he appears by diligent study to have amply made up for loss of past time and for neglected opportunities. In 1758 his name is included in the Triposes of that year, and in the same year he took his degree of B.A. With these advantages, he might reasonably hope to succeed in any one of the learned professions which he might think proper to select; and accordingly, as the bent

[1] Stephens's 'Memoirs of Tooke,' vol. i. pp. 21, 22.
[2] 'Quarterly Review' for 1812, vol. vii. p. 326.

of his genius, as well as his inclinations, pointed to the Law as holding out the most probable chances of his achieving success in life, he had, two years previously, prepared the way for gratifying his inclinations by entering himself a member of the Society of the Inner Temple. Unfortunately, however, his father, to whose affection he owed so much, was not less earnestly desirous that his son should become a clergyman of the Church of England ; and consequently, with this difficulty confronting him, he so far avoided giving offence to his father as to accept the humble and unenviable situation of usher of a boarding-school kept by a Mr. Jennings at Blackheath, and, on his retirement, by his son-in-law, a Mr. Williams. That, with a wider field for the exercise of his abilities, he might have proved invaluable as an instructor of youth, seems scarcely to be questionable. Young, indeed, as he was at this time, he appears to have inspired the pupils under his charge not merely with respect, but with awe. According to one of them, " there was something inexpressibly significant in his voice, manner, and gestures, that rendered it impossible to approach him with the same ease as an ordinary mortal."[1]

Thus unsatisfactory, notwithstanding the advantages he had enjoyed of an Eton and Cambridge education, were the worldly prospects of this remarkable man, when, most unfortunately as it

[1] Stephens's 'Memoirs of John Horne Tooke,' vol. i. pp. 23-25.

proved for his future interests and respectability, he at length consented to gratify his father's wishes by entering into holy orders; this concession being followed by his nomination to a curacy which he had obtained in Kent. It was no long time, however, before ill health compelled him to give up his charge, and, accordingly, still hankering after the Law, and having as yet been admitted into deacon's orders only, he returned to London and determined "to eat his way to the Bar" in the hall of the Inner Temple. It was at this period, apparently, that he formed the acquaintance of two individuals who subsequently rose to high eminence in the legal profession—Lloyd, afterwards Lord Kenyon, and John Dunning, afterwards Lord Ashburton, as yet however, young men of slender pecuniary means, like himself. "I have been repeatedly assured by Mr. Horne Tooke," writes his biographer, "that they [Kenyon, Dunning, and Tooke] were accustomed to dine together during the vacation at a little eating-house, in the neighbourhood of Chancery Lane, for the sum of sevenpence halfpenny each! 'As to Dunning and myself,' added he, 'we were generous, for we gave the girl who waited on us a penny a piece; but Kenyon, who always knew the value of money, sometimes rewarded her with a halfpenny, and sometimes with a promise.'"[1] This state of affairs could, however, have lasted no very long time, when,

[1] Stephens's 'Memoirs of Tooke,' vol. i. p. 33.

yielding to the entreaties of his family, and probably to pecuniary necessity, he returned to his allegiance to the Church; was admitted to priest's orders in 1760; and, in the course of the same year, was inducted to the chapelry of New Brentford, in the county of Middlesex, which had been purchased for him by his self-sacrificing father.

Considering the reluctance with which this remarkable man had entered the service of the Church, as well as the discredit which he subsequently reflected on his sacred profession, his exemplary behaviour on his first taking possession of his new preferment no less takes us by surprise than it calls forth our commendation. His sermons, especially, regarded as plain, practical expositions of the leading and vital truths of Christianity, are stated to have been almost models. He was not only charitable to his poorer parishioners, and ungrudging of his time to the sick, but carried his philanthropy to the length of studying the art of medicine for the express purpose of ministering to the infirmities of those whom he knew could ill-afford to call in the services of an apothecary. "To attain this end," we are told, "he carefully studied the works of Boerhaave, and the best practical physicians of that day; and having learned to compound a few medicines, he formed a little dispensary at the parsonage-house, whence he supplied the wants of his numerous and grateful patients." [1]

[1] Stephens's 'Memoirs of Tooke,' vol. i. p. 39.

Of the success which he claimed for his work of humanity, he seems to have been not a little proud. It was his belief, he used often to say, that his medical were far more efficacious than his spiritual labours.[1]

During the earlier years of his spiritual ministration, the young incumbent of New Brentford was twice enabled to gratify his craving for foreign travel by visiting the Continent as a travelling tutor; his companion each time being the son of a man of fortune. The first occasion on which he was thus absent from his duties was in 1763, at the age of twenty-seven, when his pupil was a son of the eccentric miser, John Elwes, Member of Parliament for Berkshire, with whom he continued in France for considerably more than a year. The next time he crossed the British Channel was in 1765, in charge of the son of a neighbour, a Middlesex gentleman of the name of Taylor, with whom, to his infinite delight, he was empowered to extend his wanderings to the sunny skies and classic soil of Italy. At Calais he was introduced to Thomas Sheridan, the lexicographer and father of the author of the 'School for Scandal;' while at Paris commenced his friendship with the celebrated democrat and libertine, John Wilkes, whose gratitude, before having quitted England, he had earned by zealously taking his part in a recently published and

[1] Stephens's 'Memoirs of Tooke,' vol. i. p. 40.

impetuously written political pamphlet. As may be supposed, this intimacy with so notorious a delinquent neither improved his morals nor accorded with his holy calling. Not satisfied with having discarded, as he had done, his clerical costume before sailing from Dover, he now went so far as, with a miserable affectation of wit, to ridicule the sacred profession of which he was a member, in language which even Wilkes, to whom it was addressed, could scarcely have read without a feeling of disgust.[1] Parting from Wilkes, with whom he agreed to carry on a correspondence, he journeyed to Switzerland, where he was introduced to Voltaire; at Lyons he spent a week with the author of 'Tristram Shandy;' and, having crossed the Alps, visited the principal cities of Italy, with the advantage of enjoying the carnival in all its perfection at Venice.

It was during this visit to Italy that, being at an entertainment at which he seems to have been a stranger to almost every one present, the guests, on discovering him to be a clergyman, treated him, if not rudely, at least with coldness. In the course of the evening, however, so completely did he succeed in establishing himself in their good graces, that the party, fascinated by his conversation, insisted, when they broke up, on seeing him home to his lodgings, accompanied by a band of music.[2] His

[1] Letter to Wilkes of January 3, 1776; Stephens's 'Memoirs of John Horne Tooke,' vol. i. p. 76.
[2] Earl Russell's 'Memoirs of Thomas Moore,' vol. vi. p. 287.

conversational powers, indeed, especially at a later date when he had acquired an intimate knowledge of the world and of human nature, must have been of a high order. According to the 'Quarterly Review' of sixty years since—a source little likely to be unduly biassed in his favour—" He never appeared to greater advantage than in conversation. He was naturally of a social and convivial turn. His animal spirits were strong; the promptitude of his understanding was equal to its vigour; and he was by no means too proud to receive with satisfaction the small but immediate reward of approbation and goodwill which is always cheerfully paid to the display of agreeable qualities in society. He possessed," continues the same writer, "an inexhaustible fund of anecdotes, which he introduced with great skill, and related with neatness, grace, rapidity, and pleasantry. He had a quick sense of the ridiculous, and was a great master of the whole art of raillery, a dangerous talent, though the exercise of it in his hands was always tempered by politeness and good humour. No man, we believe, ever provoked him by hostile attack without having reason to repent of his rashness."[1]

On the return to England of the subject of these observations, in the summer of 1767, he not only resumed his clerical habit and the performance of his clerical duties at New Brentford, but having in due

[1] 'Quarterly Review' for 1812, vol. vii. pp. 326, 327.

time succeeded in establishing for himself the reputation of a popular preacher, was frequently solicited to preach in the pulpits of the different London churches, and more especially in that of St. Paul's, Covent Garden, in the immediate vicinity of the home of his infancy. Before a year, however, had passed away, an event occurred which had the effect of working a notable revolution in his habits and feelings. In the month of February, 1768, on the eve of the usual excitement and violence of a general election, Wilkes, setting all risks of pains and penalties at defiance, not only ventured to return to England, but took the world by surprise by declaring himself a candidate for the representation of the county of Middlesex in Parliament. By the majority of the electors this announcement of the audacious democrat was received with satisfaction; by the masses of the people with enthusiasm. On the day that the election commenced, the agitation which prevailed was extraordinary. At an early hour in the morning, the different thoroughfares leading to Brentford having been taken possession of by his partisans, no person was allowed to pass unless wearing a blue cockade in his hat, or furnished with a ticket declaring for Wilkes and Liberty. Sir William Beauchamp Proctor, one of the rival candidates, had his carriage broken to pieces, while another unpopular person, Mr. Cooke, son of the City Marshal, was pelted at Hyde Park Corner, and thrown from his horse. "Squinting Wilkes and Liberty," writes Gilly Williams to George Selwyn, "are everything with us. It is scarce safe to go to the other side of Temple Bar without having that obliquity of vision." So familiar, indeed, were the words "Wilkes and Liberty" to every ear, that a wit of the day commenced one of his letters: "I take Wilkes and Liberty to assure you," &c.[1]

South Brentford, it is scarcely necessary to observe, stood in the very centre of the approaching contest, and accordingly its minister, intrepid, eloquent, enthusiastic in favour of free institutions, as well as being now the personal friend and partisan of Wilkes, was little likely to shrink from applying all his talent and influence to insure the triumph of the popular cause. "Scarcely," we are told, "allowing himself time for the usual refreshment which Nature requires, he was employed, sometimes on foot, and sometimes on horseback, in canvassing the county, enumerating the merits and the sufferings of Mr. Wilkes, palliating his errors, and apologizing for his follies." "It was he," according to the same writer, "who infused a portion of his own spirit and ability into the committees for managing the contest; it was he who, sometimes in company with the popular candidate, and sometimes by himself, addressed large bodies of the electors, who had been collected in

[1] 'Selwyn Correspondence,' vol. ii. p. 275; Walpole's 'Letters,' vol. v. p. 111.

different places for that purpose."[1] In the heat of his enthusiasm, he had even, to the amount of all he was worth in the world, rendered himself liable for the payment of expenses, without incurring which, Wilkes, whose fortunes at this time were nearly desperate, would have been unable to commence the struggle. "In a cause so just and so holy," were his unhallowed words in the hearing of his own parishioners, "he would dye his black coat red."[2]

From this period, politics, for a long time to come, continued to be the prevailing consideration in the mind of this restless and energetic man. "The Ishmael of literature and politics," to use the words of the 'Quarterly Review,'[3] "his hand was against every man's hand, and every man's hand was against him." Debarred from exercising his eminent talents on the arena which he would willingly have chosen for their display, his mind appears to have become soured by disappointment and neglect; thus tending to whet his appetite for political discord, and to render him one of the most formidable and indefatigable abettors of the cause of democracy of his day. He was not only the suggester and principal founder, in 1769, of the Society for Supporting the Bill of Rights, but is stated, on more than one authority of no mean credit, to have composed and foisted upon the public the celebrated "volunteer

---

[1] Stephens's 'Memoirs of Tooke,' vol. i. pp. 94, 95.
[2] Ibid., vol. i. pp. 94, 97.   [3] Vol. vii. p. 316.

speech," said to have been addressed by Alderman Beckford to George III. at St. James's in 1770; the same speech which was subsequently thought worthy of being engraved on the pedestal of Beckford's statue in the Guildhall of the City of London. Lastly, he not only became a prolific writer of ephemeral political strictures and diatribes, but, what redounded much more to his fame, was his well-known controversial encounter with Junius in 1771, in which, in the use of wit, sarcasm, and terseness of style, he unquestionably bore hard upon his formidable anonymous antagonist. It was in this year, it may be mentioned, and not till this year, that, triumphing alike over the odium which he had incurred, and the sturdy opposition of the celebrated divine, Dr. Paley, he was allowed to take his degree as M.A. at Cambridge.

It was at this period also that the public was diverted by the once memorable dispute and correspondence, which took place in 1770 and 1771, between the minister of New Brentford and his former idol and ally, Wilkes. The great offence, it appears, given by the former, had been the utterance of some expressions of indignation at discovering, as he believed he had done, certain attempts being made to render the Society for Supporting the Bill of Rights instrumental to the discharge of Wilkes's private debts, expressions which Wilkes and his friends had met by imputing counter offences to their brother democrat. True it is that the latter appears to have passed through this ordeal without having entailed any additional discredit on himself, yet it was certainly not without having suffered a sensible diminution of his former popularity. So differently, indeed, at this period were the respective merits of the two democrats rated by the public, that when, on the 1st of July, 1771, Wilkes was elected one of the sheriffs of London, it was by a large majority of voters, whereas, at nightfall of the same day, his former ally was burnt in effigy opposite the Mansion House.

The subject of these observations was apparently approaching his thirty-eighth year, when his anxiety to exchange a profession which he disliked, and for which he was deplorably unsuited, for one which he not only preferred, but in which he was eminently qualified to shine, returned to him with increased force. He had, indeed, reached a time of life which renders the exchange of an old for a new profession a matter for serious consideration; but, on the other hand, not only was he bereft of his parents, to whom, if living, he would doubtless have shrunk from thus causing pain, but, personally speaking, every inducement which interest or ambition could suggest incited him to hazard the experiment. It was under these circumstances then, that, in the year 1773, he took the decided step of resigning his New Brentford benefice, and, having divested himself as much as lay in his power of his clerical vocation, took up his abode in a house which he hired in the neighbourhood of Brentford, and there, by sedulous study, prepared himself for the future practice of the Law. Unfortunately, however, he encountered an unexpected difficulty which he failed to overcome. The period of five years, which it was requisite for him to pass before he would be eligible to be called to the Bar, having expired in 1779, he applied in the month of June that year to the authorities of the Middle Temple for admission to their society, but, on the ground that he was a clergyman in full orders, was pronounced to be ineligible.[1]

Happily, the disappointment which he must have felt was not without its attending advantage. In 1774, for instance, the knowledge which he had obtained of the Law enabled him to render eminent service, in a case of disputed inclosure rights, to Mr. William Tooke, a gentleman of considerable property residing at Purley, near Godstone, in Surrey, who in return, besides paying him well, left him a legacy of 500*l*., and assigned him his now more familiar surname of Tooke.

In the mean time, absorbed though his thoughts had been in his legal studies, politics had unfortunately far from lost their charms for the excitable patriot. Enthusiastically sympathizing with the

[1] It may be mentioned that the appeal was finally rejected by a majority of only one, and that the judgment has in our time been in more than one instance reversed.

Americans in their pending struggle for their rights, it was not unnatural perhaps that when, in April, 1775, the fatal collisions at Lexington and Concord occasioned the first effusions of American blood, he should have deduced, from the imperfect evidence which had as yet reached England, that the blame rested entirely with the troops of the mother country. When, however, on the same insufficient grounds, we find him, as a member of the Constitutional Society, proceeding to the length of proposing, carrying, and taking upon himself the sole responsibility of inserting in the newspapers, with his name affixed to it, a resolution of that society, subscribing the sum of one hundred pounds for "the relief of the widows, orphans, and aged parents of our beloved American fellow-subjects," who, preferring death to slavery, were "inhumanly murdered by the King's troops at or near Lexington and Concord, in the province of Massachusetts," we can scarcely feel surprised at such language having laid him under government proscription, and subjected him to a criminal prosecution. Accordingly, on the 4th of July, 1777, he was brought to trial for sedition before Lord Chief Justice Mansfield at Guildhall, on which occasion, notwithstanding the spirit and ability with which he conducted his defence, was sentenced, not only to be imprisoned for the space of twelve months, but to pay a fine of two hundred pounds.[1] " I hope," said

[1] Stephens's 'Memoirs of Horne Tooke,' vol. i. pp. 435, *note*, 476.

Dr. Johnson, "they did not put the dog in the pillory for his libel; he has too much literature for that."[1] The period of imprisonment to which he was sentenced was passed by him in the King's Bench Prison.

The first step of any importance taken by Horne Tooke after his release from prison was to purchase, in 1780, a small estate at Witton, near Huntingdon, for the purpose of devoting himself to the pursuit of agriculture. Here, however, he would appear to have resided no very long time when, finding himself becoming a martyr to the ague, he beat a somewhat speedy return to the more congenial locality of London, where he hired and furnished a house in Richmond Buildings, Dean Street, Soho. Literature now claimed his diligent, if not undivided, attention. In 1786 he published the first volume of his celebrated philological work, 'Epea Pteroenta ; or, the Diversions of Purley,' the elements of which had appeared some years previously, in a letter addressed by him to Mr. Dunning on the construction put by the judges on some words in his indictment in 1777.

"Were I," said Dr. Johnson, "to make a new edition of my dictionary, I would adopt several of Mr. Horne's etymologies."[1] This publication was followed, in 1788, by his once scarcely less celebrated treatise, 'Two Pairs of Portraits,' in which the four persons who figured in it are, on the one hand, Lord

---
[1] Croke 's 'Boswell's Life of Johnson,' p. 616.

Chatham and his illustrious son; and, on the other hand, the two Foxes, Lord Holland and his no less gifted offspring, Charles James Fox. The preference is given to the Pitts. But more stirring times were now again in store for the still restless politician. The lawyers of the Middle Temple had, as we have seen, pronounced him to be a clergyman in full orders, and therefore debarred from practising as a barrister; but, though thus declared to be disentitled, the same rule had yet been made applicable to clergymen in the event of their being returned to the House of Commons, and accordingly the success which he had failed to acquire at the Bar he now hoped to have an opportunity of achieving in the Senate. Accordingly it was under these circumstances that, in the month of June, 1790, he stood forward, in opposition to Mr. Fox and Lord Hood, as a candidate for the representation of Westminster, on which occasion, so greatly did he ingratiate himself with the voters, partly by the popular sentiments which he advocated, and partly by the rich vein of humour which characterized his addresses from the hustings, that, though ultimately compelled to yield to the combined influence of the Treasury and the Whig Club, he not only polled no fewer than sixteen hundred and seventy-nine votes, but polled them without having solicited, much less bribed, a single voter; without having kept open a single public-house for the entertainment of the electors, and without having given away a single cockade. It could not have been very long after this period that he formed the acquaintance of the celebrated Talleyrand, then in England. "As for M. Talleyrand," writes Mr. James Bland Burges to Lord Auckland, in May, 1792, "he is intimate with Paine, Horne Tooke, Lord Lansdowne, and a few more of that stamp, and generally scouted by every one else."[1]

But a much more critical event, which befell this remarkable man during the autumn of his long life, was his memorable committal to the Tower of London, on charges of high treason, on the 16th of May, 1794. It was a period, it should be remembered, when the horrors of the French revolution were still vividly impressing men's minds, and accordingly a period when the fears of the timid easily tortured the advocacy of parliamentary reform by bolder spirits into a design to subvert the Government, and to plunge the country into the miseries of civil war. At all events, the veteran political agitator, for such he had now become, found himself a proscribed and imperilled man. On the 6th of October, a true bill was found against him by the grand jury, and, on the 17th of November, he was brought to trial at the bar of the Old Bailey. Among the witnesses examined for the defence was the then Tory First Lord of the Treasury, Mr. Pitt, the object in requiring his testimony being to show that the practices and

[1] 'Auckland Correspondence,' vol. ii. p. 410.

principles of the reformers of 1780, with whom he had then been actively associated, were quite as advanced as those of the reformers of 1794. At first, his memory conveniently failed him during the searching interrogation to which he was subjected; but having apparently had it refreshed by the straightforward evidence of Sheridan, who was the next witness examined, it was elicited from him, on his being allowed to revise his evidence, that at least on one occasion he had assisted at a meeting of delegates deputed by several counties to take measures for procuring parliamentary reform. The result of the trial, which lasted six days, was the delivery, after a deliberation of only a few minutes by the jury, of a verdict of "Not Guilty;" a verdict received with applause within the walls of the court, and with acclamations by the vast multitude assembled in its precincts.

In the mean time, the presence of mind, wit, subtlety, and coolness which, during the last few eventful days, had been displayed by the "great grammarian," as Lord Brougham designates Horne Tooke, had not more satisfied the expectations of his friends, than his courage, political as well as personal, had excited the admiration of his enemies. A false rumour, indeed, had obtained currency at the time, that, on his being committed to the Tower, his spirit had not only failed him, but that he had burst into tears. Wilkes, however, on its reaching his ears, expressed much surprise, if not incredulity. "I knew he was a knave," he said, "but I never thought him a coward."[1] Moreover, his habitual pleasant humour had continued to sparkle no less cheerfully than in less anxious and perilous days. One cold night, for instance, during his trial, he was traversing, after the day's proceedings, the short distance between the Old Bailey and Newgate, to which latter prison he had recently been transferred, when a lady contrived to approach near enough to him to fold a silk handkerchief round his neck. "Pray, madam, be careful," was his gay address to her, as he felt her hand performing the operation, "for I am rather *ticklish* at present about that particular place."[2]

On the 27th of May, 1796, the "great grammarian" stood a second time on the hustings as a candidate for the representation of Westminster in Parliament; but, though he polled a far more considerable number of votes than on the last occasion, he was again unsuccessful. It seems to have been on one of these two occasions that a scapegrace of the opposite party observed sneeringly to him at the hustings—"Well, Mr. Tooke, you have all the blackguards with you this morning;" he replied, "I am delighted to hear it, sir—and from such *excellent* authority too."[3]

[1] 'Quarterly Review,' vol. vii. p. 328.
[2] Stephens's 'Memoirs of Tooke,' vol. ii p. 150.
[3] Earl Russell's 'Memoirs of Thomas Moore,' vol. ii. p. 252.

The final result of the continued endeavours of Horne Tooke to get returned to Parliament was, to say the least of it, though successful, far from satisfactory. In the month of February, 1801, for example, this fierce denouncer of rotten boroughs and warm advocate of the purity of election so far compromised his character for political consistency and credit, as to accept a seat in the House of Commons as representative of the notoriously corrupt borough of Old Sarum; the occurrence being rendered the more amazing from the fact of his patron being a wild young nobleman, Lord Camelford, who, three years afterwards, fell by the pistol of a brother duellist. To Horne Tooke the attainment of the object he had so long had in view proved of little value. Had he been less advanced in years at the time he entered Parliament, his oratorical efforts might in all probability have achieved for him all the success which was augured from his great abilities, and which, on repeated occasions, he had already brilliantly established for himself on the hustings. As it was, however, the effect which they produced was neither such as to heighten the enthusiasm of his admirers, nor to excite the uneasiness of his political opponents. Not only, it should be stated, was he now in his sixty-fifth year, but increasing bodily infirmities, though they failed to subdue his indomitable spirit, threatened materially to interfere with his regular attendance in Parliament.

But he had another and an insurmountable difficulty to contend against. He had not long taken his seat, when an attempt was made to effect his exclusion from the House of Commons, on the plea that he was a clergyman in full orders; an attempt which was, indeed, wisely turned aside for the present by Lord Sidmouth, then Prime Minister, but for which he subsequently substituted a Bill, which passed into law, declaring persons in holy orders to be ineligible in future Parliaments to sit in the Lower House. The effect of this measure on the future of the member for Old Sarum it was of course easy enough to foresee. He was relieved, indeed, from the operations of the Bill so long as the present Parliament continued to exist, but, on its early dissolution, his senatorial career came to an end, and he retired into private life. One valid cause the public may be said to have had for congratulating itself on his emancipation, inasmuch as it afforded him ample time to complete his famous work, the 'Diversions of Purley,' the second part of which he published in 1805.

The closing years of Horne Tooke's long life were passed by him in easy circumstances in a pleasant and roomy villa at Wimbledon, in Surrey, where his garden and his library severally contributed their share in providing him with occupation and entertainment. A martyr, during those years, to periodical attacks from more than one acute disorder, few

men would seem to have endured pain with more
exemplary patience and fortitude, or, when free from
pain, to have enjoyed existence with a truer zest.
His villa, moreover, during these closing years, was
the constant resort of a crowd of admiring visitors
and friends, to whom his delightful conversation was
an unfailing attraction, and whom he entertained
with a hospitality which almost amounted to pro-
fuseness. Among these favoured guests was his
biographer, Stephens, who has bequeathed us a
tolerably graphic portrait of the philologist, in the
aspect in which he seems to have usually presented
himself to his guests in the days of his Wimbledon
hospitalities. "When I first saw him," writes the
former,[1] "he had already passed the meridian of life,
and his dress, which savoured of the old school,
seemed to add an air of dignity to his conversation.
His coat, which consisted of a dark brown English
broad-cloth, was calculated for Court, as it was
destitute of the modern appendage of a collar; while
his cuffs were adorned with a large row of steel
buttons. His small-clothes exactly corresponded both
in cut and colour; his waistcoat was handsomely
tamboured; his stockings were of silk; he wore long
ruffles at the wrist; while his hair was tied and
powdered in the manner of former times. In the
midst of conversation, he generally recurred to the
contents of a large snuff-box, containing rappee; and

[1] 'Memoirs,' vol. ii. p. 234.

I thought I could perceive that he managed this in such a manner as to render it serviceable to his wit and repartee. His house and table denoted great plenty, if not great opulence, and the view towards the lawn, which was terminated by a distant wood, always appeared delightful to me."

Horne Tooke expired on the 18th of March, 1812, at his villa at Wimbledon, in the seventy-sixth year of his age. He had desired that his remains should be interred in his own garden, without any funeral service being performed over them, but, owing to the house being about to be sold, his executors deemed themselves justified in deviating from his injunctions, and accordingly he was buried in his sister's tomb in Ealing Church.

JONATHAN DAVIES, D.D.

THE simple and abstract fact of an obscure individual having, solely by his own merits, raised himself to be successively Head Master and Provost of Eton School, entitles him, we conceive, independent of all other claims to consideration, to a notice in any biographical work devoted expressly to Eton worthies. Dr. Jonathan Davies, to whom this remark refers, was apparently born in the year 1737. The child of parents of humble origin, he early attracted the favourable notice of Provost Barnard, who, it has been said, was at the cost of placing and maintaining him at Eton, and to whom he subsequently owed his successive steps of advancement through life. From Eton he passed, in 1755, to King's College, whence, in due time, he returned to Eton as an Assistant Master. In 1773, he succeeded Dr. Foster as Head Master; in 1781, he was appointed a Canon of Windsor, and on the 14th of December, 1791, on the death of Dr. Roberts, succeeded him as Provost of Eton, on which he resigned his canonry. He died on the 5th of December, 1809, in his seventy-third year, and was buried at Eton. To Eton College, besides a provision for Task and Declamation Prizes, he bequeathed an exhibition for a superannuated Eton scholar ; to King's College he bequeathed an exhibition, and also founded a university scholarship at Cambridge, similar to the Craven scholarships, of one of which he had formerly been in the enjoyment.

CHARLES MARQUIS CORNWALLIS.

CHARLES, first Marquis Cornwallis, though neither a soldier nor an administrator of the highest rank, must, nevertheless, be admitted to have performed sufficiently valuable service for his country in each of those capacities to entitle him to figure prominently in its biographical literature. If, for instance, his military career in America was clouded by a great disaster, on the other hand, his conduct of affairs in India, while filling the double appointment of Governor-General and Commander-in-Chief, was an admitted and eminent success; while the judgment, firmness, and wise and amiable spirit of conciliation displayed by him as Lord Lieutenant of Ireland, during the critical period of the rebellion in that country, seem entirely to merit the warm praise which they have been thought to deserve. "Cornwallis," said the first Emperor Napoleon at St. Helena, "was a man of probity, a generous and sincere character; *un très-brave homme*. He was the man who first gave me a good opinion of the

English; and," the Emperor added, "I do not believe that he was a man of first-rate abilities, but he had talent, great probity, and sincerity."[1] Chivalrous in his views of honour, and eminently brave, Lord Cornwallis, in the field, was vigilant, cautious, and indefatigable, while, in social life, he was not less distinguished by the amiability of his disposition, by his unostentatious comportment and unassuming manners.

Born in Grosvenor Square, London, on the 31st of December, 1738, Charles Viscount Brome, as was his earlier title, was the eldest son, though the sixth child, of Charles, first Earl Cornwallis, whom, in June, 1762, at the age of twenty-three, he succeeded as second Earl. Of his Eton days, we are at least able to relate that he went there at an early age; that, while playing at hockey, he was accidentally struck in the eye by his schoolfellow, Shute Barrington, the future excellent Bishop of Durham, by which mischance he sustained a slight, though permanent, obliquity of vision; and, thirdly, that in the Eton School List for August, 1754, his name stands as that of the fourth oppidan in the Sixth Form. It has been usual for his biographers to represent him as having passed from Eton to Trinity College, Cambridge; but the registers of that society have been searched, and searched in vain, for any record of his having been one of its members.

[1] O'Meara's 'Napoleon in Exile,' vol. i. p. 496.

Devoting himself to the army as a profession, the young lord had not completed his eighteenth year, when, on the 8th of December, 1756, he was appointed to an ensigncy in the 1st Guards, now the Grenadiers. Twenty months afterwards, in August, 1758, he was promoted to be a Captain of the 85th Foot, and appointed aide-de-camp to the Marquis of Granby, under whom he fought at the battle of Minden, and in other actions. In January, 1760, immediately after his having come of age, he was elected member for Eye, in Suffolk, a borough for which he continued to sit in Parliament till his succession to the peerage, in June, 1762; on the 1st of May, 1761, he was appointed Lieutenant-Colonel of the 12th Foot; in 1765, George III. nominated him to be one of the Lords of his Bedchamber, and, on the 2nd of August, in that year, to be one of his aides-de-camp. On the 21st of March, 1766, he was appointed Colonel of the 33rd Regiment, and, on the 8th of December, 1770, Constable of the Tower. In the mean time he had married, on the 14th of July, 1768, Jemima Tullikens, daughter of Colonel James Jones, of the 3rd Foot Guards, by which lady he became father of two children, Charles, afterwards second and last Marquis Cornwallis, and of Lady Mary, married to Mark Singleton, Esq., then in the 1st Guards.

It was to the credit of Lord Cornwallis that, in his seat in the House of Lords, he had strongly opposed, and uniformly voted against, the principle of American taxation; and accordingly when, on the 1st of January, 1776, he was appointed, with the local rank of Lieutenant-General, to one of the divisions of the British army about to embark for the projected subjugation of the American colonies, it was probably not without some feelings of compunction that, as a military man, he felt himself bound to draw his sword against a section of his fellow-subjects whom he considered to have been treated with injustice. His position, indeed, must at this period have been a very trying one. If, for instance, as is probable, it was thus with a painful reluctance that he undertook the discharge of his new duties, greatly must that reluctance have been aggravated by his approaching separation from a loving and beloved wife and her young children. The sight, indeed, of Lady Cornwallis's distress, such as it has been described to us, must have been hard for him to witness. So overcome was she by her husband being called into active service, that she flew, it is said, to his uncle, Dr. Cornwallis, Archbishop of Canterbury, and so affected him by her tears as to induce him to solicit and obtain the King's permission for her husband to renounce the appointment and remain in England. Satisfaction, however, was not the prevailing sensation in Lord Cornwallis's mind on his being apprised of this well-meant, but unauthorized interference with his professional obligations.

Sacrificing, therefore, his feelings to the calls of duty and honour, he instantly waited on the King, and expostulated with him so warmly on the danger to which such a step would expose his honour, that the royal consent was withdrawn; and, accordingly, on the 10th of February, 1776, the Earl embarked for America, leaving Lady Cornwallis to bewail his absence in the cheerless solitude of his family seat, Culford Hall, near Bury St. Edmunds. He returned to England, indeed, on furlough, in January, 1778, but re-embarked at St. Helens on board the *Trident* on the 21st of April following; Lady Cornwallis, with her children, accompanying him as far as Portsmouth, whence, after he had sailed, she returned to her former solitude at Culford. "Poor Lord Cornwallis," runs a letter addressed to George Selwyn by another noble passenger on board the *Trident*, Frederick Earl of Carlisle—"Poor Lord Cornwallis is going to experience, perhaps, something what I have felt, for he has brought with him his wife and children, and we embark to-morrow if the wind serves. My heart bleeds for them."[1] Lady Cornwallis survived only till the 14th of February, 1779, when she expired the victim, as she had always predicted to her confidential attendant, of a broken heart. Agreeably with her expressed wish, a thorn-tree, emblematical of the sorrow which terminated her existence, was planted above the vault at Culford,

[1] 'Selwyn Correspondence,' vol. iii. p. 276.

in which her remains lie, and as nearly as possible over her heart.[1]

The earlier period of the military career of Lord Cornwallis in America, while serving under the orders of Generals Howe and Clinton, was far from being undistinguished by success and renown. More than one, for instance, of his encounters with the American generals must be admitted to have been brilliant affairs; while his administration of civil power in the province of South Carolina proved no less sagacious than his conduct in the field had been spirited. Having previously distinguished himself at the battle of Brandywine, in 1777, and afterwards at the siege of Charlestown, the next notable service performed by Lord Cornwallis was the victory won by him at Camden, on the 16th of August, 1780, on which occasion, at the head of two thousand men, he defeated General Gates with an army of upwards of four thousand. The battle of Camden was followed by the signal advantage obtained by him on the 15th of March, 1781, at Guildford Court-House, where, with a very inferior force, he again succeeded in worsting the Americans, besides capturing four of their field-pieces. But by this time the unnatural war between Great Britain and her colonies was gradually drawing near its untoward close. Well, indeed, might Lord Cornwallis have exclaimed after his late successes—as Pyrrhus had exclaimed after

[1] 'Cornwallis Correspondence,' vol. i. p. 14.

having vanquished the Romans at Asculum—" One more such victory and we are undone." By the time that autumn had set in, so heavy had become the losses in killed and wounded sustained by the British force in South Carolina, as to render it no longer available for service in the field. When, for instance, Washington and De Rochambeau commenced their famous march to give battle to Lord Cornwallis at York Town, the combined American and French army numbered as many as eighteen or nineteen thousand men, whereas Lord Cornwallis could muster under his command no more than seven thousand.

On the disheartening story of the investment and capitulation of Lord Cornwallis at York Town, we have no occasion to linger. For the credit of the high-minded Cornwallis, sufficient it is to mention that it was not till his small army had been deplorably reduced by disease and by the casualties of war—not till he found himself enfiladed at every point—not till his shells were nearly expended, and his defences half demolished and tumbling to pieces, that he could be prevailed upon, on the 17th of October, to despatch a flag of truce to General Washington, admitting that his post was no longer tenable, and proposing a cessation of hostilities. The articles of the memorable capitulation which followed were signed by the respective generals on the 19th of October, at two o'clock on which day the British troops, nominally amounting to six thousand men, laid down their arms in the face of the enemy.

On the return, it may be mentioned, of Lord Cornwallis to England, early in 1782, a change of ministry deprived him of his appointment of Governor of the Tower, which post, however, was restored to him in 1784, and from that time was retained by him to the close of his life. Active service, in the mean time, he would in all probability have preferred, but, though not immediately re-employed, he was not forgotten in his retirement at Culford. In 1785, for instance, he was sent on a short mission to Frederick the Great of Prussia, and, on the 2nd of June, 1786, was elected a Knight of the Garter. At length, in 1786, he was appointed Governor-General of, and Commander-in-Chief of the forces in, India, in which double capacity he conducted and concluded an administrative career of eminent sagacity and vigour, with the further distinction of having subdued, in 1792, the powerful Sultan of the Mysore, Tippoo Saib, invaded his dominions, besieged his capital, Seringapatam, and compelled him to sue for peace at the cost of a vast amount of territory and treasure. Nor, in his hour of triumph and greatness, was Lord Cornwallis forgetful of old ties and old friends in England, nor regardless of the claims of the widow and the orphan. To Lady Ossory, for instance, Horace Walpole writes on the 7th of July, 1792—" I have this moment received a letter from

Lady Waldegrave, acquainting me with one she has just had from Lord Cornwallis, expressing his affectionate remembrance of his great friend, her lord, and assuring her that for his sake he will, while he lives, perform every office of friendship and assistance in his power to her and her children. How very amiable in the moment of victory to find Alexander, the conqueror of India, thinking of writing a consolatory letter to a widow at the other end of the world, and tying up a branch of cypress with a bundle of laurels and boughs of olive!"[1]

At the conclusion of the war in the Mysore, Lord Cornwallis returned to England, where he was honoured with fresh distinctions. He was made a Privy Councillor; was advanced to the rank of Marquis on the 15th of August, 1792; on the 13th of February, 1795, he was appointed Master-General of the Ordnance; and, on the 13th of June, 1798, Lord-Lieutenant of Ireland. In this latter year, the critical year of the rebellion in Ireland, and of the futile invasion of that country by the French, he not only distinguished himself by the promptitude with which he met the one and quelled the other, but, as has already been intimated, displayed a combined

---

[1] Walpole's 'Letters,' vol. ix. p. 378. The Lady Waldegrave here referred to was Elizabeth Laura, cousin and wife of George, fourth Earl of Waldegrave, who, on the 17th of October, 1789, had left her a widow with five children. Of these, the eldest son, George, the fifth Earl, was unhappily drowned in the Thames near Eton, on the 29th of June, 1794, when only in his eleventh year.

amount of judgment, firmness, and spirit of conciliation which reflected the highest credit alike on his head and on his heart.

In Ireland, Lord Cornwallis remained till March, 1801, when, having been succeeded by Lord Hardwicke, he was soon afterwards sent to France to sign the Treaty of Amiens. Of the punctilious sense of honour evinced by him at the congress on this occasion, an interesting anecdote was related by Napoleon when in exile at St. Helena. "At Amiens," said the Emperor, "the treaty was ready, and was to be signed by him [Cornwallis] at the Hôtel de Ville at nine o'clock. Something happened which prevented him from going; but he sent word to the French ministers that they might consider the treaty as having been signed, and that he would sign it the following day. A courier from England arrived at night, with directions to him to refuse his consent to certain articles, and not to sign the treaty. Although Cornwallis had not signed it, and might have easily availed himself of this order, he was a man of such strict honour, that he said he considered his promise to be equivalent to his signature, and wrote to his Government that he had promised, and that having once pledged his word, he would keep it. That if they were not satisfied, they might refuse to ratify the treaty."[1]

In January, 1805, on the recall of Marquis

[1] O'Meara's 'Napoleon in Exile,' vol. i. p. 496.

Wellesley from the East, Lord Cornwallis was again selected to fill the high appointments of Governor-General and Commander-in-Chief in India. His valuable existence, however, was now drawing near its close. On reaching Calcutta, where he arrived with failing health, he proceeded by water to take the command of the upper provinces of his vice-regal dominions, but, while pursuing his projected progress, sank into a foreign grave. Succumbing, apparently, to a gradually and fatally increasing debility, rather than to any positive disorder, he expired at Ghazepore, in the province of Benares, on the 5th of October, 1805, in the sixty-seventh year of his age. India honoured his memory with statues and a mausoleum, while, in England, the House of Commons voted him a monument in St. Paul's Cathedral.

INDEX.

₊ The names of the subjects of Memoirs are printed in small capitals.

Abergavenny, Lord, ii. 105, 106.
Abernethy, John, i. 111.
Adam, —— ii. 264.
Addington, Dr., i. 160.
Addison, Joseph, i. 162; ii. 267.
Aiguillon, Duc d', ii. 172.
Albans, Charles Duke of, ii. 287.
Allen, Ralph, i. 79, 88.
Almon, John, i. 268.
Altamont, John Dennis, Lord, ii. 193.
Altamont, Lady, ii. 186.
Amelia, Princess, i. 277, 278.
Amherst, Jeffrey Lord, i. 149; ii. 141.
Ancaster, Duke of, ii. 74, 75.
Anglesey, Richard Earl of, i. 90.
Anne, Queen, i. 105, 177, 302.
Annesley, James, i. 90.
Anson, Admiral Lord, i. 166; ii. 59, 171.
Anspach, Margrave of, i. 171.
Anstey, Ann, ii. 163.
ANSTEY, Christopher, ii. 162–7; 15.
Anstey, Rev. Christopher, ii. 162.
Anstey, Mary, ii. 162.
Antrobus, Mary, i. 364.
Antrobus, Robert, i. 352, 353.
Arbuthnot, John, ii. 5.
Argyle, Archibald Duke of, i. 252.
Argyle, John Duke of (4), i. 71; ii. 126.
Argyle, John Duke of (5), i. 259.
Arne, Cecilia, i. 207.
Arne, Edward, i. 203.

ARNE, Thomas Augustine, i. 203–9.
Ashburton, John Dunning, Lord, ii. 306, 318.
Ashton, Mrs., i. 335.
ASHTON, Rev. Thomas, D.D., i. 332–6; 302, 342; ii. 23, 39.
Ashton, Thomas, i. 335.
Aston, Molly, i. 180.
Aubrey, John, i. 333.
Auckland, Lord, ii. 278, 284, 320.
Augusta of Saxe-Gotha, Princess, i. 44, 46.
Austria, Anne of, i. 281.
Aylesbury, Charles Bruce, Earl of, ii. 126.
Aylesbury, Countess of, ii. 126, 127, 128, 137.

Bailey, Nathaniel, i. 111.
Baker, George, ii. 157.
Baker, Rev. George, ii. 157.
BAKER, Sir George, ii. 157–61; i. 81.
Baker, Lady, ii. 157.
Balls, John, ii. 52.
Balmerino, Lord, ii. 106, 109.
Barker, Anne, i. 14.
Barker, Henry, i. 14.
BARNARD, Dr. Edward, ii. 10–16; i. 321; ii. 55, 231, 232, 327.
Barré, Colonel, i. 104, 160, 161; ii. 241, 250, 281.
Barrington, John Viscount, ii. 286.
Barrington, Mrs., ii. 287, 289.
BARRINGTON, Dr. Shute, ii. 286–93; 330.

INDEX. 341

Barrington, William Viscount, i. 123, 270; ii. 243, 292.
Barrow, Sir John, ii. 170, 173, 190, 216.
Bates, ——, ii. 81.
Bates, Mrs., ii. 81.
Bath, Lord, ii. 72.
Bath, William Pulteney, Earl of, i. 3, 39, 166, 259.
Bathurst, Allen Lord, i. 81; ii. 57.
Bathurst, Peter, i. 81.
Battie, Rev. Edward, i. 18.
BATTIE, William, M.D., i. 18–25; 30; ii. 25.
Bayham, Viscount—*see* Camden, Earl.
Beattie, Dr., i. 192; ii. 282, 283.
Beauclerk, Lady Diana, ii. 44, 287.
Beaulieu, Earl of, i. 169, 170.
Beckford, William, i. 122, 125; ii. 314.
Bedford, John Duke of, i. 27, 44, 45, 71, 125, 238, 259, 260, 270, 274; ii. 59, 60, 222, 238.
Bedingfield, Philip, ii. 53.
Bedingfield, Susan, ii. 53.
Bellenden, Mary, ii. 127.
Bennet, Mrs., ii. 264.
Bentham, James, i. 290.
Bentley, Dr. Richard, i. 2.
Bentley, ——, ii. 34, 39.
Berkeley, Charles Earl of, i. 212.
Berkeley, Lady Mary, i. 212.
Bernini, J. L., ii. 138.
Berry, Agnes, ii. 43, 44.
Berry, Mary, ii. 42, 43, 44, 45, 47, 120.
Berry, ——, ii. 44.
Bessborough, Earl of, i. 138; ii. 55.
Bethell, S., ii. 110.
Blackstone, Sir William, i. 297.
Bland, Dr., i. 19, 97.
Blandford, George Marquis of, i. 321, 322.

Blencowe, Sir John, i. 92.
Blencowe, Joyce, i. 92.
Blount, Martha, i. 61.
Boerhaave, Herman, ii. 307.
Boissy, Louis de, ii. 141.
Bolingbroke, Henry St. John, Viscount, i. 87, 112, 167, 182; ii. 63.
Boothby, Miss, i. 180.
Boscawen, Mrs., i. 351.
Boswell, James, i. 16, 166, 361; ii. 7, 196, 198, 295.
Bothwell, ——, i. 264.
Boughton, Mrs., i. 178.
Bowyer, William, ii. 292.
Braddock, General, i. 101.
Brenton, Captain, ii. 75.
Bright, Thomas, ii. 230.
Bristol, Earl of, ii. 19.
Brocket, ——, i. 371.
Brookes, Dr. H., ii. 94, 95.
Brougham, Lord, i. 277; ii. 248, 321.
BROUGHTON, Rev. Thomas, i. 26–9; 30.
Browne, Rev. James, i. 375.
Bruce, James, ii. 114.
Brunswick-Wolfenbuttel, Duchess of, i. 255.
BRYANT, Jacob, i. 320–31; 30, 302; ii. 16, 55, 91.
Brydges, Sir Egerton, i. 372.
Buckingham, George Villiers, Duke of, i. 97; ii. 89.
Buckingham, George Marquis of, i. 46, 58, 116, 229, 232.
Buckingham, Marchioness of, i. 227, 228.
Bulkeley, Lord, ii. 271.
Bunbury, Sir Charles, i. 53; ii. 297.
Burges, James Bland, ii. 320.
Burke, Edmund, i. 112, 120, 134, 144, 161, 226, 235; ii. 96, 115, 134, 177, 225, 226, 250, 251, 283.
Burnet, Bishop, i. 337.

342   INDEX.

Burney, Dr. Charles, i. 206, 207, 208; ii. 1.
Burney, Frances—*see* D'Arblay.
Bute, Countess of, i. 64, 71.
Bute, James Earl of, i. 252.
BUTE, John Earl of, i. 252–85; 42, 44, 46, 49, 106, 116, 117, 118, 119, 123, 125, 126, 129, 216, 218, 220, 231, 232, 233, 238, 297, 370, 371.
Butler, Charles, ii. 61, 289.
Butler, Dr. Joseph, ii. 50.
Byng, Admiral, i. 101; ii. 40.
Byron, Lord, i. 63; ii. 35.
Byron, Vice-Admiral, ii. 183.

Calcraft, ——, ii. 241.
Calvert, Felix, ii. 163.
Calvert, John, ii. 163.
Cambridge, Mrs., ii. 3.
CAMBRIDGE, Richard Owen, ii. 1–9; 55.
CAMDEN, Charles Pratt, Earl, i. 302–19; 5, 30, 112, 135, 140, 156, 158, 159, 194, 195; ii. 255.
Camden, Countess, i. 307.
Camden, John Marquis, i. 308.
Camelford, Lord, ii. 323.
Camoens, Lewis de, i. 167.
Campbell, Lady Anne, i. 252.
Campbell, Lady Caroline, ii. 126.
Campbell, Lord, i. 159, 307, 311.
Canning, George, i. 162.
Carlisle, Frederick Earl of, ii. 101, 118, 121, 333.
Caroline, Princess, i. 37.
Caroline, Queen, i. 15; ii. 90, 91, 127.
Carraccioli, ——, ii. 116.
Castlereagh, Lord, ii. 244.
Cathcart, Lord, ii. 216.
Catherine, Empress, i. 172; ii. 34.
Cavendish, Admiral Philip, i. 48.
Cavendish, Lord John, ii. 261, 265, 272.

Chamber, Thomas, i. 212.
CHAMPION, Anthony, ii. 168–9.
Champion, Peter, ii. 168.
CHAPMAN, Dr. John, i. 30–2; 90.
Chapman, Rev. William, i. 30.
Charles I., i. 34; ii. 39, 97, 98.
Charles II., i. 34, 37, 302.
Charles V., i. 63.
Charles Edward, Prince, i. 346; ii. 59.
Charlotte, Queen, i. 121, 326; ii. 157.
Chatham, Countess of, i. 101, 142, 145, 147, 149, 163, 211, 213, 216, 226, 227.
Chatham, John Earl of, i. 163.
CHATHAM, William Pitt, Earl of, i. 96–163; 36, 40, 50, 59, 60, 178, 179, 195, 211, 213, 214, 216, 217, 218, 219, 220, 221, 222, 223, 224, 225, 226, 228, 231, 237, 238, 239, 240, 259, 260, 261, 263, 281, 303, 306, 312, 314; ii. 29, 58, 151, 237, 240, 244, 319.
Chatterton, Thomas, i. 29, 300; ii. 39.
Chesterfield, Lord, i. 44, 99, 107, 135, 145, 224, 255, 269, 273, 283, 347; ii. 4, 11, 62, 89, 108, 122, 226, 227.
Chevenix, Mrs., ii. 29, 30.
Choiseul, Duc de, ii. 103.
Churchill, Rev. Charles, i. 54, 215, 267; ii. 68, 72.
Chute, ——, ii. 24.
Cibber, Colley, i. 369.
Cibber, Mrs., i. 203, 206.
Clinton, General Sir Henry, ii. 212, 215, 217, 334.
Clive, Lord, ii. 150.
Cloberry, Robert Glynn—*see* Glynn, Robert.
Coalston, Lord, ii. 195.
Cobham, Lord, i. 296.

Cobham, Richard Viscount, i. 58, 101, 210, 211, 212, 230, 231.
Cocchi, Dr., ii. 27.
Coignie, Madame de, ii. 103.
COLE, Rev. William, i. 286–95; 13, 286, 296, 302, 322, 332, 363, 368, 376; ii. 23, 91, 98, 297.
Colebrooke, Sir George, i. 107.
Coleman, ——, i. 22.
Collins, Anthony, i. 32.
Colman, George, ii. 89.
Conflans, Admiral de, ii. 175.
Congreve, William, i. 67, 368...
Coningsby, Lady Frances, i. 165.
Coningsby, Thomas Earl of, i. 165.
Conolly, Rt. Hon. William, ii. 204.
Conway, Charlotte Lady, ii. 123.
Conway, Francis Lord, ii. 18, 123.
Conway, Henry, ii. 23, 30.
CONWAY, Field-Marshal the Rt. Hon. Henry Seymour, ii. 122–42; 46, 135, 137, 146, 148, 187, 240, 260, 276, 328, 332; ii. 18, 38, 91, 96, 143, 172, 259.
Cooke, Catherine, i. 200.
Cooke, ——, ii. 311.
Cooke, Rev. John, ii. 56, 82.
COOKE, Dr. William, i. 199-202; 33.
Cornwallis, Caroline, i. 247.
Cornwallis, Charles Earl, i. 245; 330.
Cornwallis, Charles Lord, i. 245.
CORNWALLIS, Charles Marquis (1), ii. 329–39; i. 245; ii. 212, 215, 256.
Cornwallis, Charles Marquis (2), ii. 331.
CORNWALLIS, Frederick, Archbishop of Canterbury, i. 245–51; 195, 197; ii. 332.
Cornwallis, Lady Mary, ii. 331.
Cornwallis, Marchioness, ii. 331, 332, 333.
Courtown, Lady, ii. 187.

Coventry, Lady Anne—see Foley.
Coventry, Lord, ii. 100, 118.
Coventry, Maria Countess of, ii. 113, 118.
Coxe, Archdeacon, i. 40, 173.
Craddock, Charlotte, i. 69.
Cradock, ——, ii. 80, 82, 85.
Creasy, Professor, i. 114.
Crillon, Duc de, ii. 155.
Cromwell, Oliver, i. 105; ii. 84.
Cumberland, Richard, i. 344, 346, 347, 348, 351; ii. 281.
Cumberland, William Duke of, i. 2, 48, 159, 167, 219, 220, 240, 264, 276; ii. 25, 125, 126, 144, 200, 220, 223, 227.
Cummins, ——, i. 113.
Curtis, Sir Roger, ii. 184, 186, 190, 192.
Curzon, Assheton, Viscount, ii. 193.

Dalrymple, Sir James, ii. 194.
Damer, Anne Seymour, ii. 137, 139, 141.
Damer, Hon. John, ii. 137, 138, 139.
Damiens, ——, ii. 106, 107.
Dampier, Thomas, ii. 13.
Daniel, Mrs., i. 85.
D'Arblay, Madame, i. 326, 327, 329; ii. 1, 159, 160.
Dartmouth, William Earl of, i. 117, 258.
Dashwood, Catherine, i. 178.
Dashwood, Sir Francis, ii. 67.
DAVIES, Rev. Jonathan, D.D., ii. 327–8.
DAVIES, Rev. Sneyd, D.D., i. 194–8; 246, 307.
Deffand, Madame du, ii. 38, 39, 103.
Delany, Mrs., i. 183, 189, 326, 329, 351.
De Lizy, M., i. 211.
Denbigh, Earl of, i. 271.
Denbigh, Susan Countess of, i. 97

Derby, Countess of, ii. 141.
Derby, Lord, ii. 74, 141.
Desnoyers, ——, i. 16.
Devonshire, William Duke of, i. 11, 46, 48, 103, 259, 369; ii. 132.
Dibden, Dr., ii. 298, 299, 300.
Dickens, Dr., ii. 25.
Disraeli, Isaac, i. 295.
Doddridge, Dr., i. 57.
Dodington, Bubb, i. 265.
Dodsley, Robert, ii. 165, 368.
Dorset, Duke of, i. 259.
Dorset, Lord, ii. 89.
Draper, Joe, i. 367.
Draper, Lady, ii. 154.
DRAPER, Lieut.-Gen. Sir William, ii. 150-6; i. 31; ii. 143.
Drury, General, ii. 173.
Ducarel, Dr., i. 290.
Dundas, Henry, ii. 270.
Dunk, Thomas, i. 345.
Dutens, M., i. 262, 264, 272, 273.

Eden, ——, ii. 160.
Edgecombe, Lord, i. 33, 137.
Egmont, Lord, i. 241.
Egremont, Charles Earl of, i. 232, 237, 271, 310.
Eliot, Hon. Edward James, i. 163.
Eliot, Lady Harriet, i. 163, 226.
Eliot, Lord, i. 163.
Elizabeth, Queen, i. 249.
Elliot, Sir Gilbert, ii. 176.
Elliott, G., i. 264.
Elwes, John, ii. 308.
Essex, ——, i. 295.
Essex, Frances Countess of, i. 175.
Essex, William Anne, Earl of, i. 175.
Estaing, Count d', ii. 182.
Ewer, Dr. John, i. 30.

Falkener, Sir Everard, ii. 113.
Fane, Charles Viscount, ii. 59.

Fanshawe, ——, ii. 101.
Farmer, Dr., ii. 297.
Farrington, General, ii. 90.
Ferdinand, Prince, i. 120; ii. 145, 147.
Festing, Michael, i. 204.
Fielding, Beatrix, i. 63.
Fielding, Catherine, i. 63.
Fielding, Lieut.-General Edmund, i. 63.
Fielding, Eleanor, i. 64.
FIELDING, Henry, i. 62-88; 97,182, 228.
Fielding, Sir John, i. 64, 82, 84, 88; ii. 79.
Fielding, Mrs. Sarah, i. 63.
Fielding, Miss Sarah, i. 63.
Fielding, Ursula, i. 63.
Fielding, William, i. 88.
Fielding and Co., Messrs., i. 85.
Finch, Hon. Edward, i. 10.
Fitzpatrick, ———, ii. 114.
Fitzwilliam, William Earl, ii. 230.
Flaxman, John, ii. 193, 301.
Foley, Lady Anne, ii. 118.
Foote, Samuel, ii. 89.
Forbes, Admiral, i. 47.
Fordyce, Dr., ii. 297.
Forster, Elizabeth, ii. 49.
FORSTER, Nathaniel, D.D., ii. 49-53.
Forster, Rev. Robert, ii. 49.
Forster, Susan, ii. 52.
FOSTER, Rev. John, D.D., ii. 231-3, 327.
Fountaine, Miss Anne, i. 8.
Fox, Charles James, i. 56, 101, 126, 128, 129, 162, 179, 195, 260, 262, 267, 316; ii. 73, 74, 75, 76, 80, 114, 115, 137, 141, 262, 268, 269, 270, 271, 273, 274, 275, 276, 283, 297, 319.
Fox, Henry, i. 56.
Fox, General Henry Edward, i. 56.

Fox, Sir Stephen, i. 34.
Franklin, Benjamin, i. 111; ii. 176, 177, 180, 181.
Frederick, Sir Charles, i. 103.
Frederick the Great, i. 105, 171; ii. 336.
Frere, Mrs., ii. 105.
Furnese, Miss, ii. 114.

Gage, General Thomas, ii. 201, 202, 203, 204, 208.
Galissonière, ——, i. 101.
Garrick, David, i. 16, 369; ii. 14.
Garrick, Mrs., ii. 142.
Gates, General, ii. 334.
Geminiani, Francesco, i. 207.
George, Dr., i. 1, 31.
George I., i. 10, 114, 302; ii. 20, 21, 90, 170, 185.
George II., i. 6, 10, 15, 37, 40, 41, 59, 96, 100, 112, 116, 171, 172, 217, 245, 255, 296, 302; ii. 51, 60, 90, 91, 127, 175, 221, 286.
George III., i. 41, 42, 44, 46, 49, 50, 60, 153, 178, 214, 217, 219, 232, 238, 239, 244, 249, 250, 255, 257, 277, 314, 326, 371; ii. 13, 135, 157, 158, 172, 184, 185, 186, 192, 219, 221, 222, 227, 234, 235, 238, 239, 245, 267, 268, 279, 287, 314, 331.
George IV., ii. 13.
Germaine, Lady Betty, i. 212.
Germaine, Lord George, ii. 74, 210, 257.
Giardini, Felix, ii. 78.
Gibbon, Dr., i. 328.
Gibbon, Edward, i. 62, 73; ii. 7, 250, 251, 279, 280, 297.
Gisborne, Dr., i. 374.
Gisburne, Colonel, ii. 153.
Glenberrie, Lady, ii. 284.
GLYNN, Robert, M.D., ii. 86-8; 91, 376.

Godolphin, Dr., i. 21.
Godolphin, ——, ii. 224.
Goldsmith, Oliver, ii. 199.
Goodall, Provost, ii. 170.
Goode, Barnham, i. 21.
Gordon, Lord George, ii. 115, 116.
Gough, Richard, i. 201, 290, 295, 301.
Gould, Sir Henry, i. 63.
Gower, Earl, i. 259; ii. 112, 224, 239, 274.
Gower, Hon. Richard Leveson, ii. 93.
Grafton, Augustus Henry Duke of, i. 46, 48, 50, 134, 142, 143, 145, 146, 148, 149, 150, 152, 156, 158, 221, 222, 223, 240, 256, 259, 310, 312, 317, 318, 371, 373; ii. 227, 238, 240, 245, 255.
Grafton, Charles Fitzroy, Duke of, ii. 17.
GRAHAM, Rev. George, ii. 198-9.
GRANBY, Lieutenant-General John, Marquis of, ii. 143-9; 128, 150, 153, 154, 331.
Grandison, John Lord, i. 97.
Granger, Rev. J., i. 290.
Granville, Earl, i. 119.
Grattan, Henry, i. 162.
Gray, Dorothy, i. 352, 365.
Gray, Philip, i. 352.
GRAY, Thomas, i. 352-77; 54, 183, 332, 333, 337, 338, 339, 341; ii. 19, 23, 26, 32, 34, 39, 55, 70, 71, 91, 123, 157, 165.
Greene, General, ii. 210.
Gregory, Elizabeth, i. 302.
Grenville, Elizabeth, i. 232.
GRENVILLE, Rt. Hon. George, i. 230-44; 42, 43, 58, 129, 133, 145, 195, 211, 217, 218, 219, 220, 224, 226, 228, 229, 264, 266, 271, 273, 274, 275, 297, 308, 313, 349; ii. 40, 59, 62, 63, 64, 115, 131, 132, 134, 135, 140, 222, 226, 236, 237, 238, 243.

Grenville, Grenville, ii. 222.
Grenville, James, i. 216.
Grenville, Lord, i. 119.
Grenville, Richard, i. 211.
Grenville, Thomas, i. 232; ii. 75.
Grenville, William Lord, i. 232; ii. 274.
Grey, Lady, i. 4.
Grose, Francis, i. 290.
Guilford, Francis Earl of, ii. 234, 235, 268.
Guilford, —, see North.
Guise, Sir John, ii. 287.
Guise, Sir William, ii. 287.

Haberden, Dr., i. 376.
Hackman, ——, ii. 78, 80.
Haddington, Thomas Earl of, ii. 195.
Hailes, Ann Lady, ii. 195.
HAILES, David Dalrymple, Lord, ii. 194-7.
Hailes, Helen Lady, ii. 196.
Hales, John, i. 333.
Hales, Dr. Stephen, i. 187.
Halifax, Lady Anne, i. 346.
Halifax, Catherine, i. 200.
Halifax, Countess of, i. 345, 348, 350.
Halifax, Dr., i. 376.
Halifax, Lady Frances, i. 346.
HALIFAX, George Montagu, Earl of, i. 344-50; 201, 237, 310; ii. 54, 55, 57, 235.
Halifax, Dr. Samuel, i. 200.
Hallam, Henry, i. 378.
Halley, Dr. Edmund, i. 187.
Hallifax, Dr., ii. 84, 85.
Hamilton, Lady Archibald, i. 99.
Hamilton, Lady Christian, ii. 194.
Hammond, James, i. 99, 178.
Hanbury, Albinia, i. 164.
Hanbury, Charles—see Williams, Sir Charles Hanbury.

Hanbury, John, i. 164.
Handel, George Frederick, i. 14, 27, 28.
Hanover, Ernest King of, ii. 186, 267.
Hardinge, Rev. Gabriel, i. 1.
Hardinge, George, i. 2, 4, 5, 9, 18, 194, 196, 197, 305; ii. 10, 14, 16, 24, 39, 42.
Hardinge, Henry Viscount, i. 5.
HARDINGE, Nicholas, i. 1-5; 6, 8, 9, 194, 197.
Hardwicke, Philip Earl of (1), i. 257, 259, 275, 278; ii. 50, 51.
Hardwicke, Philip Earl of (2), ii. 51, 70, 73.
Hardwicke, Philip Earl of (3), ii. 338.
Harrington, ——, i. 34.
Harrington, William Earl of, i. 6, 259.
Harris, James, ii. 7.
Harris, Thomas, i. 28.
Hartop, Chiverton, ii. 174.
Harvey, Lord, ii. 89.
Hawke, Sir Edward, i. 120; ii. 175.
Hawkins, Sir John, ii. 41.
Hawkins, Letitia, ii. 41, 298, 299.
Hayter, Dr., ii. 53.
Henault, President, ii. 102, 103.
Henley, Robert, i. 305.
Herbert, ——, i. 34.
Herries, Lady, ii. 43.
Herring, Archbishop, ii. 50.
Hertford, Francis Marquis of, i. 332; ii. 18, 23, 123.
Hertford, Lady, ii. 103.
Hertford, Lord, i. 221; ii. 100, 129, 130, 132.
Hertford, Maria Marchioness of, ii. 118, 121.
Hertford, Marquis of, ii. 118.
Hervey, Carr Lord, ii. 19.
Hervey, John Lord, i. 38, 39, 180; ii. 19.
Hervey, Lady, i. 263.

INDEX. 347

Heton, Bishop, i. 249.
Hill, Aaron, i. 206.
Hinchinbroke, Edward Richard Viscount, ii. 54.
Hogarth, William, i. 14, 16, 17, 54.
Holdernesse, Earl of, i. 117, 258.
HOLLAND, Henry Fox, Lord, i. 34–56; 65, 104, 116, 165, 170, 257, 265; ii. 98, 319.
Holland, Henry Richard Vassall, Lord, ii. 264.
Holland, Henry Rich., Earl of, ii. 105, 106.
Holland, Lady, i. 36, 37, 38, 55, 56.
Holland, Stephen Fox, Lord, i. 56.
Hollis, Thomas, i. 151.
Home, Rev. John, i. 262, 279, 284.
Hood, Lord, ii. 319.
Hook, Theodore, ii. 89.
Horne, Benjamin, ii. 303.
Horne, John, ii. 302.
Horne, John—*see* Tooke, John Horne
Horne, Thomas, ii. 303.
Hough, Bishop, i. 296.
Howard, Lady Frances, ii. 187.
Howe, Lady Charlotte Sophia, ii. 193.
Howe, Emanuel Scrope, Viscount, ii. 170.
Howe, George Augustus Viscount, ii. 174.
Howe, Lady Louisa Catherine, ii. 193.
Howe, Lady Mary, ii. 186, 190, 193.
Howe, Mary Countess, ii. 174, 184.
Howe, Mrs., ii. 177, 180, 184, 185, 191, 192.
HOWE, Admiral Richard Earl, ii. 170–93; 200, 209, 218.
HOWE, General Viscount, ii. 200–18; 176, 178, 334.
Howe, Viscountess, ii. 170, 185, 201.
Huntingdon, Selina Countess of, i. 249.

Hurd, Bishop, i. 298, 369; ii. 50.
Hutton, Archbishop, i. 250.

Ilchester, Countess of, i. 167.
Ilchester, Stephen Fox, Earl of, i. 35, 167.

Jeffreys, Lord Chancellor, i. 269.
Jeffreys, Nicholas, i. 307.
Jennings, ——, ii. 305.
Jodrell, Paul, i. 90.
Johnson, Dr. Samuel, i. 57, 59, 60, 61, 79, 111, 140, 166, 176, 177, 179, 180, 187, 188, 190, 263, 371; ii. 7, 41, 196, 197, 198, 199, 295, 296, 318.
Jones, Colonel James, ii. 331.
Joyeuse, Admiral Villaret, ii. 184.

Kames, Henry Horne, Lord, i. 190.
Kendal, Duchess of, ii. 20, 21.
Kenyon, Lord, ii. 306.
Keppel, Lord, ii. 74, 183.
Kerrick, Rev. Thomas, ii. 88.
Kilkerran, Lord, ii. 196.
Kilmarnock, Lord, ii. 106, 109.
Kinnoul, Earl of, i. 192.
Knowles, Lady, i. 198.
Knyphausen, ——, ii. 217.

La Condamine, C. M. de, ii. 107.
La Harpe, Jean Frs. de, i. 77.
Lampe, John Frederick, i. 206.
Lansdowne, Lord, i. 262; ii. 320.
La Roche, ——, ii. 242.
Laud, Archbishop, i. 289.
Lawrence, Lord, ii. 151.
Le Despencer, Thomas Lord, i. 321; ii. 73.
Lee, General, i. 133, 141, 313.
Legge, Hon. Captain Edward, ii. 171.
Legge, Henry Bilson, i. 117, 258.
Lennox, Lady Sarah, i. 37, 52, 53.

348 INDEX.

Lens, Bernard, ii. 25.
Lever, Sir Ashton, ii. 4.
Lexington, Robert Sutton, Lord, ii. 143.
Ligonier, ——, ii. 99.
Lincoln, Earl of, ii. 26, 27.
Lindsay, Lady Charlotte, ii. 248, 263, 283, 284.
Liotard, John Stephen, ii. 55.
Lisburne, Lord, ii. 74.
Lobb, Stephen, ii. 220.
Lombe, ——, i. 295.
Londonderry, Robert Marquis of, i. 308.
Londonderry, Marchioness of, i. 308.
Lort, Dr., i. 292; ii. 297.
Louis XIV., ii. 216.
Louis XV., ii. 103, 107.
Lovat, Lord, ii. 106, 109.
Lowther, Sir James, i. 371; ii. 258.
Luxborough, Lady, ii. 127.
LYTTELTON, Dr. Charles, i. 296-8; 299, 300; ii. 93.
Lyttelton, Christian Lady, i. 177, 211.
Lyttelton, Elizabeth Lady, i. 186.
LYTTELTON, George Lord, i. 176-93; 59, 65, 71, 75, 78, 122, 141, 195, 224, 228; ii. 66.
Lyttelton, Sir George, ii. 97.
Lyttelton, Lucy Lady, i. 182, 193.
Lyttelton, ——, i. 81.
Lyttelton, Sir Thomas, i. 177, 186, 296.
Lyttelton, Thomas Lord, i. 182, 193.
Lyttelton, William Henry Lord, ii. 168.

McArdell, James, i. 336.
Macartney, Lord, i. 55.
Macaulay, Thomas Babington Lord, i. 114, 115, 116, 139, 162, 163, 210, 211, 216, 269; ii. 270.
Macdaniel, Mary, i. 75.

Macintosh, Sir James, i. 361.
Mackenzie, Stuart, ii. 222.
Mackie, ——, ii. 114.
McLean, ——, ii. 32, 33.
Macnamara, ——, ii. 79.
Macpherson, James, i. 262.
Mahon, Lord, i. 155, 160.
Mallet, David, i. 87, 181, 207, 262.
Manchester, Isabella Duchess of, i. 167, 168, 169, 170.
Mann, Sir Horace, i. 37, 214, 356; ii. 30, 37, 59, 126, 127, 137, 240.
Manners, Lord Robert, ii. 147.
Mansfield, Lord, i. 106, 159, 162, 241, 271, 312; ii. 317.
Marchmont, Earl of, i. 159.
Marlborough, Charles Duke of, i. 37, 58, 63, 120, 211, 321, 322; ii. 90.
Marlborough, Sarah Duchess of, i. 37, 98, 130.
Martin, ——, i. 49.
Mascove, Professor, ii. 236.
Mason, George, i. 14, 338, 353, 357, 358, 364, 368, 369, 372; ii. 39, 203.
Masters, ——, i. 292, 293.
Mathias, Thomas James, i. 199, 328.
Mazarin, Cardinal, i. 281.
Meredith, Sir William, ii. 242.
Michalin, Pierre, ii. 121.
Middlesex, Lady, i. 254.
Middleton, Dr. Conyers, i. 32.
Millar, ——, i. 80.
Milles, Edith, i. 300.
MILLES, Dr. Jeremiah, i. 299-301; 297.
Milles, Dr. Thomas, i. 299.
Milton, John, i. 151, 361.
Milton, Joseph Lord, ii. 137.
Mirepoix, Madame de, ii. 103.
Mitchell, Sir Andrew, i. 270; ii. 222.
Mitford, Rev. John, i. 357, 372.
Monboddo, James Burnet, Lord, i. 77.

INDEX. 349

Montagu, Charles, ii. 23, 24.
Montagu, Duke of, i. 259; ii. 60.
Montagu, Edward, ii. 24.
Montagu, General Edward, ii. 23.
Montagu, Edward Wortley, i. 252, 271.
Montagu, George, i. 189, 332, 333; ii. 22, 23, 24, 25, 39, 116, 165, 236.
Montagu, John, ii. 24.
Montagu, Lady Lucy, ii. 235.
Montagu, Lady Mary Wortley, i. 64, 67, 68, 71, 75, 77, 80, 252.
Montagu, Mrs., i. 190.
Moore, Thomas, i. 167.
More, Arthur, ii. 105.
More, Hannah, ii. 43.
Morell, Mrs., i. 19, 20.
MORELL, Dr. Thomas, i. 13-17; 27.
Morgan, Thomas, i. 32.
Morton, ——, i. 110.
Mount-Alexander, Countess of, i. 89.
MOUNTENEY, Richard, i. 89-91.
Mounteney, Richard, i. 89.
Mountford, Lord, ii. 33.
Mountnorris, Countess of, i. 192.
Mountnorris, Earl of, i. 192.
Mountstuart, Lord, i. 276.
Mudge, ——, i. 111.
Muntz, ——, ii. 39.
Murphy, Arthur, i. 84, 262.
Murray, Lieut.-General James, ii. 154, 155, 156.

Napoleon I., ii. 329, 338.
Nepean, Sir Evan, ii. 276, 277.
Newcastle, Duke of, i. 46, 48, 100, 106, 107, 162, 240, 246, 257, 258, 259, 260, 261, 275; ii. 57, 223.
Newton, Bishop, i. 236, 248.
Newton, Dr., ii. 95.
Nichols, John, i. 1, 15, 23, 89, 90, 290, 297, 370, 371; ii. 12, 158, 198.

Noble, Rev. Mark, ii. 84.
Norfolk, Duke of, ii. 100, 222.
Nortgeth, ——, i. 364.
North, Francis Lord, ii. 113.
NORTH, Frederick Lord, ii. 234-85; i. 316, 349; ii. 73, 102, 136, 137, 139, 140, 141, 227.
North, Lady, ii. 263, 276, 277, 278.
North, ——, ii. 278.
North, Miss, ii. 278.
Northington, Lord, i. 242, 305; ii. 227.
Norton, Sir Fletcher, i. 233.
Nugent, Robert Earl, i. 227.

Oglethorpe, General James Edward, i. 203.
Oliver, Rev. ——, i. 64, 65, 80.
Oliver, Dr., i. 94.
Onslow, George, i. 223.
Orford, George Earl of, i. 46; ii. 34, 46, 224.
Orford, Robert Earl of, ii. 29.
Orford, Earl of —, see also Walpole.
Ossory, Lady, i. 24, 189; ii. 6, 44, 45, 47, 83, 116, 120, 336.
Ossory, Lord, ii. 111.
Owen, Thomas, ii. 2, 5.

Paine, Thomas, ii. 320.
Paley, Dr., ii. 314.
Palliser, Sir Hugh, ii. 74.
Palmerston, Lord, i. 162; ii. 244.
Park, Thomas, i. 51.
Parker, Archbishop, i. 251.
Patrick, Miss Penelope, i. 7.
Patrick, Dr. Simon, i. 7.
Pelham, Henry, i. 11, 36, 100, 236; ii. 113.
Pembroke, Lady, i. 326.

Pembroke, Lord, ii. 112.
Pepys, Sir Lucas, ii. 160.
Percival, Lord, i. 367.
Pergolesi, J. B., i. 302.
Phillips, T., ii. 110.
Phillpotts, Dr., ii. 289.
Piazza, Signor, ii. 25.
Pitt, Anne, i. 112.
Pitt, Hon. Charles James, i. 163.
Pitt, Robert, i. 96.
Pitt, Thomas, i. 97.
Pitt, William, i. 150, 155, 162, 163, 226, 316; ii. 28, 75, 96, 135, 136, 227, 272, 274, 320.
Platen and Darlington, Sophia Charlotte, Countess of, ii. 170.
Plumptre, Professor, i. 376.
Plunket, ——, ii. 33.
Plymouth, Earl of, i. 334.
Poland, Poniatowski King of, i. 172, 173.
Pole, Cardinal, i. 250.
Pomfret, Earl of, i. 271.
Ponsonby, ——, ii. 113.
Pope, Alexander, i. 58, 61, 79, 80, 178, 211, 296; ii. 5, 19, 29, 31.
Portland, Duke of, i. 138, 273, 274, 275.
Potter, Dr. John, i. 31, 300.
Powys, Thomas, ii. 258, 271.
Poyntz, ——, i. 167.
Pratt, Elizabeth, i. 302.
Pratt, Sir John, i. 5, 302, 304.
Prescott, Colonel William, ii. 204, 205, 207, 208.
Pringle, Harriot, i. 163.
Pringle, Lieut.-Colonel, i. 163.
Pritchard, Mrs., i. 267.
Proctor, Sir William Beauchamp, ii. 311.
Pynsent, Sir William, i. 130.

Queensberry, Duchess of, i. 253; ii. 31.

Queensberry, Duke of, ii. 65, 98, 99, 103, 117, 118, 119, 121.
Quin, James, i. 345.

Rafa, ——, i. 64.
Ramsay, Allan, i. 5.
Ray, Miss, ii. 75, 77, 78, 79, 81.
Reed, Isaac, ii. 295, 296.
Reynolds, Sir Joshua, i. 112, 311, 336; ii. 7.
Rich, Sir Robert, i. 186.
Richard, William, i. 345.
Richardson, Samuel, i. 76, 77; ii. 198, 298.
Richmond, Duke of (1), ii. 105.
Richmond, Charles Duke of (2), i. 37, 71.
Richmond, Duke of (3), i. 154, 156, 158, 259, 275, 276; ii. 273.
Rigby, Richard, i. 81, 106, 238; ii. 92, 238.
Roberts, Dr., ii. 327.
Rochambeau, J. B. D. de, ii. 335.
Rochester, John Wilmot, Earl of, ii. 54, 89.
ROCKINGHAM, Charles Watson Wentworth, Marquis of, ii. 219-30; i. 129, 240, 275; ii. 183, 234, 243, 266.
Rockingham, Marchioness of, ii. 230.
Rockingham, Thomas Marquis of, ii. 219.
Rogers, Mrs., i. 360.
Rous, Sir John, ii. 76, 261.
Rowe, Nicholas, i. 253.
Roxburgh, Duke of, i. 71.
Russell, Earl, i. 139; ii. 224.
Rutland, Bridget Duchess of, ii. 143.
Rutland, Charles Duke of, ii. 147.
Rutland, John Duke of, i. 260; ii. 143.

Sackville, Lord George, ii. 145, 146.

INDEX. 351

Sandwich, Edward Montagu, Earl of, ii. 54.
Sandwich, Elizabeth Countess of, i. 346.
SANDWICH, John Montagu, Earl of (4), ii. 54–85; i. 259; ii. 91, 175, 224.
Sandwich, John Earl of (5), i. 346; ii. 59.
Sandwich, Judith Countess of, ii. 59.
Saunderson, Professor, ii. 25.
Sawbridge, Alderman, ii. 252.
Scarborough, Earl of, i. 138.
Schultz, ——, i. 47.
Schwellenberg, Madame, i. 327.
Scott, Lord Charles, ii. 93.
Scott, Sir Walter, i. 82, 84; ii. 40, 41.
Secker, Archbishop, ii. 50.
SELWYN, George Augustus, ii. 89–121; i. 11, 50, 51, 52, 55, 56, 139, 164, 235, 332; ii. 23, 38, 84, 312, 333.
Selwyn, John, i. 164; ii. 96.
Selwyn, Colonel John, i. 11; ii. 90, 91, 96.
Selwyn, Mary, i. 11; ii. 90.
Seward, Anne, i. 196.
Seward, William, i. 96.
Seymour, Lady Frances, ii. 147.
Seymour, Lord George, ii. 115.
Shakespeare, William, i. 112, 151, 375; ii. 12, 264, 284, 295, 296.
Shannon, Henry Earl of, i. 175.
Sharp, Rev. John, i. 366.
Sheffield, Lady, ii. 279.
Sheffield, Lord, ii. 160, 278, 279.
Shelburne, Lord, i. 97, 135, 139, 142, 145, 149, 151; ii. 228, 243, 255, 268, 272, 273, 274—see also Lansdowne.
Sheridan, Richard Brinsley, ii. 283, 321.
Sheridan, Thomas, ii. 308.

Sherlock, Bishop, i. 7, 8, 27, 287.
Sherlock, Mrs., i. 7, 8.
Shorter, Sir John, ii. 18, 123.
Sidmouth, Lord, ii. 324.
Singleton, Mark, ii. 331.
Skrine, William, ii. 109.
Sleech, Dr. Richard, i. 200.
Sleech, Dr. Stephen, ii. 15.
Sligo, Marquis of, ii. 193.
Smith, Sydney, ii. 89.
Smollett, Tobias, i. 75, 184, 185, 188, 262.
Snape, Dr., i. 19.
Sneyd, Rev. John, i. 194.
Somerset, Charles Duke of, i. 93, 94; ii. 147.
Spence, Rev. Joseph, ii. 26, 27.
Spencer, Lord Charles, i. 321.
Spencer, Earl of, i. 131.
Spencer, Lady Elizabeth, i. 328.
Spencer, Hon. John, i. 130.
Spenser, Edmund, i. 112.
Spilsbury, ——, i. 336.
Stair, Lord, ii. 125.
Stanhope, Countess, i. 131, 163, 225, 226.
Stanhope, Charles Earl, i. 163.
Stanhope, Philip Henry Earl, i. 139, 178, 318; ii. 70, 151, 155.
Stanislaus, King, i. 133, 141, 313.
Stanley, Major, ii. 74.
Stapylton, Sir Thomas, i. 321.
STEEVENS, George, ii. 294–301.
Stephens, Alex., ii. 303.
Storer, ——, ii. 284.
Stormont, Lord, ii. 283.
Stowell, William Scott, Lord, ii. 193.
Strafford, Thomas Earl of, ii. 201, 219.
Strangford, Lord, i. 167.
Stuart, Sir Charles, i. 284.
Sturgeon, William, ii. 230.
Suffolk, Henrietta Countess of, i. 212.

Suffolk, Earl of, i. 244.
Sumner, Archbishop, i. 245.
SUMNER, Dr. John, i. 33; 30, 201; ii. 12, 232.
Surrey, Earl of, ii. 261, 262, 264.
Swift, Jonathan, ii. 5.
Sydney, Thomas Viscount, i. 9; ii. 11.
Sykes, Dr. Arthur Ashley, i. 32.

Talleyrand, M., ii. 320.
Taylor, ——, ii. 308.
Temple, Anna Countess, i. 212.
Temple, Hester Countess, i. 210, 211, 228, 230.
Temple, George Grenville, Earl, ii. 271, 273, 275.
TEMPLE, Richard Earl, i. 210-29; 58, 101, 118, 120, 122, 124, 131, 132, 133, 134, 136, 138, 159, 276, 230, 231, 237, 310; ii. 241.
Temple, Sir Richard, i. 177.
Temple, Rev. W. J., i. 361, 368.
Thackeray, Rev. Francis, i. 96, 116.
Thicknesse, Rev. John, i. 92.
Thicknesse, Philip, i. 92; ii. 225.
Thicknesse, Philip, i. 93.
THICKNESSE, Ralph, i. 92.
Thirlby, Dr. Thomas, i. 251.
Thompson, Anthony, ii. 162.
Thomson, James, i. 182.
Thurlow, Dr., ii. 287.
Thurlow, Lord, ii. 228, 250, 256.
Tindal, Matthew, i. 32.
Tindal, Nicholas, ii. 49.
Tippoo Saib, ii. 336.
Tomline, Bishop, i. 150.
TOOKE, John Horne, ii. 302-26.
Tooke, William, ii. 316.
Townshend, Audrey Harrison, Viscountess, ii. 116.
Townshend, Charles, i. 135, 144, 145, 146, 148, 149, 224; ii. 29, 112, 121, 226, 237.

Townshend, Charles Viscount, i. 6, 9, 11, 247.
Townshend, Henry, i. 11.
Townshend, Lieut.-Col. Henry, ii. 11.
Townshend, Lord John, ii. 283.
Townshend, Lord, i. 58, 284.
Townshend, ——, ii. 289.
TOWNSHEND, Hon. Thomas, i. 9-12; 59, 225; ii. 11, 67.
Townshend, Colonel William, ii. 18.
Townshend, Hon. William, i. 247.
Trenchard, George, ii. 3.
Trevigar, ——, ii. 25.
Tyson, ——, i. 201.

Vansittart, Miss, i. 282.
Vattel, Emmerich de, i. 112.
Vertue, George, ii. 36.
Villiers, Sir George, i. 97.
Villiers, Harriet, i. 97.
Voltaire, F. M. A. de, i. 368, 375; ii. 309.

Wade, Marshal, ii. 125.
Waldegrave, Lady, ii. 38, 187, 337.
Waldegrave, Lord, i. 179, 254, 261.
Wales, Princess Charlotte of, ii. 292.
Wales, Frederick Prince of, i. 16, 91, 99, 181, 182, 253, 254; ii. 25, 231, 235.
Wales, George Prince of, ii. 159.
Wales, Princess of, i. 216, 220, 254, 255, 268, 275, 280.
Waller, Sir Jonathan Wathen, ii. 193.
Walpole, Sir Edward, i. 89, 93.
Walpole, Horace, i. 2, 14, 21, 24, 30, 32, 37, 40, 49, 50, 51, 81,'99, 107, 117, 119, 127, 136, 139, 141, 147, 152, 159, 165, 166, 174, 178, 180, 185, 187, 188, 189, 212, 214, 215, 221, 233, 247, 253, 256, 261, 262,

265, 280, 282, 288, 290, 292, 296, 332, 333, 334, 337, 338, 339, 341, 347, 350, 351, 355, 357, 358, 359, 363, 364, 369, 374, 376; ii. 6, 13, 17, 48, 55, 59, 61, 70, 77, 83, 91, 96, 98, 100, 101, 103, 104, 105, 106, 111, 113, 116, 120, 123, 125, 126, 127, 129, 130, 131, 132, 135, 136, 137, 138, 139, 140, 142, 146, 148, 165, 172, 175, 203, 225, 236, 240, 244, 260, 266, 271, 278, 336.
Walpole, Horatio, ii. 17.
Walpole, Lady, ii. 20, 25, 123.
Walpole, Sir Robert, i. 3, 4, 11, 36, 89, 90, 98, 100, 165, 166, 167, 170, 179, 181, 182, 236; ii. 17, 19, 29, 57, 219, 261.
Walsingham, Admiral, ii. 81.
Walsingham, Charlotte, i. 175.
Walsingham, Countess of, ii. 20, 21.
Walsingham, Mrs., ii. 81.
Walsingham, Captain Robert Boyle, i. 175.
Walter, Peter, i. 80.
Warburton, Bishop, i. 7, 112, 265, 298, 369; ii. 50, 52, 64, 66.
Warner, Rev. Dr., ii. 108, 119.
Warren, Dr., ii. 284.
Warton, Dr. T., i. 370.
Washington, George, ii. 179, 180, 211, 212, 213, 334.
Waterland, Dr. Daniel, i. 32.
Watson, Bishop, ii. 229.
Watt, Robert, i. 28, 32.
Wedderburn, Lord, ii. 250.
Wellesley, Marquis, ii. 339.
Wentworth, Lady Anne, ii. 201.
Wentworth, Lady Henrietta Alicia, ii. 230.
West, Benjamin, i. 58.
West, Elizabeth, i. 337.
WEST, Gilbert, i. 57-61; 176, 183; ii. 23, 55, 91.
West, Mary, i. 211.

WEST, Richard, i. 337-43; 332, 333 335, 354, 356, 361.
West, Dr. Richard, i. 58.
West, Rt. Hon. Richard, i. 337, 342.
Weston, Rev. Charles, i. 7, 201.
WESTON, Rt. Hon. Edward, i. 6-8 10, 59.
Weston, Dr. Stephen, i. 6.
Weymouth, Lord, ii. 239.
Wharnecliffe, Lord, ii. 19.
Wharton, Dr., i. 363, 371, 374, 375; ii. 70, 165.
Whately, ——, i. 113, 141.
Whitaker, Dr., ii. 51.
Wilberforce, William, i. 162; ii. 99, 100.
Wilkes, John, i. 214, 215, 216, 267, 268, 308, 309, 310, 311, 349; ii. 63, 64, 65, 66, 68, 70, 89, 241, 308, 309, 311, 312, 313, 314, 315, 321.
William Rufus, i. 161.
Williams, Charles, i. 164.
WILLIAMS, Sir Charles Hanbury, i. 164-75; 37, 38, 65, 71, 80, 81, 94, 179, 181, 195, 228; ii. 89, 92, 108.
Williams, Lady Frances, i. 173.
Williams, Gilly, i. 139; ii. 38, 101, 104, 312.
Williams, ——, ii. 305.
Willis, Dr. Francis, ii. 159.
Willis, Rev. Thomas, i. 288.
Willoughby of Parham, Hugh Lord, i. 297.
Wilson, Rev. Hugh, i. 302.
Winchilsea and Nottingham, Daniel Earl of, ii. 220.
Windham, William, ii. 283.
Winnington, Thomas, i. 165, 167, 170.
Wolfe, General, ii. 172, 179, 200.
Woodcock, Ebro, ii. 121.
Woodfall, William, ii. 211.
Woodhouselee, Lord, ii. 194.

Wraxall, Sir Nathaniel, i. 227, 228; ii. 102, 107, 111, 117, 252, 257.
Wyndham, Sir William, i. 232.

York, Edward Augustus Duke of, i. 46; ii. 97, 159, 172, 174.

Yorke, Charles, i. 265.
Young, Anthony, i. 207.
Young, Edward, i. 364.
Young, Dr. Philip, i. 247.
Young, Rev. William, i. 80.
Young, Sir William, i. 111.

THE END.

www.ingramcontent.com/pod-product-compliance
Lightning Source LLC
Chambersburg PA
CBHW020241240426
43672CB00006B/601